D0180523

F L A S H P O I N T S

Environmental Restoration

Ethics, Theory, and Practice

edited by

William Throop

Humanity Books

an imprint of Prometheus Books
59 John Glenn Drive, Amherst, New York 14228-2197

Published 2000 by Humanity Books, an imprint of Prometheus Books

Inquiries should be addressed to
Humanity Books
59 John Glenn Drive
Amherst, New York 14228–2197
VOICE: 716–691–0133, ext. 207
FAX: 716–564–2711

04 03 02 01 00   5 4 3 2 1

Library of Congress Cataloging-in-Publication Data

Environmental restoration : ethics, theory, and practice / edited by William
    Throop.
        p.   cm. — (Flashpoints series)
    Includes bibliographical references.
    ISBN 1–57392–818–6 (paper)
    1. Restoration ecology—Philosophy. I. Throop, William.
QH541.15.R45 E56 2000
333.95'153—dc21   99-058010
                                                                      CIP

Printed in the United States of America on acid-free paper

Flashpoints

Series Editor: Roger S. Gottlieb
Worcester Polytechnic Institute

Preserving Wildlife: An International Perspective
edited by Mark A. Michael

Environmental Restoration

For my parents,
and for my daughter, Laura

Contents

Acknowledgments

Many friends and colleagues provided support during the production of this book, and I am very grateful for all of their contributions. Roger Gottlieb supplied the impetus for the project. The advice and encouragement that I have received from colleagues at St. Andrews College and Green Mountain College, especially Tom Benson, Mel Bringle, and Dick Prust, have been invaluable. Over the past several years, I have discussed many of the issues addressed in this book with Ned Hettinger and Steve Schwartz. Their insightful comments and occasional expressions of incredulity have tempered my views and refined my appreciation of the issues. Jennifer Oleszkowicz and Barbara Root ably and cheerfully performed many tasks which were essential to the production of the anthology.

Introduction

THE PRACTICE OF ENVIRONMENTAL RESTORATION

L ike most species, humans alter their environment, often resetting succession or sending ecosystems onto new trajectories. Even early in human history, many of these alterations had dramatic effects on other species and on future
generations of humans. The widespread deforestation of ancient Greece permanently altered that landscape and contributed to the decline of powerful civiliza-
tions. The pattern of resource depletion, ecosystem degradation, and resultant
cultural change has been all too frequently repeated. Contemporary humans are
merely following a time-honored tradition, but with a significant difference: The
modern global economy recreates the pattern on a much larger scale.

As the human population has increased and as the tools with which we
modify the environment have become more powerful, environmental degradation has become more widespread and more severe. Now we must worry about
global decline of biodiversity, global depletion of energy resources, global
warming, and the gradual poisoning of the global environment. Because the
consequences of our actions have become so far-reaching, traditional responses—making do with whatever new ecosystem arises, moving on to other
lands—no longer suffice. The ecosystems that evolve in response to our impact
tend to be much less hospitable than earlier systems, and fewer places invite
migration. It seems that we must clean up our mess.

Environmental restoration is an increasingly popular way of "cleaning up"
and, consequently, a burgeoning field of scientific inquiry. While restoration
projects are as varied as the kinds of environmental damage they address, they
all involve minimizing some prior human impact by restoring a system to a
healthier state, typically a state involving the species and processes that characterized the predisturbance ecosystem.

11

Much restoration involves returning species to an area. As a response to deforestation in Scotland, volunteers attempt to replant the oaks, rowans, and scots pines of the ancient Caledonian forest. Because of government-sponsored programs to eradicate prairie dogs in the Western United States, the black-footed ferrets who prey on them were driven to the brink of extinction. When an isolated population of ferrets was discovered in Wyoming in 1981, a restoration project was initiated which involved captive breeding of ferrets and their subsequent reintroduction to protected prairie dog colonies.

Often, restoration involves the elimination of exotic species. In the 1920s, mountain goats were introduced to the Olympic Mountains of Washington. Their dramatic population growth has significantly affected the indigenous vegetation in alpine and subalpine regions. Restoration efforts have involved removal of goats through live-trapping, but the completion of the project appears to require shooting the remainder of the population.

At its most complex, restoration requires large-scale landscape alteration. After the Army Corps of Engineers straightened the Kissimmee River in Florida to control flooding and increase agricultural land, water quality declined, and the Everglades ecosystem suffered. After much debate and planning, restoration of the river and the surrounding wetlands has begun. The cost of putting the curves back in the Kissimmee, approximately $372 million, is at least one hundred times the cost of the initial straightening, and much more will be needed to fully recover the hydrological cycles on which the Everglades depend. Projects like this mark the coming of age of restoration.

The roots of contemporary restoration practice have been traced to nineteenth-century Midwest prairie landscape architects Jens Jensen and Ossian Cole Simonds, who used natural designs for their work.[1] Early in this century, the U.S. government recognized the importance of some kinds of restoration; the Lacey Act of 1900 aimed to preserve and restore game birds and other wild birds.[2] In the 1930s, at the University of Wisconsin–Madison Arboretum, Aldo Leopold led efforts to restore patches of tallgrass prairie. Most of the key U.S. environmental acts of the 1960s and 1970s cited restoration as an explicit goal.[3] As a result, the volume of restoration projects in the United States increased dramatically.

By 1982 there was enough interest in environmental restoration to justify a journal devoted to the field. *Restoration and Management Notes*, edited by William Jordan, one of restoration's most visionary practitioners, has included articles on topics ranging from current restoration projects to the social, political, and philosophical issues raised by these projects. Increasingly, restoration practice is seen as an important contributor to the growth of ecological knowledge. A. D. Bradshaw maintains that "the acid test of our understanding of ecosystems is not whether we can take systems to bits on pieces of paper, however scientifically, but whether we can put them back together in practice and make them work."[4] The Society for Ecological Restoration was formed in 1989, and under its auspices a new journal, *Restoration Ecology*, was initiated in 1993. Although the science of restoration is still in its infancy, demand for practitioners far outstrips the availability of those formally trained in related fields. Fortunately, large restoration projects often make use of many volunteers.

On summer Saturday mornings in Chicago, small armies of volunteers hack away at brush to help recreate the oak savannas that once characterized the area. Along the Mattole River in northern California, members of the Mattole Restoration Council wrestle boulders into midstream to restore salmon spawning pools, and schoolchildren help transport salmon fry to suitable spots in the river. William Jordan has argued that with enhanced public participation in restoration and with its ritualization, the practice can become a new paradigm for environmentalism, replacing wilderness preservation. If current trends continue, the rhetoric of restoration will take its place alongside sustainability and wilderness preservation as a central feature of twenty-first-century environmental debate.

PHILOSOPHICAL ISSUES

As the practice of environmental restoration becomes more prominent, the philosophical issues to which it gives rise become more immediate. Many of these issues cluster around key decisions we must make in evaluating restoration projects. We must decide what goals are appropriate for restoration projects, what values motivate and justify restoration, what means are acceptable to achieve these goals, and what overall attitude we should have toward restoration.

First, let us consider the questions of goals. What should we attempt to achieve in restoration? Should we seek to return a degraded ecosystem to some predisturbance structure, or would just any healthy structure do? If the former, how far back should we try to turn the environmental clock? Many restorationists have attempted to return ecosystems to a historic structure which predates a human disturbance. Since "restoration" is usually defined in terms of its goals, this goal is ensconced in standard definitions, such as that accepted by the Society for Ecological Restoration prior to 1994. Restoration is "the intentional alteration of a site to establish a defined indigenous, historic ecosystem. The goal of the process is to emulate the structure, functioning, diversity and dynamics of the specified ecosystem."[5]

Distinctions are commonly drawn between restoration, rehabilitation, and reclamation, though the lines between these are blurred and variable. Rehabilitation encompasses a range of options which do not aim at exact fidelity to a predisturbance system, though the resulting systems often have functions and species similar to earlier states. Reclamation typically involves significantly enhancing the health of a system, often by radically shifting its structure, as in cases of reclamation of strip mines through converting them to agricultural land. To such standard distinction, Stephanie Mills adds reinhabitation, which involves integrating humans sustainably into a renewed landscape. Finer distinctions are sometimes useful; John Cairns outlines eight classes of restoration ranging from "resetting the ecological clock" to letting natural processes repair an ecosystem.[6]

The standard "predisturbance structure" goal of restoration raises a number of problems, both empirical and normative. Often it is very hard to determine what the predisturbance structure was like. This is especially true in cases where the disturbance occurred far in the past and few, if any, similar systems have been preserved undisturbed. If we want to restore the forests of Scotland which were cut hundreds of years ago, we must look to Norway for model forests that we presume to be similar.[7] Furthermore, serious limitations in our knowledge of ecosystems often make it unlikely that we will be able to duplicate the original exactly even if we have access to similar systems. Even if our knowledge were adequate, our ability to restore all parts of an ecosystem might not be up to the challenge. Such empirical problems raise doubts about the rationality of seeking a return to a predisturbance structure.

The empirical challenge of restoration is amplified if the surrounding landscape has changed. We may need to manage an area intensively if some essential ecosystem processes are blocked by changes in contiguous land. Thus, efforts to restore oak savanna and prairie in the Midwest involve repeated controlled burns, because the use of surrounding land requires suppression of "natural" fires. Ecosystems are dynamic, and the attempt to return to an earlier structure can appear as a naive attempt to stop history or as mere nostalgia for a more innocent past. Minor modifications of the standard goal may adequately address some of these concerns. For example, we may seek to return an ecosystem to a structure it would have had if it had not been disturbed—perhaps a structure far different from any prior structure because of other changes in the land. Although this modification respects the dynamic nature of ecosystems, it multiplies the epistemic problems. Often, we may be able merely to speculate about what a system would have been like if we had not degraded it.

The predisturbance structure goal is also beset with metaphysical and evaluative problems. It is not clear why we should value return to a predisturbance structure over creation of a new, healthy structure. Often the model of art restoration is invoked to illustrate and motivate the predisturbance goal. When a painting is damaged, we often want to return it too its predamage state. The analogy to environmental restoration is threatened, however, because the identity conditions for ecosystems are extremely muddy. With paintings, the restorer works on the original and seeks exact fidelity to the predamage state. In environmental restoration, it is not so clear that the original system remains after disturbance. Moreover, it seems ridiculous to attempt exact duplication of vegetation patterns, rock distribution, and so on. If we reasonably respond that the goal is the same *kind* of ecosystem, then the analogy with art restoration is weakened, and it yields rather different conclusions. Ecosystem restorations may be more like art forgeries than art repairs, as Robert Elliot argues. A common response is to focus on restoring the processes that characterized an earlier system, rather than the precise structure, but why should we prefer these to some other processes?

Of course, sometimes return to a predisturbance structure may be the least risky way of returning a system to health; we may not know enough about a system to be confident about the success of other changes. But this argument makes the standard goal contingent on our current limitations and suggests that this goal should change as knowledge grows. A deeper justification of the predisturbance objective maintains that human alteration of natural processes decreases some value which can only be recovered if the alteration is reversed. Some early childhood lessons suggest that when we have done something wrong we should rectify the situation by putting things back the way they were. Such an intuition may lie at the heart of the standard goal. Yet this rationale works only if the predisturbance structure has some special value. What could this value be? Nature does not have intrinsic preferences for some states over others; her modus operandi seems to be "whatever works."

One answer to the value question, an answer which has a good pedigree, is that the predisturbance structure was more wild and hence more valuable than the disturbed state. Restoration may recover lost value by returning some of the original wildness. For example, a Yellowstone with restored wolves may be wilder than it was without them. This justification confronts a serious paradox, however. "Wildness" is typically defined in terms of lack of human alteration. If so, how can the additional human alteration of an ecosystem involved in restoration enhance wildness? Furthermore, the appeal to the value of wildness ill accords with the theme of much restoration literature that humans are parts of nature. This leads us back to the troubling question of what values, if any, make restoration preferable to other responses to degradation.

Partly in response to some of these problems, the Society for Ecological Restoration has recently accepted a much broader definition of restoration: "Ecological restoration is the process of repairing damage caused by humans to the diversity and dynamics of indigenous ecosystems."[8] This definition makes defending restoration easier because few will argue against repairing damage. On the other hand, the definition gives much less guidance on goals, hence the deep philosophical questions remain. Even if one allows considerations of feasibility to dominate discussions about what goals to pursue in a situation, value judgments about the preferability of certain results will play an essential role in decision making. In practice, many restorationists continue to pursue the goal of a predisturbance structure while acknowledging that the result is likely to fall far short of the goal.

In addition to the problems of justifying goals for restoration, there is an issue about the comparative value of undisturbed and restored ecosystems. If we succeed in completely restoring a damaged ecosystem to a predisturbance structure, have we recovered all of the value lost through the damage? The answer to this question has important implications for environmental policy. If the answer is "yes," then there is little argument against activities like mining and logging, which degrade an area, as long as mechanisms exist to ensure that the area will be completely restored. The loss of value is only temporary and usually offset by important human gains. If the answer is "no," however, then policies that protect areas from human disturbance will be much easier to justify.

The debate about this issue usually revolves around metaphysical claims which support different value judgments. If an ecosystem restoration is comparable to an art forgery, then its metaphysical differences from the original support significant value differences. Someone who unwittingly trades an original for a forgery had lost a great deal. Restorations have also been compared to artifacts, which are essentially different from predisturbance "natural" ecosystems, because the nature of a restoration is determined by our purposes, not by purposeless evolutionary mechanisms. Such contentious metaphysical claims have spawned a small industry of defining key aspects of the identity conditions for ecosystems.

Comparative value judgments affect the more general issue of what attitude we should take toward restoration. Should we wholeheartedly embrace restoration as a new paradigm for environmentalism? Or would an ambivalent attitude be more appropriate? Perhaps restoration does involve value loss, but in a world such as ours, it may constitute the best response to a bad situation. Or perhaps, worse, it is yet another manifestation of the human impulse to dominate nature, which has been responsible for many of our environmental problems. If so, maybe we should reluctantly resort to restoration only when we have made messes that nature cannot clean up on its own.

The issue of attitude highlights the following two related themes which unite many of the articles in this book: the search for the appropriate relation of humans to nature and the evaluation of the natural. A sanguine attitude toward restoration can be justified in part by observations that humans are a part of nature and that our alterations of nature are essentially no different in value from the alterations made by other species. According to this attitude, restoration reconnects people with nonhuman nature, and it is among the most benign of human alterations of nature. Thus, it should be championed as a way of life that fruitfully integrates humans into ecosystems in a world where human activities all too often isolate us from nature.

In contrast, more ambivalent attitudes may be justified by emphasizing the ways in which human activity differs from the processes of wild nature. Although biologically, humans may be a part of nature, in other senses we have removed ourselves from natural processes. Technological developments release us from some of the severity of natural selection and shield us from many environmental fluctuations. Our abilities to transmit information to others around the globe transcend communication systems we find elsewhere. We modify nature on a scope and at a speed unknown among other species. Under such circumstances, it seems peculiar to propose that we are, or should be, plain members of the biotic community.

If some wedge can be driven between humans and the rest of nature, we can reasonably ask whether some ecosystem states and some human behaviors are more natural than others, and if so, whether these are more valuable by virtue of being more natural. On the one hand, restoration seems to attempt to return an ecosystem to a more natural state; thus a positive attitude toward it may be justified by the value of the natural. On the other hand, restoration often involves invasive human alteration and control, which seems the antithesis of the natural. Some see more than irony in the use of bulldozers, chain saws, and rifles in pursuit of the natural. To such people, the radio-collared restored wolves of Yellowstone National Park reduce its naturalness rather than enhance it.

The issue of determining the acceptable means for achieving restoration goals has received relatively little treatment by philosophers. However, if one values a predisturbance structure in part because it reduces human impact, then one may be required to limit how invasive the means can be. At some point, the disvalue of the human modifications involved in restoration will outweigh the value achieved through mitigating earlier impact. Highly invasive means may create a system more closely approximating a zoo than a natural system, even if the structure of the system is the same as a predisturbance system.

Restoration activities almost inevitably involve the death of individual organisms. If these organisms have any moral standing, then another factor enters into the evaluation of means. Under what circumstances is it permissible to cause death to achieve the goals of restoration? Sometimes restoration inadvertently causes death, as in the transportation of a reintroduced species. Often, however, the death is deliberate. It may be indirect, as when a reintroduced predator kills members of a prey species, or it may consist in the direct elimination of exotic species. The latter case involves special issues about the disvalue of exotic species.

Exotic species are traditionally defined as species that have been introduced to an environment by humans. If humans are fully parts of nature, however, human introduction is not essentially different from other forms of species migration. On this assumption, it seems hard to justify the disvalue of exotics per se. Of course, some exotics dramatically alter an environment and endanger other species, as does the zebra mussel in the Great Lakes. But does this alteration justify the species' removal? On what basis do we prefer indigenous species to their introduced rivals?

The trade-off between the death of individuals and the restoration of ecosystems becomes particularly troublesome when the individuals are sentient animals. Feral pigs are killed to restore and protect ecosystems in Hawaii. Many feral goats on San Clemente Island are live-trapped at great expense. Others are shot, at less expense, to restore the island's ecosystems and to protect three endangered species of plants. What principles can we use to evaluate comparatively the good of preserving endangered species or ecosystems and the value of lives that may be sacrificed in the process? In restoration projects where no endangered species are protected, it may appear that nonhuman lives are sacrificed for our mere preference for historical ecosystems. Can this practice be justified?

The nest of issues surrounding environmental restoration contains many of the central metaphysical and normative questions facing environmentalists. Thus, the systematic evaluation of restoration can be a fruitful first step toward developing a coherent environmental philosophy and a stiff test of existing philosophies. Since these issues often have far-reaching implications for environmental policy, we can expect the debates they spark to engage a broader public. In the struggle to extend ethics so that it covers human interaction with nonhumans, we must address these issues.

THE SELECTIONS

I have used the need for decisions about goals, values, attitudes, and means as a guide in structuring the anthology. The articles in part I initiate the discussion of goals by describing a variety of restoration projects and raising questions about the predisturbance structure goal shared by many restorationists. As we have seen, our appraisal of goals depends in part on our decision about how much value to place on restored ecosystems; this is the focus of part II. In part III, more specific issues about goals are addressed and issues about means are broached. Part IV returns to issues of value, but focuses on larger questions about our general attitude toward restoration.

In the first selection, Margaret Holloway describes the recent degradation of the Everglades ecosystem and the steps that are proposed to remedy the situation. The remedies include diverting water back into the old channels cut by the Kissimmee River, reestablishing wetlands which will attract native wildfowl, and eliminating exotic species. Along the way, she wonders about the indeterminacy of the goals of many restoration projects and muses about their high costs. The question "Is it worth it?" hovers in the background. Several other examples of wetland restoration suggest that we do not know enough to recreate wetlands, and this prompts a discussion of the challenges facing multidisciplinary areas like restoration ecology. Researchers in disciplines ranging from hydrology to botany and zoology must work to integrate their knowledge if large-scale restoration projects are to be successful.

Stephanie Mills approaches restoration from a social perspective in her description of the Mattole River salmon restoration activities. She shows how people from a wide variety of backgrounds—loggers and ranchers, teachers and environmental activists—have been brought together in pursuit of returning a healthy salmon population to the degraded river. She interviews leaders of the project and explores their motivations. The personal fruits of participating in restoration emerge as powerful by-products of the activities. Volunteers *feel* their connection to the land, they acquire intimate knowledge of some of its facets, and they have a sense of contributing rather than just taking from the earth. Mills's enthusiasm for the way of life revealed by these activities provides material to justify an unmixed positive attitude toward restoration.

The historical perspective provided by Susan Power Bratton suggests a more mixed appraisal of restoration as it is presently conceived. She outlines several early examples of restoration which reflect the goals of enhanced productivity and recovered "natural balance," before turning to the current emphasis on recreating predisturbance states that can be sustained with minimal human management. Although she finds this "natural past" orientation appropriate in some cases, she argues that it unduly narrows the range of acceptable restoration projects. To preserve endangered species or reestablish populations, humans may need to manage actively a system or to create a new system that avoids problems which beset the populations in their original habitat. She argues that an awareness of the dynamic nature of ecosystems and the role humans have played in many systems also supports the expansion of restoration goals to include "seminatural" ecosystems.

Part II begins with Robert Elliot's now-classic article "Faking Nature." In 1982, Elliot was among the first to raise concerns about guarantees of restoration as a justification for increased land degradation. His article attempts to undermine such justification by pointing to the ways in which the value of something often depends on its history. The value of a work of art is, in part, of function of its having been produced by a particular artist. If such a work were lost, its value could not be returned by acquiring a qualitatively identical work. Instead, we would call such a work a "fake." Similarly, he argues, an ecosystem's value is in part determined by its history, in particular, its evolving out of natural processes. Since this history is not recovered in restoration, the resultant ecosystem has diminished value.

Eric Katz discusses some of the limitations of Elliot's art analogy, but supports his main conclusion with new arguments. He sees restored ecosystems as artifacts whose natures are determined by human purposes; in this way, they are essentially different from natural ecosystems. As a result, restoration of the original is impossible. According to Katz's argument, the claim that we can restore nature presupposes an anthropocentrism and a fondness for technological fixes which have jointly played a central role in creating the environmental crisis. Far from being part of the solution, the restoration mentality is part of the problem. Katz hastens to add that he is not disparaging attempts to improve damaged ecosystems, but he is urging that we alter the way we think about these attempts. As he sees it, restoration is like "putting a piece of furniture over a stain in the carpet." One improves appearances, but one does not eliminate the underlying problem.

The largely negative appraisal of restoration that many people find in Elliot and Katz has generated heated debate. The three selections that follow attempt to show why their arguments are misguided and to provide more attractive views of the achievements of restorationists. In recent books, Elliot and Katz have continued the discussion and refined their views.[9] Andrew Light applies a pragmatic perspective to the issues at hand. He distinguishes between benevolent and malicious restorations and argues that Elliot's charges of "faking nature" apply only to the latter case, where the promise of restoration is used as an excuse for degrading the environment. Benevolent restorations heal a breach between humans and nature and thereby restore what Light calls "the culture of nature." This goal of reconstructing a positive relationship with nature is compatible with Katz's view that restorations are artifacts, but not with his argument that restorations count as more human domination of nature. Light provides a detailed analysis of this argument and develops a series of examples designed to show why restorations need not involve domination.

In the course of his extended meditation on the natural and its value, Robin Attfield identifies different limitations to the Elliot/Katz critiques of restoration. He agrees that it may be conceptually impossible to restore wilderness, given the standard definition of wilderness as land unaltered by humans. However, he notes that this definition leaves us with very little genuine wilderness since humans have altered most ecosystems. In his judgment, restoration of nonwilderness areas seems neither impossible nor undesirable, for the overall value of the system may be enhanced through reintroducing native species or restoring ecosystem processes. Indeed, he maintains, the full value of a predisturbance system can be recovered if the same species are allowed to flourish in accordance with their own nature. In conclusion, Attfield argues that our roles as preservers and restorers of the natural must be combined with our role of "making nature habitable," that is, of sustainably altering nature so that we can flourish as well as other species.

Holmes Rolston, one of the foremost defenders of "natural" values, points to a significant difference between restored ecosystems and works of art or artifacts. In the former, natural processes do much of the work, though humans may jump-start some processes and contribute some planning. In contrast, paintings and other artifacts are comparatively passive; all repairs are brought about by the artist's intervention. Thus, in nature, the degree to which a restoration is a human creation diminishes over time. While the historical continuity with unaltered ecosystems cannot be recovered, the naturalness can. Restoration can be justified in terms of the natural values that do return. However, Rolston notes that in practice restorations often lack the value of the predisturbance system because they lack some of its diversity or complexity.

The essays in part III return to concrete cases as they raise specific issues about ends and means. The first two articles focus on the restoration of oak savannas in areas outside of Chicago which have become thick woodlands. Jon Mendelson and his colleagues raise a series of objections to this highly visible project. They contend that savannas are not distinct ecosystems, that the restoration is attempted in some areas where savannas have probably never existed, that the heavy use of fire and toxic chemicals is inappropriate, and that the ecosystems being destroyed in the process are natural. In their eyes, this case illustrates the dangers of restoration that is based on inadequate information and that attempts to reproduce transitional biotic communities, that is, those that occupy intermediate points on a continuum between distinct ecosystems. Human preferences for certain ecosystems fill the gaps in our knowledge and invasive techniques are often required to achieve the goals. Even in places where savannas once existed, they argue, an appreciation of the dynamic nature of ecosystems should deter us from seeking a return to some idealized past.

Steve Packard, who has been spearheading the oak savanna projects for more than a decade, systematically responds to these objections. He argues that the concerns about goals and means in the oak savanna project stem from inferior concepts of "nature" and the "natural." If what is natural in an area is defined as "complex assemblages of species as they have evolved in their environments over the ages," then savannas are natural systems, even if Native American burning played a role in their creation. By this definition, they will still be natural even if invasive means are required to recover them. Indeed, the succession of these systems to thick woods is artificial, since it involves the loss of historically important periodic burning. If what is natural has value, then restoring oak savannas enhances value.

Donald Scherer objects to the standard practice of trying to eliminate from a system all species introduced by humans. He sees this goal as unacceptably misanthropic and ecologically unsound. The unintentional human transportation of a species is ecologically just one way species migrate. To single it out and to label its products with the negative term "exotics" is to presuppose that human alterations of ecosystems are ipso facto bad. Yet not all nonindigenous species are harmful to ecosystems. An ecologically sound approach to exotics would focus only on species that harm the community into which they are introduced. Scherer closes with some suggestions for how restoration should be conceived if we see humans as fully parts of ecosystems.

In contrast to Scherer, I defend the standard practice of eliminating exotics. My essay focuses on the case of the exotic mountain goats in Olympic National Park and asks whether the park service proposal to shoot the remainder of the goats is morally acceptable. My defense of an affirmative answer involves three steps. First, I argue that the differences between human and nonhuman introduction of species are sufficient to justify the disvalue of exotic species. Second, I show how restoration can return the value lost through human alteration of the ecosystem. Third, I argue that it is reasonable to weight the value returned more than the disvalue of the death of the goats. If eliminating the goats can be justified, then many other restoration practices which involve the death of individuals are also likely to be justified.

Part IV focuses on the broader outlines of our emerging environmental ethic. In the first two selections, Frederick Turner and William Jordan argue that environmental restoration sets a fruitful new paradigm for ethics. In the essay that follows, G. Stanley Kane worries that it would be more dangerous than fruitful. Turner wants to diminish the current gap between humans and the rest of nature, and he proposes "gardening" as a promising way of integrating humans into nature. His focal example of the "gardening" is prairie restoration at the University of Wisconsin Arboretum. Here, volunteers create a Midwestern Arcadia. Responding to the charge that the resulting prairie is a fake, Turner argues that nature is copying itself and that humans are merely playing the role of pollinators who permit a system to evolve through their activities. Turner closes with the optimistic image of humans creating their gardens on other planets and thereby serving as vectors for enhancing life.

Jordan fills in many of the details of the argument that restoration is the most promising way for humans to achieve a healthy relation to the environment. He shows how restoration engages a much wider range of our abilities than other paradigms of environmental ethics, such as wilderness preservation: It involves an active relation with nature where goods are exchanged; it stretches us intellectually, physically, and emotionally; it connects us with the past; and it can be a social enterprise which, when properly ritualized, can express our spiritual dimension. He notes that though we are of nature, our self-awareness separates us from nature. We therefore need ways of reconnecting with it. By ritualizing restoration, we not only return nature; we return ourselves to nature as well.

If restoration à la Jordan begins to look like the centerpiece of a new nature religion, through Stanley Kane's eyes, it looks more like a continuation of the human domination of nature. History suggests that the human control presupposed in Turner's metaphor of gardening is a manifestation of hubris. Our intellectual and physical capabilities are far more limited than the metaphor suggests. According to Kane, a more appropriate attitude toward nature would be trust, a trust that the biotic community will thrive if humans reduce their impact. This trust can be coupled with an appreciation of the mystery of nature that contrasts with the ideal of "maker's knowledge" implicit in restoration and in the gardening metaphor. The emphasis on trust and mystery strongly suggests a wilderness ethic, which Kane believes is not a competitor to restoration, but rather a counterbalance.

A brief epilogue clusters the positions defended in the articles into two competing gestalts: restoration as a key element of sustainability or restoration as an expansion of a wilderness ethic. These gestalts magnify some argumentative threads and minimize the significance of others. The issues are so complexly interwoven, however, that different patterns might emerge from a shift in perspective. The debates about restoration have just begun, and it is too soon to speak with authority about how the patterns of response should be cast. These papers provide a broad range of entry points into the debates, as well as many of the important touchstones in the emerging literature. Collectively, they illustrate both how philosophically rich the area of environmental restoration is and how much work remains to be done.

NOTES

1. John J. Berger, "Ecological Restoration Comes of Age," *Forum for Applied Research and Public Policy* 10 (1995): 90–99.

2. John J. Berger, "The Federal Mandate to Restore: Laws and Policies on Environmental Restoration," *Environmental Professional* 13 (1991):195–206.

3. Ibid.

4. A. D. Bradshaw, "The Reconstruction of Ecosystems," *Journal of Applied Ecology* 20 (1983): 1–17.

5. J. Aronson et al., "Restoration and Rehabilitation of Degraded Ecosystems in Arid and Semi-Arid Lands: A View from the South," *Restoration Ecology* 1 (1993): 8–17.

6. John Cairns, "The Status of the Theoretical and Applied Science of Restoration Ecology," *Environmental Professional* 13 (1991): 186–94.

7. William Jordan IV, "Forests of Caledon," *Restoration and Management Notes* 10 (1992): 132–36.

8. Laura Jackson, Nikita Lopoukhine, and Deborah Hillyard, "Ecological Restoration: A Definition and Comments" *Restoration Ecology* 3 (1995): 71–75.

9. Robert Elliot, *Faking Nature* (New York: Routledge, 1997); Eric Katz, *Nature As Subject* (New York: Rowman and Littlefield Publishers, 1997).

REFERENCES

Aronson, J., et al. "Restoration and Rehabilitation of Degraded Ecosystems in Arid and Semi-Arid Lands: A View from the South." *Restoration Ecology* 1 (1993).

Berger, John J. "The Federal Mandate to Restore: Laws and Policies on Environmental Restoration." *Environmental Professional* 13 (1991).

———. "Ecological Restoration Comes of Age." *Forum for Applied Research and Public Policy* 10 (1995).

Bradshaw, A. D. "The Reconstruction of Ecosystems." *Journal of Applied Ecology* 20 (1983).

Cairns, John. "The Status of the Theoretical and Applied Science of Restoration Ecology." *Environmental Professional* 13 (1991).

Elliot, Robert. *Faking Nature.* New York: Routledge, 1997.

Jackson, Laura, Nikita Lopoukhine, and Deborah Hillyard. "Ecological Restoration: A Definition and Comments." *Restoration Ecology* 3 (1995).

Jordan, William, IV. "Forests of Caledon." *Restoration and Managment Notes* 10 (1992).

Katz, Eric. *Nature As Subject.* New York: Rowman and Littlefield Publishers, 1997.

Part I

Cases and Questions

1

Nurturing Nature

Marguerite Holloway

They used to stretch for hundreds of miles as a tawny sea of saw grass. Metallic-looking plankton added a golden patina to the shallow, slowly moving water that flowed between hammocks of tall grasses and stands of white-barked, high-kneed cypress trees. Even now, at half their original size, the Everglades appear to stretch forever—gilded, green, punctuated by the white of an ibis or a pink roseate spoonbill. Nothing could seem more natural.

Yet the most important aspect of this unique ecosystem is anything but natural. Four great gates at the northern end of Everglades National Park and fourteen hundred miles of canals and levees determine the quantity of water that can enter the area. Sugarcane plantations and vegetable farms to the north and east use fertilizers and pesticides that determine the quality of that same water. Demands for agriculture, urban living, and flood control have made the Everglades too wet in the wet season, too dry in the dry season, too rich in nutrient phosphorus, and therefore too close to extinction.

Because control has undone the Everglades, it seems appropriate that chaos be their salvation. Biologists and engineers will try to recreate some of the irregularity of nature by, among other things, delivering water on an erratic schedule, putting uncontrolled, meandering curves into a straight canal, and fostering botanic biodiversity rather than biomonotony. Thus, the formerly watery wilderness will be the locus of the largest and most expensive attempt at ecological restoration yet undertaken.

The fact that restoration is being attempted on such a grand scale is testament to the growing status and popularity of ecological restoration, a young field that already carries a heavy burden. Environmentalists, government officials, and business managers increasingly perceive restoration as a way to undo

Marguerite Holloway, "Nurturing Nature," *Scientific American* (April 1994). Reprinted by permission of *Scientific American*.

ecological damage and to compensate for development. The practice encompasses such diverse efforts as removing nonindigenous plants, reintroducing endangered fauna, transforming canals that replaced rivers back into rivers, and donning scuba gear to plant sea grass on the ocean floor. Converts have swelled the ranks of the Society for Ecological Restoration to twenty-two hundred; when it was established in 1989 the group had a mere three hundred members. A peer-reviewed journal, *Restoration Ecology*, was launched in 1993.

Despite its newfound prominence, restoration remains controversial because it has raised profound and unresolved questions. The idea of restoration seems disarmingly simple at first, but the goals are elusive. If, for instance, scientists want to return an environment to its "natural" state, they need a full understanding of what that is, how the particular ecology is constantly changing, and how human beings fit into it. No one has, or is likely to have, such insight. Given, then, that an exact reconstitution is not possible, should researchers—and society—be content with achieving a semblance? Should a restored system be self-sustaining, or should it be managed? Given such uncertainties, how is one to judge success?

These fundamental complexities are further complicated by political strategy and public policy. Some biologists believe the promise of restoration fuels destruction. They argue that such pledges encourage thoughtless development and exploitation: If people believe nature can be rebuilt, there is no harm in losing more of it. Other researchers see restoration as the only possible way society can respond to an already irreversibly impaired environment.

The Everglades will serve as the testing ground and battlefield where business leaders, government officials, biologists, and the rest of the population address these questions on a vast scale. "The issue is so prominent, no one can afford not to have their name on it," comments Thomas V. Armentano, acting director of research at Everglades National Park. "If it works, it will be unprecedented."

JUST ADD WATER

The starting point for restoration in southern Florida is water. As many conservationists working on the matter joke, the solution to the Everglades' problem is perceived as a *Field of Dreams* theme: If you water it, they will come. This sea-monkey, just-add-water approach derives from the hydrologic history of the region. Efforts at restoration began in the 1980s, when it became evident that the Everglades were drying up. Only one-fifth of the water that used to reach the ecosystem at the turn of the century was getting there, often at the wrong times. Only 5 percent of the wading birds that used to nest in the wetlands were still doing so.

Development, which began in the early 1900s as areas were drained for farming in the peat-rich soil, has been, and continues to be, rapid and intense. Southern Florida has one of the fastest-growing populations in the country;

domestic water consumption is also high at an average of 123 gallons per person per day. (The national average is 108 gallons per person per day.) The remaining two million acres of the Everglades are contained in the park, Big Cypress National Preserve, the Arthur R. Marshall Loxahatchee National Wildlife Refuge, and several water conservation areas. Each site abuts residences or farms.

Most of the chaos that has been introduced into the ecosystem so far has been political, not scientific. In the years since the ecological threats became widely known, nearly every agency and special-interest group has been on one side or another of at least one lawsuit to promote or stall restoration. The largest case was brought in 1988 by the federal government against the state for failing to protect the water supply. Although the parties reached an agreement in 1991, sugar growers opposed it. A new compromise fell through in December 1993. (Ironically, because sugar is federally subsidized at between $1.4 billion and $3 billion a year, it appears that the federal government has paid many of the court costs against itself.)

Despite the haggling about who will pay and the unresolved, baroque questions about which agency will control what, several restoration projects are under way. The South Florida Water Management District. which regulates water use in the watershed and oversees the water conservation areas, has constructed a thirty-seven-hundred-acre wetland to remove nutrients from agricultural water.

This runoff currently drains southeast into the wildlife refuge, where erect stands of cattails along the northern border attest to the influx of phosphorus. Although scientists debate the source of the mineral at some sites, the nutrient clearly fosters the growth of cattails. Cattails, in turn, replace saw grass and other indigenous plants, reducing floral diversity and habitat for waterfowl. The constructed marsh will turn cattails to advantage, using them to remove 75 percent of the phosphorus from incoming water.

The Everglades Nutrient Removal Project, as the marsh is called, constitutes the largest cleansing wetlands created in the United States. Cattails and other plants used in the project are commonly employed in smaller-scale managed wetlands to purify water. Although conflicts in the approval process have held up the release of water, it is intended to serve as a demonstration. Similar facilities, covering a total of forty thousand acres, are also being planned to cleanse storm water.

Cleanup is not cheap. The cost of these efforts could reach $465 million or more, and it is this figure that makes many of the large sugar companies and farmers balk: Under the most recent proposal, they would have been responsible for a total of between $232 million and $322 million over the next two decades. In January, however, Flo-Sun, Inc., reached an independent settlement and agreed to finance part of the cleanup. Given that many farms may not be around in several decades, the position of the holdouts makes some sense. Because growers keep the soil drier than it would normally be, the peat is being oxidized and blown away at the rate of anywhere between one and three centimeters a year. Within a lifetime, many farmers may reach the limestone bed rock of southern Florida—at which point sod restoration may become the new focus of the region.

Scientists disagree on the relative importance of removing nutrients from the water or just getting the water back into the Everglades. Water formerly traveled over the area in a sheet that was sometimes as many as sixty miles wide and as much as a foot deep. Now it is ushered through a labyrinthine network of canals, pumping stations, locks, and gates. Because the region's hydrology is so disturbed and there are so many demands for water, efforts to fix flow seem even more daunting than those designed to remove pollutants. Despite all the attention directed at the Everglades, the park only just recently received increased amounts of water. Armentano says the strategy is not working: The added water, which is coming into a slough from a canal to the east, is seeping right back out again.

Regional agencies have devised several long-term plans to address the hydrologic problems. Modelers at the South Florida Water Management District are writing computer programs to reconstruct how water traveled before the region was crosshatched by canals and levees. Once finished, this so-called natural system model will be superimposed on an existing model of how water currently flows. Researchers are also working to predict how hydrologic changes will affect vegetation.

Using these tools, experts hope ultimately to devise a politically acceptable and environmentally sound way to divide water in southern Florida, explains Jayantha T. B. Obeysekera, an engineer for the district. Such answers will not be available for a while. Models inevitably reveal the many gaps in data that have to be filled in by fieldwork. Furthermore, the graphic results must be viewed for what they are and with the same careful scrutiny that all the conflicting climatic change models garner. "It is like Disney World: It looks natural, but you go outside, and you realize it is not," Obeysekera cautions.

While modelers are trying to anticipate how the system could be manipulated, field engineers and biologists have been examining the feasibility of restoring the Kissimmee River. The Kissimmee was formerly a 103-mile-long rambling river that flowed south into Lake Okeechobee, which, in turn, sloshed into the Everglades. Together the river and the lake were responsible for the unique hydrology of the region. Like many rivers, the Kissimmee was unruly, inundating the wetlands adjacent to it, overflowing the lake after heavy rains, flooding farms, damaging property. So, between 1962 and 1972, the Army Corps of Engineers straightened it out. The Kissimmee is now a subdued, fifty-six-mile canal called C-38.

Public opinion, however, proved less amenable to control. The army had only just completed its work when several groups, including the Fish and Wildlife Service and the Audubon Society—which had opposed the alignment in the first place—called for restoration. The conservationists, public and private, won their case, and the South Florida Water Management District was required to determine the feasibility of putting the curves back into the

Kissimmee and water back onto its floodplains. The resulting study, as well as others, revealed that the loss of thirty thousand acres of wetlands on either side of the river had diminished bird and fish habitat and had degraded water quality.

Between 1984 and 1989 the South Florida Water Management District conducted a demonstration project on twelve miles of the river to determine if restoration was indeed possible. "It would be the purest restoration project that I am aware of because it would eliminate any of man's interference in this area," yells Louis A. Toth, who directed the project. He and several colleagues are hovering above the project site in a helicopter, recording changes in vegetation that have taken place since they finished monitoring the project several years ago. A line of oaks a mile or so inland sketches the upper limit of the floodplain. The researchers see the succession they expected: In some sites, switchgrass is giving way to wax myrtle; willows are replacing woody species.

Toth is careful to emphasize that the project has not restored the floodplain—rather it shows that there is ecological benefit in trying to restore. As a pair of sandhill cranes dash through a marsh trying to escape the downdraft of the helicopter, Toth remarks that there was a 1,000 percent increase in the number of wading birds after reflooding: "It indicates that the species will return if there is further restoration." He also explains that it took nearly twenty years to develop a definitive goal for the project—a span that exceeds the lifetime of most restoration efforts and most political administrations.

The full-scale project will bring back 26,500 acres of wetlands. To obviate demands for flood control, the district will also have to purchase farms. In total, restoration of the Kissimmee will cost at least $372 million. "It is the new environmental pork barrel," comments Daniel E. Willard of Indiana University. "It will cost one hundred times as much to put the curves in as it did to take them out."

EXORCISTS OF EXOTICS

The last big piece of the restoration work in southern Florida has not received as much press as have pollutants and hydrology. Nevertheless, that element—the removal of nonindigenous plants, sometimes referred to as exotics—has become a pressing concern. According to a recent report by the Office of Technology Assessment, more than two thousand plant species that came from somewhere else thrive in the United States today. Fifteen of them have caused over a half a billion dollars' worth of damage since 1906. But even committed restorationists are divided on the necessity of destroying them. Some feel any growth in a disturbed area is better than nothing. "In some places, we have phragmites, which are hated by everyone," Willard says, describing a marsh plant that can grow rife in areas outside its natural habitat. "But black night herons nest in phragmites. Is it a failure if we have them there?"

The exorcists of the exotics counter that native ecosystems and biodiversity cannot truly be restored as long as foreign species are present. "I am very anti–exotic species, even when they are not causing a problem," says Peter White, director of the North Carolina Botanical Garden. "They are the most irreversible of all human effects: We can clean the air, we can clean the water, we can restore wetlands, but exotic species are difficult to get rid of."

In the Everglades the most unwanted aliens are a Brazilian pepper plant and melaleuca, an Australian tree imported to help drain marshes. Both tend to grow in very dense stands, as do cattails, driving out other plants and reducing wildlife habitat. Keeping melaleuca controlled in the Everglades requires vigilance. Thick forests of the trees can be seen running along the canal bordering the eastern boundary; inside the saw-grass fields, hundreds of white corpses of the poisoned trees reveal the scope of the seek-and-destroy mission. In addition, two insect pests are being imported from Australia to control the pines.

At a site called the hole-in-the-doughnut, an even more dramatic campaign is being waged against the Brazilian pepper. Situated in the middle of the park, the hole-in-the-doughnut was farmed until the 1970s. It is now the location of the park's hurricane-decimated research center. The soil the farmers had broken up and tilled for so many years proved to be ideal for the pepper plant. So park biologist Robert F. Doren, who started the Exotic Pest Plant Council ten years ago, decided to remove the topsoil the farmers had worked. Doren found that the pepper plants did not return to areas from which the soil had been stripped. But what will take their place remains unclear—the results of the succession experiment will become evident only in the next few decades. In that time, $44 million will be invested in clearing one hundred acres of topsoil each year for fifteen or twenty years, at a cost of $16,500 an acre, while the hole-in-the-doughnut is rehabilitated. "One of the questions is, What do you actually get?" Armentano says.

Whether it is used by scientists to play gardener and weed out exotics or to play God and part the waters, information about the effects of restoration is in great demand in southern Florida—and elsewhere. Knowledge is inadequate in all areas of science, including the interaction between hurricanes, fire, and nutrient recycling in the Everglades, the characteristics of the soil and its microbial communities, and the effects of sea-level rise on the ecosystem. In addition, basic components of the hydrology are not understood. What is the role of changed water patterns and drainage on bird nesting and feeding habits? Has reducing the flow of fresh water through the Everglades caused the demise of Florida Bay?

But because there is little precedent for restoration of this magnitude, many scientists are advocating a one-day-at-a-time approach. Such a strategy would allow experts to experiment and revise plans if a particular line of attack did not seem to be working. "We have to take an adaptive approach. We are not going to have the degree of predictability that we want," explains Steven M. Davis of the South Florida Water Management District, an editor of the book *Everglades: The Ecosystem and Its Restoration*. Davis thinks this concept is difficult for some researchers to accept. Many want to set targets for certain species: Restoration is working if, say, the anhinga population increases by x percent. "We may have the illusion of control," he notes. "But no matter what we do, we are not going to put the Everglades back to the way they were. There are going to be surprises."

Indeed, many biologists argue that the flexible approach Davis champions should be the key element of restoration. Its absence is one of the biggest flaws in efforts to compensate for economic development, says Charles A. Simenstad of the University of Washington. Simenstad has done extensive work on the restoration of rivers and fish habitats in the Pacific Northwest. He found that when the failure of some aspect of a plan becomes apparent there is often little chance to correct the mistake. An inappropriate goal, dear to the agency granting the permit, is often the source of constraint.

To make matters worse, many of these compensatory efforts do not yield information, because they are not framed in the context of experimentation and are not monitored. In an attempt to make projects more sound and more adaptive, Simenstad is encouraging multistage plans: try a few approaches, wait a few years, see which works best, and then follow it.

Even though Simenstad, Davis, and many other restorationists are trying to escape what may be a restricting emphasis on precise end points, this focus has arisen precisely because so many restoration projects have not had clearly defined goals. The adaptive strategy may make very good sense in places where engineers or scientists have a reasonable expectation that they can improve the functioning of an ecosystem. In those cases, perhaps rehabilitation is a better word: There is still a clear sense of what the original environment was, and getting back to it seems a somewhat reasonable feat. But a look at many past restoration projects suggests that such rehabilitation is not always possible, particularly where an entire ecosystem is being created. Furthermore, when the incentive for restoration is to compensate for development rather than to redeem an ecosystem, the lack of clearly defined goals for a project can conceal technical failure—or let a developer off the hook.

Joy B. Zedler of the Pacific Estuarine Research Laboratory at San Diego State University has conducted one of the most thorough dissections of one such restoration attempt. Since 1989 she has monitored a salt marsh that was built to mitigate the construction of a highway. The project was designed as a habitat for the endangered light-footed clapper rail. Ten years of salt-marsh building later, the rails still have not arrived. "I don't think we are ever going to get functional equivalency for the marsh," Zedler says.

Zedler also determined that for want of a bee, a marsh can be jeopardized. Some plants at the site were not setting enough seed, because pollinators were rare. The insects were not crossing the highway or making their way through urban areas to reach the wetland. "There are millions of pieces in an ecosystem, and we have looked only at a tiny fragment of them," Zedler cautions. "It is not as easy to restore these systems as developers would have us think. When you are trying to improve conditions, I think you can do a lot, but you can never get back what we lost."

This conclusion fits into a national pattern of restoration failures. Mary E. Kentula, director of the Environmental Protection Agency's Wetlands Research Program, and Jon A. Kusler, director of the Association of State Wetland Managers, edited a 1990 report on the status of the science of wetlands restoration. As Kentula notes, they determined that "the efficacy of restoration and creation methods remains uncertain. The technology is unproved for many types of wetlands, and the quality of completed projects is inconsistent."

Kentula also conducted a study of 150 young restoration projects in Oregon. She found that most of the new wetlands were very wet indeed. They were in fact about 90 percent open water. The natural sites they were meant to substitute were only 20 to 22 percent water; the rest was vegetation and wildlife habitat. The reason is that creating ponds is easier and cheaper than ensuring all the species that should be there are there, Kentula explains. But "wetlands are where we have the most experience in restoration, and we see the same mistakes being made over and over again." According to Kentula and Kusler, one of the hardest features of a project to get right is its hydrology.

Correct hydrology is precisely what Zedler ultimately found to be the most crucial missing element in the San Diego marsh. Zedler's observations have led her to be very outspoken about the dangers of mitigation—a position that has earned her the epithet "Joyless Zedler" among some of her colleagues. Zedler confines most of her concern to southern California. This region has lost more than 75 percent of its coastal wetlands—leaving only 31,700 acres of estuarine habitat, of which 18,600 are open water. Ninety-four animal and 187 plant species are endangered or threatened in the state. "California shows that if losses continue, you eventually get to a point where they cannot rebound if there is a catastrophic event," Zedler says. "Species have to come back from somewhere, and there is not enough habitat left so that they can recover."

Zedler and others believe science may not yet be up to the task of ecosystem duplication. The field is so young that it is lacking the quality control that it needs, states John Cairns Jr., distinguished professor at the Virginia Polytechnic Institute and State University. Cairns chaired the committee that produced a 1992 National Research Council report on restoring aquatic ecosystems. Restoration needs "the kind of control in which ludicrous statements and publications are immediately pounced on and eliminated," he says. "The reason the new journal was founded was because of all the aggravation people in the field go through dealing with reviewers who do not know the existing literature, small as it is."

Other ecologists think these conclusions are unwarranted. They believe the shortcomings of many restoration projects are often perfectly explainable for several reasons. Regulations are one of the culprits. "For those projects that clearly failed, I would take the perspective that it is an agency's failure," argues Dennis M. King of the Center for Environmental and Estuarine Studies at the University of Maryland.

King makes a strong case. The surge in contemporary restoration activity was set in motion by changes in federal wetlands legislation in the 1980s.

Before then, restoration in the United States had been largely nostalgic, such as the creation of a prairie because this symbol of the American landscape had disappeared, or practical, such as the prevention of erosion in a pit mine. Ten years or so ago mitigation was introduced. It is the process of last resort: compensating for development by creating, restoring, or rehabilitating an ecosystem if destruction was unavoidable. If, for instance, a company wanted to build a mall on a marsh, it was unlikely to get a permit to do so from the Army Corps of Engineers unless it made a marsh elsewhere.

A MALL FOR A MUD PUDDLE

In 1981 President Ronald Reagan's Task Force on Regulatory Relief pushed the Army Corps of Engineers to speed up the approval process. According to a 1990 study by William L. Kruczynski, then at the Environmental Protection Agency (EPA), the new rules limited the power of the EPA, the Fish and Wildlife Service, and the National Marine Fisheries Service to review permits. The three agencies, charged with commenting on the environmental impact of development, increasingly recommended mitigation because it was clear that they could not influence the army's judgments.

But there were no mechanisms in place to monitor compliance. "The regulations had not been enforcing quality control," King explains. "And the market has been for low-cost permits, not high-quality restoration." One of King's favorite examples is a developer who chose a site on which to construct a wetland after receiving his permit to build a shopping center. He hit granite one foot below the surface at the site of the proposed marsh. Rather than go back through the permit process, the contractor blasted the granite and built a mud puddle that King says has no ecological value. The cost of the "restoration" was $1.5 million an acre.

With the right amount of money and follow-up, King says, anything is possible. "You see all those statistics on failure rates, and you talk to all the scientists and scratch below the surface and ask them why they failed, and they always know," he argues. "It is not a failure of science. The institutions are not holding the scientists' feet to the fire."

Mark S. Fonseca, a research ecologist at the National Marine Fisheries Service, agrees. He has been working on the restoration of sea-grass beds on the eastern seaboard for more than a decade. "The technical ability is there," Fonseca says. "It is more a problem of the scale of the losses." Fonseca explains that to be successful, restoration has to take place within the context of the preservation or rehabilitation of an entire ecosystem. He notes that he can restore an entire bay, even replant the entire seafloor with sea grass, but if the water column is not cleaned up and pollution persists, the grass will die all over again.

The importance of the Everglades plan derives from the fact that this vast wetlands provides such a context. The region is one focus of the attention of the National Biological Survey (NBS), a new agency established within the

Department of the Interior to inventory all animal and plants as well as to study and identify areas at risk. The NBS will attempt to consider entire ecosystems rather than individual species, such as the northern spotted owl.

Because every gallon of water that flows through the Everglades is tracked by the South Florida Water Management District or the Army Corps of Engineers, the bureaucratic structure needed to monitor the region as a whole appears to be already in place. "Kusler and Kentula were looking at much smaller systems," Davis says. "You can set up end points when you have smaller areas. You have captive ecosystems: They are so highly managed they are like circuses. But the Everglades are huge. They will be less predictable in their responses."

The NBS approach, which embodies the prevailing ethic of sustainable development, resembles the perspective from which landscape architects and some western Europeans have traditionally viewed restoration. "They are used to looking at much larger systems than most ecologists are," Cairns says. "Most ecologists in the American and British mold try to find places where humans are not part of the system. The Europeans assumed that humans are always in the landscape. They are not running off to the Galápagos to find some untouched ecosystem."

Achieving that kind of perspective at the level of the evolving science is also crucial. At the moment, the field appears to be missing the very quality that ecologists are demanding from restoration projects: integration. The discipline is by its nature broadly based: Good restoration includes information on soil, microbes, botany, hydrology, and population ecology, to name a few aspects of any ecosystem. But specialists rarely come together because of what Cairns describes as tribal language and an intellectual electric fence. At meetings, some scientists "want to talk about the number of bugs they had after using a certain fertilizer. It is almost like gardeners talking to each other," King laments. "The perspective has got to widen."

It is also clear that a degree of snobbishness exists on the part of people dealing with landscape-based projects toward those working on fragments of ecosystems. But doing one without taking the other into consideration may be useless, as the death of the pines in southern Florida attests. Barren pines, some with dead needles swinging from nearly naked branches, protrude from plush undergrowth on a 3.5-acre plot in Miami. Until Hurricane Andrew ripped through in 1992, this fragment was one of the last remnants of a coastal forest that covered southern Florida decades ago. Every tree on the site is now dead, as are most of the small pine forests in the region—only an 11,000-acre stand in the park remains.

No one knows what happened to the pines. Was it the force of the hurricane? Had the size of the forests made them vulnerable? Had municipal changes in water flow diminished the amount of sap the trees usually produced to push insect pests out of boreholes? "Everyone is watching the park, waiting to see what happens there," says George D. Gann-Matzen, president of Eco-Horizons, a restoration firm, as he gazes at the dead trees. He was hired to remove an exotic Asian vine that had been smothering the pines, camouflaging them as great green druids, and to manage the tiny woods as if it were still wild, when the hurricane struck. Absent trees, Gann-Matzen is unsure whether to burn or plant seedlings.

Gann-Matzen's restoration and management problems appear isolated. But without this forest fragment in downtown Miami, the pines in Everglades National Park, just to the south of the city, could be in jeopardy. Ten of some twenty-six species of birds that inhabited the park's forest have not been seen in the past several years, or longer. And biologists speculate that the disappearance of the last few woods destroyed an arboreal corridor that these birds traveled southward along, down into the park.

So few large tracts of untouched land are left that restoration must work in tandem with preservation. Areas of conservation are needed to ensure that species can survive, particularly as the human population explodes and the pressures that regions such as southern Florida experience increase. There seems to be tacit agreement that most of nature is hardly natural anymore—the orchestration of water in the Everglades is but one example. Ultimately, the state of the science does not matter to the majority of restorationists. Their attitude is just do it, do something.

REFERENCES

Berger, John J., ed. *Environmental Restoration: Science and Strategies for Restoring the Earth*. Washington, D.C.: Island Press, 1990.

Douglas, Marjory Stoneman. *The Everglades: River of Grass*. Sarasota, Fla.: Pineapple Press, 1988.

Kusler, Jon A., and Mary E. Kentula. *Wetland Creation and Restoration: The Status of Science*. Washington, D.C.: Island Press, 1990.

McPhee, John. *The Control of Nature*. New York: Farrar, Straus & Giroux, 1989.

National Research Council. *Restoration of Ecosystems: Science, Technology, and Public Policy*. Washington, D.C.: National Academy Press, 1992.

2

Salmon Support

Stephanie Mills

Water flows downhill and salmon swim upstream. Half a century ago in the Mattole River watershed, water made its way down thousands of nameless rills, then scores of creeks, to become the Mattole River and to wind its sixty-two miles to the Pacific. Before the time when nine-tenths of the watershed was logged, the water's movement was governed just enough by the forest of Douglas fir and tan oak and myriad plants of the understory that there was an equilibrium in the Mattole's tributary streams and riverbed. There were shaded creeks, clean spawning gravels, deep pools, and a cool estuary whose brushy banks harbored an abundance of insect life, all of these conditions being necessary to good salmon habitat. So the Mattole, like virtually all the rivers pouring into the Pacific, from Hokkaido to Monterey Bay, supported a good population of wild salmonids—native races of king and silver salmon, and steelhead trout. Descriptions of Pacific Northwest salmon runs beggar the imagination with their abundance, like the tales of flights of passenger pigeons numbering in the hundreds of millions or of bison herds blanketing mile upon mile of the plains.

"Stories have been handed down to us," wrote Janet Morrison, chairwoman of the Mattole Restoration Council, "of streams teeming with salmon, spooking horses at crossings, and of men with pitchforks standing on shore and pitching the salmon into wagons."[1] The situation is different today. In 1991 so few king salmon returned to the river that no salmon eggs could be harvested for the Mattole Watershed Salmon Support Group's hatch-box project. (The hatch boxes, where salmon fry can be reared, are a crucial part of a holistic effort to keep the river's native salmon run from extinction.)[2] In 1992 there were a few adult spawners. Their race may yet be facing the fate of the passenger pigeon.

Whenever we try to pick something out of the universe, said John Muir, we find it hitched to everything else. Some years ago, when these Mattolian back-to-the-landers, or "New Settlers," took it upon themselves, for reasons both mythopoetic and practical, to foster the resurgence of the Mattole's native race of king salmon, they learned they had to follow the salmon's existential logic right up into the root hairs of the watershed's upland forest. A precious remnant of once-great diversity, the Mattole king salmon are among the few scores of wild populations remaining of the thousands of races that had enlivened the tributaries of the North Pacific.

To the uninitiated a salmon is just a salmon: lox, maybe. To the aficionado, the five species of Pacific salmon spawning in North America—king, silver, red, humpbacked, and dog—have distinct identities and seasons and flavors, all arising from their home streams. Like characters in Russian novels, their names vary from situation to situation, and from phase to phase. Those same five species also are known as chinook, coho, sockeye, pink, and chum salmon. From hatching through maturity they are called alevin, then fry, then parr, then smolt, and finally adults—spawners. All that language bespeaks the character and complexity of these anadromous fish which run back to the river from the ocean to mate and bind together the land and the sea in the course of their existence.

The salmon was to the first peoples of the Pacific Northwest what the bison was to the peoples of the prairies. Salmon were a staple of existence, but no mere meat. Among the Indians who caught them, a ceremonial relationship to the salmon was virtually universal. They were regarded as conscious, immortal beings. Throughout the region, the taking of the first salmon was a ritual act, with prescribed formulas of address: "I am glad I caught you. You will bring many salmon into the river. Rich people and poor people will be happy. And you will bring it about that on the land there will be everything growing that there is to eat. . . ."[3]

Taboos dictated which persons might partake of the first salmon, and how the offal was to be disposed of, especially the heart—that there should be no mutilation of it by scavengers. The purpose of these courtesies was to show respect to the salmon and to ensure its return from the sea and thus the people's well-being throughout the year. The salmon were addressed by many different names: "Chief Spring Salmon," "Quartz Nose," "Two Gills on Back," "Lightning Following One Another," and "Three Jumps."[4]

It is not so difficult to understand why these totem fish (and of them, the king is the biggest, and the mightiest traveler) enjoyed such great respect. Their lifeway is a heroic evolutionary saga of wild Nature and place. The great silver bodies hurtling headlong up rushing torrents to mate; the careful excavation, in her natal stream's gravels, by the spawning female making her redd, or nest; the arching, simultaneous expression, by female and male, of eggs and milt into the redd's pockets; and the wasting and death of the spawned-out fish whose corpses feast the bears and bald eagles streamside—it all is nothing short of Wagnerian.

Unlike Atlantic salmon and steelhead trout, Pacific salmon species mate once only and then die. They hatch and grow to a degree of maturity upstream from the sea. The length of time they spend in the freshwater pools and riffles of their origin varies by species. At some point, though, a change in the endocrine system creates an absolute need for salt, and the young salmon, now called smolt, commit themselves to the trip downstream to the ocean.

There, again depending on the species, they spend one to five years eating, trying not to be eaten, and growing from six inches to a yard or more long and accumulating from six to sixty pounds of rich flesh. Their movements in the Pacific are presumed to be great northwesterly gyres. The distance they venture off the continental shelf is a matter for speculation. As the salmon approach sexual maturity their bodies prompt the return to the home stream. By means largely olfactory and perhaps geomagnetic, they navigate the cloud-locked Pacific, enter rivers as vast and contaminated as the Columbia, Sacramento, and Willamette, and, where the way is not barred by a dam, return to a home stream, one watercourse among thousands, to reproduce.

This inexorable longing for and loyalty to a natal spawning stream that can call across a thousand miles of stormy sea means that the various races of salmon that return to all these rivers and creeks have over time—a long time—become genetically distinct. Of the thousands of native races of Pacific salmon, a few hundred remain. The American Fisheries Society has declared 124 races of Pacific salmon to be in some degree of danger of extinction. Among these is the Mattole king, which is at "high risk" of perishing.

Epic traits of the Pacific salmon's life cycle—the glinting infancy in streams and maturation at sea, the dramatic return, full-grown, to the same spawning grounds they hatched in—are also what make the salmon almost a self-catching fish. It's an obvious trick to spread a net or weir across the stream and haul them in. Because the various salmon runs occur at about the same time each year and because the fish arrive en masse, an entrepreneur can just about catch himself an entire generation of fish. After all the spawners are taken over several consecutive years (five years being old for a salmon and about the longest time a stream's cohort of fish might be at sea), that stream's race is extinct. This practice of trapping a stream's whole run annihilated numerous races of salmon before the turn of the nineteenth century, when it was outlawed. It comes under the general heading of "overfishing," which by other means continues to this day. Now the netting is done offshore. High seas driftnets—miles-long webs hovering in the open ocean, indiscriminately capturing all manner of marine life that comes their way before being hauled aboard factory ships—are being eyed as a culprit in the radical decimation of the salmon, and a great many other marine creatures as well.

The development of the American West has meant the deconstruction of the salmon's world. Dam building, in this century, especially the construction of high dams, decimated salmon runs throughout Idaho, Oregon, Washington, and northern California by flooding river valleys and drowning their spawning streams or simply by rendering the streams inaccessible. Fish ladders were supposed to enable spawning salmon to continue upstream past these great concrete obstacles, but they have not been very useful. Most grotesque is the mangling of salmon that are sucked into the turbines of power dams. During the California gold rush, hydraulic mining swept whole landscapes worth of sediment into stream channels, destroying fish habitat by clogging the gravels that harbor eggs, alevin, and fry, and leaving behind a lunar landscape. In many once-forested places, among them the Mattole, converting forests to pastures, clear-cutting and the road building that goes with it (as well as with every new homestead), and poorly managed grazing all have degraded lands upslope and salmon habitat downstream. Thus it develops that if you want to restore the fish you have to heal a whole watershed: vegetation, erosion, social fragmenta-tion—the works. For the better part of this century, the palliative response to the widespread destruction of salmon spawning grounds has been to stock rivers and creeks with generic, hatchery-bred salmon fingerlings. In his essay "Salmon of the Heart," writer Tom Jay says fishermen refer to these hatchery products as "rag." He himself calls them "homeless seagoing spam."[5]

In order to get next to some of these charismatic fish, albeit the spam ver-sion, I drove twenty miles from my home over to the seventeen-year-old Platte River Anadromous State Fish Hatchery, largest in Michigan, and a source of some of the millions of Pacific salmon fingerlings that are planted in rivers throughout the state. In the mid-1960s the salmon fishery was created to use the exotic, carnivorous salmon to check the plagues of alien fish species in Lake Michigan, particularly alewives. Later the sporting possibilities of salmon fishing were grasped, and the outdoor recreation dollars fishing licenses bring to the states bordering the lake argue for its continuation. Whatever their provenance, salmon are big and exciting to catch. (They're also fatty enough that scientist James Ludwig mordantly refers to them as a clever means of cap-turing the toxic fat-soluble polychlorinated biphenyls [PCBs] that contaminate Lake Michigan's waters. People should be very cautious about eating Great Lakes fish, he allowed. "Anyone who wants to reproduce had better be damn careful," was the way he put it.[6]) Despite their occult toxicity, these coho salmon provide angling pleasure to fishermen and women to whom the idea of native species is no big thing (and who, given the upheavals of the aquatic fauna in the Great Lakes, would be flat out of luck if it were).

The hatchery was an Orwellian dystopia for fish—a big concrete industrial site, with elaborate hydraulics and pneumatic feeding systems and a fancy Italian-made salmon egg sorter. In the hatchery, things are tilted toward indus-trial efficiency; toward a high yield of a reasonable facsimile. The adaptations of hatchery fish are in the direction of tolerating crowding. They are bred for fast growth on pelletized food, and then for being adaptable to the live foods they'll find after stocking so that they will get bigger yet. They are virtually domesticated, deracinated, infantilized, denatured (the analogy with humans in mass society is uncomfortably clear). The worker who gave me the tour, though, really seemed to have some respect for the ethos of the salmon, an understanding of the forces that had shaped its character, and a knowledge of the conditions that these still-remarkable fish need after they are pumped out of the trucks that transport them to the streams where they are planted. From there they will enter the lake and start traveling for a few years south to the shores of Indiana, then west to Wisconsin, and finally back across Lake Michigan to their foster streams, dead-heading sixty miles east in three days.

Ever since the sea lamprey snuck into the lower Great Lakes through the Welland Canal ("The lampreys came in right after the lakes had been connected by the St. Lawrence Seaway to the Atlantic," comments David Simpson, a Mattole salmon supporter who grew up fishing on Lake Superior. "What a great parable of the subjugation of an enormous, complex ecosystem to the brutishly simplistic requirements of World Trade."), the Great Lakes' ecosystems have been like a fishbowl belonging to some kid who can't quite get the combination right. The sea lamprey, whose parasitism of the native lake trout eliminated the Great Lakes' top carnivore, have wrought havoc but are not the sole culprit in the disequilibrium. As with the Mattole, environmental degradation from logging played a part in extirpating the original lake trout populations. (Introduced lake trout are beginning to establish themselves now, however.) Overfishing was another factor that early in this century upset existing predator-prey relationships, and resulted in situations conducive to booms of alien fish like smelt and alewives. By the 1960s they were using front-end loaders to clear beaches in Chicago of alewives. These several aquatic extravaganzas have taken place over the last half-century or so, and have sent fisheries managers scurrying in attempts to arrive at a functioning species mix that will serve human and rough biological purposes, if not restore the ecosystem. Thus the hatchery system, whose primary purpose is to supply a predator to Lake Michigan's crazy, mixed-up aquatic fauna.

In contrast to the clony ignobility of hatchery fish, wild salmon embodies fealty to a particular watershed, serves to define that living place, and, inseparable from it, is shaped by it in turn, much as a red blood cell is part of a larger being, interdependent with millions of other cells and kinds of cells, constituent particles of limbs and systems. The analogy, of course, doesn't carry all the way, but the sense of the watershed as an organism with its own juices, organs, members, and health does suggest how to begin to convey a feeling of the singular identity of a life-place, and how a group of twentieth-century reinhabitors, one by one, might come to love their watershed and its most charismatic species; how they might find their lives bound up with its. In the Mattole, the prime value of the salmon is that they're wild and indigenous. The Mattole Restoration Council (MRC) respects the venerable wisdom of the fish's coevolution with the watershed, and in its restoration work the council's members strive for a high degree of fidelity to nature.

If the Mattole Restoration Council, "an organization based on watershed priorities to serve the interests of the various factions of the human community engaging in recovery,"[7] and the Mattole Watershed Salmon Support Group (MWSSG) didn't exist, bioregionalists would have had to invent them. These groups perfectly embody the reinhabitory concept of "becoming native again to place." I had been hearing stories about the MRC's work for a decade, years before people began talking about ecological or environmental restoration. The stories suggested a sensitive and strenuous remarriage of humans and entire ecosystems, a way of living-in-place that aims at redressing some of humanity's juvenile errors of land exploitation, and possibly a way of seeding a new culture out of those amends. Salmon support and watershed restoration as practiced here constitute a long-haul intention of working not merely in historic but in geologic terms.

When it began in the 1970s, the Mattole Watershed Salmon Support Group, which was a founding member of the Mattole Restoration Council, just wanted to enhance the reproductive success of the king salmon. First they made hatch boxes, simple nurseries where eggs taken from and fertilized by wild salmon trapped in the river could be incubated. In the clean filtered water flowing through the silt-free gravels in the hatch boxes and rearing pond the fry could grow, enjoying regular meals and an absence of predators, and then be released into their parent creeks.

"To enter the river and attempt to bring this strong creature out of its own medium alive and uninjured is an opportunity to experience a momentary parity between human and salmon, mediated by slippery rocks and swift currents. Vivid experiences between species can put a crack in the resilient veneer of the perception of human dominance over other creatures," writes Freeman House. "Information then begins to flow in both directions and we gain the ability to learn: from the salmon, from the landscape itself."[8]

What the salmon supporters learned was that erosion problems upstream had radically changed the seaward reaches of the Mattole River, widening its bed, stripping away shade-providing vegetation on the banks, and filling in the pools where the salmon, which love cool depths, could come to oceangoing maturity. Torrents carried away nesting gravels from creeks and silt washed down and smothered what was left. So to save the world—of the salmon, at least—the Mattole Restoration Council members began over the years to plant thousands of Douglas fir seedlings and native grasses on cut-over lands upstream; they got into "restoration geology," sometimes using heavy equipment to put structure in streams which had been rendered too simple; they sweated to armor eroding creek banks with head-sized cobbles; to transplant bits of native vegetation that could stabilize sections of eroded stream banks; to plant willow cuttings and alder seedlings alongside the river to shade the water and foster the insect life on which the fish depend.

In the Mattole Watershed Salmon Support Group's scrapbooks are snapshots of ten-gallon buckets of salmon fingerlings being packed on horseback down to streams where they'd be released. (Horseback. In places where hatchery-bred salmon are stocked in streams, the fish are transported in specially cooled and oxygenated tank trucks.) In other years, with the help of the young people in the California Conservation Corps (about whom they had much good to say), they've winched boulders around in the creeks. Most everything they do is hard work: moving rocks and breaking up log jams in these deep, steep creek bottoms. The people laboring to help the Mattole heal are so tough and committed, they're acting as though restoration was their only choice. The erosion problems they're contending with in their life-place are formidable, but no more so than their will to remedy them.

For instance, there's a landslide in the Mattole watershed that is a mile long from ridgetop to river, and a half-mile wide, 375 acres of slump or debris flow that cut loose during an intense spring storm in 1983, the rains slicing down and ruthlessly cutting into exposed, unsteady soils. That monumental Honeydew Slide didn't happen overnight, but was a consequence of many different instances of inattention, from clear-cutting to careless road building to a failure to deal with small erosion problems before they grew large. More amazing than the magnitude of the slide was the reaction of the doughty Mattole Watershed Salmon Support Group, recently formed and ready to rush to the rescue in the event that the Honeydew Slide blocked the river and cut off some of the best and most heavily visited salmon spawning and rearing areas in the whole river basin.

According to the Mattole Restoration Council's newsletter, the MWSSG "had formed emergency contingency plans with the [California] Department of Fish and Game to actually move the winter run of salmon upstream if they got stranded below the debris dam. . . . The group was ready to lug the piscine paramours upstream in buckets if necessary." (These extraordinary services proved not to be necessary to the salmon, for, the newsletter continues, "with the rains, the river rose and cut a new channel south of the debris dam, providing fish passage.")[9]

Work in the Mattole is about preserving the spark of diversity that its native races of salmon possess. It's endangered species preservation work in the real world, a place where much of the land is privately owned and can't be acquired to create refuges that may be managed at the pleasure of biologists. Members of the MRC and other such groups in the valley see restoration as an indigenous occupation, like tree cutting, farming, fishing, or ranching, a livelihood peculiar to the locale, one that might continue for generations. This is a different sensibility than hiring restoration done, or imposing a restoration design from without. It is what can be done when it's too late to conserve. The object is not to reinstate some static idyll, but to restore the dynamic of evolution in an ecosystem and to include the human in that dynamic. "It is comforting to envision what benefits might result from watershed-wide restoration work (and wise maintenance of public lands)," wrote Freeman House and David Simpson in 1983 in the inaugural issue of the *Mattole Restoration Newsletter*.

If you can, imagine starting from the ridgetops and headwaters . . . planting trees and grasses for slope stability and future timber . . . as roads get built and maintained so that erosion slows rather than increases. The river gradually flushes itself and stabilizes. Vegetation gins to seal it in a cooling shade again. Work in salmon enhancement begins to pay in visible increases in spawning runs. Slit washed off the upland slopes begins to deposit itself permanently in rich alluvial flats. Grains and vegetables grow in soil that was formerly swept to sea.

A generation from now, our children reap a harvest not only of fine timber, abundant fish, productive grasslands and rich and varied plant and animal communities—but also a tradition which will assure the same harvest for their children.[10]

Perhaps it's possible to place restoration activities along a spectrum, and also to propose some differences between restoration and reinhabitation—not an absolute distinction, certainly, but one as real as that between restoration and rehabilitation. Restoration implies an exacting fidelity to the original; rehabilitation may resort to the use of similar species in order to create a rough, but functional, semblance of the original ecosystem. Restoration presently, and in many cases necessarily, requires that access to the recovering ecosystem be restricted, rather like the burn ward in the hospital. Reinhabitation implies living in, and having an economic stake in, the place restored, not in the touristic sense of being able to charge admission at the park gate, but in being able to derive what House calls "natural provision" from one's own ground: free (but not easy) protein, fuel, and building material. Restoration does not pose alternatives to the socioeconomic system that is necessitating restoration; reinhabitation does. It means the articulation of a culture of place, and for this to come about in our time means the restoration of human community in a society whose members have wildly differing and fiercely held ideas about what land is for.

⌐⇔   ⌐⇔   ⌐⇔

Jan Morrison, the chairwoman of the Mattole Restoration Council, is a land restorationist. In her last year as a communications student at Humboldt State University, Morrison headed for the hills of Redwood National Park to be part of a small business engaging in erosion control projects. It got her outside, planting trees, and provided good camaraderie.

When we met in the Mattole Valley in the late winter of 1990, Morrison spoke about her love of restoration work, the pleasure she took in making willow wattles, bundles of willow withes to be placed In horizontal trenches with tipped-back berms cut along eroding slopes. The bundles themselves help to check the erosion, and the willows sprout, as is their wont. Morrison described hillsides that had been mended in this way as looking as though they'd been embroidered with the lines of emerging green shoots.

"I learned just by doing," she says. When the erosion control group broke up in the early 1980s, she moved to the Mattole to work for a nonprofit group that had a contract from the Fish and Game Department to do a watershed-wide survey of all streams where the salmon were spawning. "They'll pay you for walking in the streams," is what she'd heard. The prospect appealed to her. The work led to her increasing involvement with the Mattole Watershed Salmon Support Group. "Salmon people were always in the river," she said. Immersion in the watershed—field study of the fish, careful evaluation of the usefulness of different erosion-control techniques, creation of a home-grown information base—is essential in this reinhabitory work. A lot of what the salmon enhancers do is mapping. It's an essential requirement for providing a local reality check on the generalizations issuing from the larger agencies that concern themselves with land and water use. The indigenes see no evil there, simply a lack of fine-grained knowledge. Morrison spoke about all the microclimates within the watershed, for instance, and said that residents of various drainages keep their own long-term rain-gauge records of the Mattole's monsoon precipitation. If information that detailed were incorporated into the regional weather maps, Morrison said, "it would tend to make for untidy isobars." It is this very untidiness that ordains the real-life conditions in which land healing may go on. There's a lot of passionate knowledge of place among the salmon people. They're willing to do the long-range and baseline studies in order to be able to make effective comparisons and to account for what they are doing. Not only do they have to wade out into rushing streams when the salmon are running, and wrestle with these great beasts, but they also have to keep accurate records of how the many different elements of the watershed restoration are working.

"Just trying to save a watershed is a lot of work," says Morrison. It's not only physical work, although there's plenty of that. It also involves jurisdictional diplomacy. The California Department of Fish and Game basically governs the fate of the salmon and it must sanction rearing activities. Even picking up fallen logs across a stream requires a permit. The Mattole Restoration Council was formed to provide an aegis for the numerous groups throughout the watershed, for the neighborhood associations and creek councils that wished to play a part in the salmon work but lacked suitable status. More important, commented Freeman House, "decisions that affected a whole bunch of things were being made by too few people. The MRC was formed to provide a broader inhabitory decision-making base."

Several months after my visit to the valley, talking on the telephone with Janet Morrison, who had just come from one of the grueling community meetings that seem to be a staple for salmon enhancers, I began to get a sense of the tact necessary to these counterculturalists, and to admire their rhetorical self-restraint. Another thing that became clear is the considerable degree of organization in the Mattole. For about three thousand people in a three-hundred-square-mile territory, there are surprisingly many groups and associations, all with real claims to a place at the council fire. It makes Chicago's Cook County seem almost random.

In the Mattole, there are really two separate cultures, the rancher and the homesteader, living side by side, Morrison observed. As in so many rural areas, there's a historical as well as an economic stratification of residents. The first peoples were extirpated without a trace. Then came ranchers, then loggers, then hippies, then dope-growing hippies, then second-home developers, then all manner of paranoias and antagonisms to rive the community through and through. There are lots of different stripes of love-hate relationships with the government, be it federal, state, or local.

A recent government action precipitated the beginning of a watershed-wide process for developing consensus on land-use practices in the valley, and ventilated some of these passions in the process. A State Fish and Game Department memorandum on degradation of salmon habitat had urged zero net sedimentation. This meant that loggers must either prevent sedimentation as a result of their activity or mitigate erosion damage elsewhere. The memorandum became the charge of the State Department of Forestry.

To help acquaint valley residents with the new policies, the Department of Forestry called together a public roundtable. At its second meeting, said Morrison, a good turnout degenerated into a shouting match among the ranchers and homesteaders and environmentalists. "Let's go outside and settle this" was heard. Somehow an almost-too-good-to-be-true outbreak of peace occurred. Someone suggested an agenda and another meeting. A rancher and an environmentalist stood up hand in hand. It began to resemble an encounter group, she said. Dan Weaver, a retired Navy pilot skilled in conflict resolution, offered to facilitate subsequent meetings. Attendance increased from a dozen to thirty, forty, then fifty people. Increasingly, they are working together.

꒡   ꒡   ꒡

Salmon enhancers are trying hard to develop a cultural sense of place across the generations. Every year or so the valley kids paint a mural in their school. The first time they chose salmon in creeks as their theme, said Morrison, they portrayed the salmon going every which way. Other details of the mural's natural history were inaccurate as well. Over the years since the hatch-box program has been working, the valley's schoolchildren have been invited to participate in this release, trekking down to the streamside and dumping big buckets of little fishes into the flowing waters of their destiny. It's part of reinstating salmon in local culture. After the children had participated in the salmon release, they painted another mural. In this one the salmon were all headed in the right direction—upstream.

꒡   ꒡   ꒡

The Mattole River watershed lies about two hundred miles north of San Francisco, then a winding highway west maybe fifty miles through a redwood forest and over a couple of ridges of the California coast range. The place is plenty remote and, by me, primitive. Dank with coastal fogs, the Mattole is said to be the wettest place in California. The country is so steep and broken that it claws the water right out of the air and pours it down a million little creeks. The landscape is overshadowed by ridge and range, cloaked in olive-drab prairie, Douglas fir, and patches of brush. In the late winter of 1990, I made a visit to the Mattole. There I enjoyed the hospitality of Freeman House and Nina Blasenheim, who have lived and worked in the valley since 1980.

House and Blasenheim and their daughter Laurel live very simply, and this, too, is part of reinhabitation: a voluntary simplicity that asks as little of the earth as possible. They heat with wood, which appears to be plentiful. California's climate is forgiving enough that they can get away without insulating their great big barn of a house. They have an open-fronted outhouse and an outdoor shower. Their household utilizes propane, which seems really to be the salvation of the rural homesteader, running their gas refrigerator, gas lamps, gas cooking stove, and a demand gas water heater—they do have all the hot water they can afford the gas to heat. A photovoltaic cell provides the juice for additional, electric illumination. They communicate by radiotelephone. Nina Blasenheim was vegetable gardening that late winter I visited, and the chickens were roaming free through the rows.

In addition to being one of the wettest places in California, the Mattole is also probably one of the most seismic places on the planet. Three tectonic plates come together in a place offshore called the Triple Junction. They had a pretty fierce earthquake shortly before my visit in 1990. Blasenheim talked about what it felt like to be at the epicenter rather than somewhere out where the wavelength is longer. She said it was as though the earth had been playing crack-the-whip. In the course of a day's visiting, touring, and hiking, House showed me some evidence of earthquake damage in the valley: a little fissure in the earth up near the road; slides, lots of slides—saturated soil slumping down; root bundles coming undone and dragging big clumps of dirt and trees down to block the dirt roads clinging to the hillsides. It's turbulent earth. In April 1992, three earthquakes, ranging from 6.0 to 7.1 on the Richter scale, struck the Mattole, causing a meter's worth of orogeny in half a minute, changing the intertidal zone as well as life onshore, where about half the homes in the area were rendered uninhabitable. Yet this violent unpredictability of the terrain is regarded, and respected, as an aspect of character, rather like the short temper of a generous friend.

On our tour of sites where salmon restoration work was under way, House took me to a spot on Mill Creek. The MWSSG had done some work there to restore silver salmon habitat. It was surely one of the loveliest places I've ever seen, a poetically beautiful dell. It's California-steep—not quite a ravine, overhung by gnarled, leggy tan oaks, these brilliant with lime-green mosses. The canyon is lush with ferns of several kinds, sword ferns most notably, whose root systems House credits with holding up the creek banks. There is also another small plant lovable for its rhizomes. A transplanted clump of *Whipplea modesta*, said House, can help shore up an eroding patch. Fallen Douglas firs catch and bridge the glen, musical with the sound of falling water.

Logging-caused erosion had scoured the creek and steepened its fall such that its waters flowed too swiftly to drop out, or recruit, the right-sized nesting gravel for salmon redds. The structural solution was to winch a windfall log down from the cut-over north bank. The restorers hauled in a portable saw mill to quarter the log lengthwise. They placed the four pieces across the stream to catch sediment and slow it down, so the right-sized gravel fell out. The water falling over the straight edges of the dams scours out congenial pools beneath. House speculated that the six or eight people who worked one hundred hours on Mill Creek may have created habitat for perhaps thirty mating pairs of silver salmon. It seems to them a fair exchange.

Part of the value of restoration work is firsthand teaching of the laboriousness of an entropy battle—how very difficult it is to put a casually torn-apart ecosystem back together! Perhaps if more people could feel the ache of that difficulty in their bones, there'd be less tearing apart. That enchanting spot in Mill Creek was human-altered. First, for the worse, by the frenzied logging upstream. But the healing—changing the stream gradient with those Douglas fir dams—left evidence of human activity, too. Other evidence is the rock armoring, dry masonry artfully shoring up the creek banks. Now there are deliberate patterns, straight lines, right angles, planes of logs over which cascade linear waterfalls. The very music and echo of the creek has been tuned by human activity. Mill Creek is not a wilderness preserve; human artifice there aims, ultimately, at restoring natural provision so that the salmon will feed the people and the forest will supply immediate human needs again. It's bold thinking that humans could participate in the ecosystem in a benevolent, post-modern way. The "conscious gamble" of those working in the Mattole is that the interaction with a watershed could engender a moral check on the human impulse to control and determine, expand and exploit. It was in talking with House that I first began, however reluctantly, to question that convenient fictive absolute of a hands-off policy toward wild Nature. To breach that concept means relinquishing *Homo sapiens'* guilt and self-loathing over what human involvement in the landscape has resulted in thus far. And that passage will be sustained by maturing beyond remorse into reinhabitation.

Now the headwaters, says David Simpson, a founder of the Mattole Watershed Salmon Support Group, is in healing mode. As of 1993, California's drought was declared to be over, which means that one of the multiple threats to the salmon's survival is in abeyance. The threat this natural disturbance posed to the radically diminished salmon population might have been less mortal if other conditions also hadn't been so adverse. The problem is that by now we've driven so many species into tiny little corners that the natural disturbances that once developed their evolutionary strength of character no longer play a salutary role, but can instead threaten their survival.

A reinhabitory organizer might envy the Mattole people, and others in their region, the charisma of the species that is the *genius loci* of their restoration work. One might envy it all—sharing a common purpose in a beautiful surround—save for the heartbreak of facing the possibility of the creature's demise. Getting your destiny bound up with that of another species is a supremely risky form of romance. Yet the constancy of the Mattole restorers has been like that of their totem species; their endeavor to date has always been against the current of land abuse, and their loyalty to place as obdurate as the king salmon's. After a decade of dealing with the minute particulars of rearing salmon fry, of creating plunge pools and elegantly shoring up creek banks and planting thousands upon thousands of trees, the fate of the salmon remains in doubt. Yet the seed bank is there. The possibility is alive, incarnate in the sea, and a small nucleus of community is still bound together and informed by it.

Basically, said Simpson, in a phone conversation in autumn of 1992, "The question of salmon survival is by no means decided, but we're doing everything we can.

"Politically it's a whole lot better; ecologically it's unresolved," he said, and spoke of an increasing coalescence in the views of the people living there—ranchers, homesteaders, even small timber companies with whom they are enjoying "new levels of cooperation"—as a result of their meeting together as members of the watershed alliance. "All we're doing is trying to hang on to what we've got while the habitat restores itself. It's the only hope of recovery."

Simpson likened the nature of this change to the long, slow turn of a battleship. "All of human history is directed toward ecological disrepair," he said, so it is hardly surprising, although no more bearable, that redirecting our lifeway toward healing should be starting when it's nearly too late. "An enormous price has been paid for this consciousness."[11]

NOTES

1. Janet Morrison, "Landforms, Waterflow, and People of the Mattole Watershed," in *Elements of Recovery: An Inventory of Upslope Sources of Sedimentation in the Mattole River Watershed with Rehabilitation Prescriptions and Additional Information for Erosion Control Prioritization* (Petrolia, Calif.: Mattole Restoration Council, 1989), p. 12.

2. The Mattole Watershed Salmon Support Group "keeps its feet wet," says Morrison. The group attends to the fish in the river, while the restoration council concerns itself more with the Mattole watershed's uplands.

3. Quoted by Freeman House "working from A. L. Kroeber: *Indians of California*" in House's magesterial essay, "Totem Salmon," in *Home! A Bioregional Reader*, ed. Van Andruss, Christopher Plant, Judith Plant, et al. (Philadelphia: New Society Publishers, 1990), p. 69.

4. Erna Gunther, *A Further Analysis of the First Salmon Ceremony* (Seattle: University of Washington Press, 1928), p. 140.

5. Tom Jay, "Salmon of the Heart," in *Working the Woods, Working the Sea: Dalmo' Ma VI, An Anthology of Northwest Writings*, ed. Finn Wilcox and Jeremiah Gorsline (Port Townshend, Wash.: Empty Bowl, 1986), p. 102. "Salmon of the Heart" follows on House's "Totem Salmon," and is a remarkable essay, weaving together poems, myths, etymologies, and fish stories to limn the psyche of the salmon.

6. James Ludwig, "Wildlife Bioeffects and Toxic Chemicals in Great Lakes Fish:

Implications for Human Health Effects," presentation at the Backyard Eco Conference, Lake Station, Mich., 1991; for a responsible (but nonetheless alarming)general scientific survey of the condition of the Great Lakes ecosystem, Theodora E. Colborn, Alex Davidson, Sharon N. Green, et al., ed., *Great Lakes: Great Legacy?* (Ottawa, Ont.: Institute for Research on Public Policy, 1990), is peerless and makes reference to Ludwig's research as well as that of legions of other scientists.

7. Freeman House, personal communication, October 1993.

8. Freeman House, "To Learn the Things We Need to Know: Engaging the Particulars of the Planet's Recovery," in *Helping Nature Heal: An Introduction to Environmental Restoration,* ed. Richard Nilsen (Berkeley: Ten Speed Press/Whole Earth Catalog, 1991), p. 48.

9. "The Honeydew Slide Chronicles," *Mattole Restoration Newsletter* 5 (winter 1986): 3.

10. Freeman House and David Simpson, *Mattole Restoration Newsletter* 1 (1983): 4.

11. David Simpson, personal communication, November 1992.

REFERENCES

Colborn, Theodora, Alex Davison, Sharon N. Green, R. A. Hodge, C. Ian Jackson, and Richard A. Liroff. *Great Lakes: Great Legacy?* Ottawa, Ont.: Institute for Research on Public Policy, 1990.

Gunther, Erna. *A Further Analysis of the First Salmon Ceremony.* Seattle: University of Washington Press, 1990.

"Honeydew Slide Chronicles, The." *Mattole Restoration Newsletter* 5 (winter 1986).

House, Freeman. "Totem Salmon." In *Home! A Bioregional Reader,* edited by Van Andruss, Christopher Plant, Judith Plant, and Eleanor Wright. Philadelphia: New Society Publishers, 1990.

———. "To Learn the Things We Need to Know: Engaging the Particulars of the Planet's Recovery." In *Helping Nature Heal: An Introduction to Environmental Restoration,* edited by Richard Nilsen. Berkeley: Ten Speed Press/Whole Earth Catalog, 1991.

House, Freeman, and David Simpson. *Mattole Restoration Newsletter* 1 (1983).

Jay, Tom. "Salmon of the Heart." In *Working the Woods, Working the Sea: Dalmo' Ma VI, An Anthology of Northwest Writings,* edited by Finn Wilcox and Jeremiah Gorsline. Port Townshend, Wash.: Empty Bowl, 1986.

Ludwig, James. "Wildlife Bioeffects and Toxic Chemicals in Great Lakes Fish: Implications for Human Health Effects." Presentation at the Backyard Eco Conference, Lake Station, Mich., 1991.

Morrison, Janet. "Landforms, Waterflow, and People of the Mattole Watershed." In *Elements of Recovery: An Inventory of Upslope Sources of Sedimentation in the Mattole River Watershed with Rehabilitation Prescriptions and Additional Information for Erosion Control Prioritization.* Petrolia, Calif.: Mattole Restoration Council, 1989.

3

Alternative Models of Ecosystem Restoration

Susan Power Bratton

E arly attempts at restoring natural ecosystems used either an agricultural model or a climax community model emphasizing productivity and stability as indicators of ecosystem health. Current restoration efforts use community structure or ecosystem function models favoring biotic diversity, presence of rare or unique elements, system complexity, and maintenance of natural processes. Naturalness as demonstrated by the self-maintenance of the system or by the reestablishment of elements present before disturbance are also common indicators of health. Present models are inadequate to deal with seminatural landscapes and highly fragmented biotic communities, however, as well as those that have lost keystone species and those that cannot be completely restored. Our concepts of naturalness assume that health is a return to a previous state and do not consider the possibility of new permutations. Naturalness also precludes complex or repeated interactions with human managers. Examples of different philosophical approaches to restoration are provided, primarily, from projects in U.S. national parks.

ROOTS OF RESTORATION

Although humans have practiced ecosystem restoration ever since farmers recognized that allowing former fields to succeed to forest would restore fertility to the soil, the roots of the present practices of ecological restoration lie deep within the conservation and preservation movements of the nineteenth and early twentieth centuries. The two major thrusts of early restoration efforts

Susan Power Bratton, "Alternative Models of Ecosystem Restoration." © 1992 Island Press (Washington, D.C., and Covelo, California). Reprinted by permission from *Ecosystem Health*, ed. Robert Costanza, Brian Norton and Benjamin Haskell.

were regaining the "natural balance" lost by ecosystems disturbed by greedy, abusive Euro-Americans and returning badly degraded lands to a more productive state. The ability of lands and waters to produce either crops or other amenities, such as shellfish and deer, is probably one of the most venerable ways of assessing ecosystem health. Just as one wing of twentieth-century environmentalism has been dedicated to conservation—the wise use of natural resources—one of the major motives for environmental restoration has been to restore degraded lands to productivity. The bountiful harvest of softwoods, clover, or ducks then indicates the ecosystem is healthy. Economic value or lack of it is thus often an important indicator of health.

During the early decades of the twentieth century, ecologists began to emphasize and quantify processes of ecological change, particularly the process of succession. Plant ecologist Frederick Clements viewed natural succession as leading to a climax community, which, when established, was the stable and final biotic assemblage occupying a particular site. According to R. P. McIntosh, "The climax *association* was, barring external disturbance, a stable and self-reproducing collection of populations, which, in Clements' scheme, was the culmination of the developmental sequence, or seres, from which it came."[1] Climax theory implies that the final community in the successional sequence has the most biomass, the most complex nutrient cycles, the greatest productivity, and the greatest species diversity. If freed from major disturbance, it also is able to maintain itself indefinitely. To a great extent, early efforts at restoring forest, prairie, and wetland vegetation reflected the notion of the climax (and, perhaps covertly, nineteenth- and early-twentieth-century social ideals).

A typical early restoration effort is the Civilian Conservation Corps' planting of white pine (*Pinus strobus*) on former agricultural fields in the southern Appalachians. There was a recognition that the sites were no longer useful for agriculture but might be returned more quickly to a forested state if the early stages of succession were skipped. White pine is a valuable and relatively fast-growing timber species. It is found in old-growth forests in the region but can also occupy open sites. Starting a mixed hardwood forest would be far more difficult and no more economically productive. The sites might be maintained for years in white pine, via culling, harvest, and replanting, or allowed to revert to native cove and oak forest. When the plantings were done during the New Deal, there was little concern for stand diversity, long-term successional trends, or the state of the forest understory. The goals were soil recovery, timber production, and site stability. A dense stand of white pine will, in fact, inhibit reestablishment of many forest floor herb species that would naturally accompany deciduous forest succession on the same sites.

Some of the pine plantings were in what are now Great Smoky Mountains National Park and the Blue Ridge Parkway. There was no concept at the time of restoring the "natural" forest structure, other than by means of unmanipulated native plant succession. It is also notable that in the early days of the Great Smoky Mountains National Park the only mammal evaluated for restoration was the white-tailed deer, which had been reduced by overhunting to a small herd in an inaccessible valley called The Hurricane.[2] The timber wolf, eastern mountain lion, river otter, and fisher were not considered possible candidates for restoration until the 1970s and 1980s.[3]

A second, and even more telling, example of early restoration efforts was the project on Cape Hatteras National Seashore to establish an artificial dune line. The Outer Banks of North Carolina overwash frequently during hurricanes and northeasters. The natural dune and shoreline are not geographically stable and migrate relative to geophysical variables, such as changes in sea level and storm frequencies. Since successional theory suggests that stable dune lines lead to development of more stable plant communities behind them, land management agencies viewed establishment of a high and very stable fore dune as a way to prevent the sea from flooding roads and buildings. The State of North Carolina, the Civilian Conservation Corps, and the National Park Service collaborated in the construction of a high fore dune (sand on brush piles or fences) topped with a dense sward of nonnative American beach grass (*Ammophila brevigalata*). The unidirectional change of climax theory is ill applied to a barrier island system that is slowly moving landward, however. Although the beach grass did temporarily stabilize the dunes, the Atlantic is slowly encroaching on their bases. The shrub communities that have developed behind the dunes represent a type of vegetation usually found on higher ground, well outside the reaches of salt spray. They will almost certainly never reach the "stable" forested state because, sooner or later, an overwash event will kill them with salt and standing water.[4] Ironically, the shrub communities tend to block the view of both the dunes and the marshes, leaving the Outer Banks tourist driving through a tunnel of woody vegetation dependent on continuing human interference with coastal hydrology. The goal of advancing succession has failed to accommodate the dynamics of island ecosystems that support numerous disturbance-tolerant species.

NATURAL HARMONY

In contrast to the manipulative and productivity-oriented mode of ecosystem restoration, there were those who favored protection for native ecosystems and generally thought the best way to restore native biotic communities is to keep people and their activities out. This camp was also influenced by notions of natural ecosystem "balance" and the ideal of a natural climax community. John Muir, for example, saw loss of wildness or loss of system integrity as undesirable states. In *My First Summer in the Sierra*, Muir recognizes that sheep cause major changes in the flora of high-elevation meadows and laments that "almost every leaf that these hoofed locusts can reach within a radius of a mile or two from the camp has been devoured."[5] He notes that although the sheep cannot kill the trees, some of the seedlings are damaged—and if the herds become large enough, "the forests, too, may in time be destroyed." Muir cynically predicts, "Only the sky will then be safe, though hid from view by dust and smoke, incense of a bad sacrifice." The same themes appear in his petitions for the establishment of Yosemite National Park, where he complains of the lumber men and shepherds and suggests that upper-elevation watersheds as well as the areas surrounding the big tree groves be included in the park:

> For after the young, manageable trees have been cut, blasted and sawed, the woods are fired to clear the ground of limbs and refuse, and of course seedlings and saplings, and many of the unmanageable giants [trees] are destroyed, leaving little more than black charred monuments. These mill ravages, however, are small as yet compared with the comprehensive destruction caused by the "sheepmen." Incredible numbers of sheep are driven to mountain pastures every summer, and desolation follows them. Every garden within reach is trampled, the shrubs are stripped of leaves as if devoured by locusts, and the woods arc burned to improve pasturage. The entire belt of forests is thus swept by fire, from one end of the range to the other; and with the exception of the resinous *Pinus contorta*, the sequoia suffers the most of all. Steps are now being taken towards the creation of a national park about the Yosemite, and great is the need, not only for the sake of the adjacent forests, but for the valley itself.[6]

In his petition concerning the preservation of the Hetch Hetchy Valley along with the Yosemite Valley, Muir proposes "ax and plow, hogs and horses" as agents of disturbance in "Yosemite's gardens and groves" and states in conclusion: "And by far the greater part of this destruction of the fineness of wildness is of a kind that can claim no right relationship with that which necessarily follows use."[7] Muir's basic strategy for restoration was to get the people out or control their activities.

This concept of the value of naturalness came one step further and began to intrude on the notion of productivity in Aldo Leopold's work. Leopold is speaking against productivity as the best indicator of ecosystem health when he writes of wolf eradication accompanied by protection of deer:

> I have lived to see state after state extirpate its wolves. I have watched the face of many a wolfless mountain, and seen the south-facing slopes wrinkle with a maze of new deer trails. I have seen every edible bush and seedling browsed, first to anemic desuetude, and then to death. I have seen every edible tree defoliated to the height of a saddlehorn. Such a mountain looks as if someone had given God a new pruning shears and forbidden Him all other exercise. In the end the starved bones of the hoped-for deer herd, dead of its own too-much, bleach with the bones of the dead sage, or molder under the high-lined junipers.[8]

This description is not unlike Muir's description of sheep as armies of antienvironmental terrorists. Leopold, however, does not see the problem as solely humans and their livestock attacking nature. He also sees it as wild nature damaging wild nature when a critical element of the "land community" is extirpated. The goal of increasing the productivity of the wild, when taken to extreme, is little different than direct degradation by humans. Leopold, in fact, equates too many cows with too many deer:

> I now suspect that just as a deer herd lives in mortal fear of its wolves, so does the mountain live in mortal fear of its deer. And perhaps with better cause, for while a buck pulled down by wolves can be replaced in two or three years, a range pulled down by too many deer may fail replacement in as many decades.
> So also with cows. The cowman who cleans his range of wolves does not realize that he is taking over the wolf's job of trimming the herd to fit the range. He has not learned to think like a mountain. Hence we have dustbowls, and rivers washing the future into the sea.[9]

Leopold changed the temporal perspective and recognized the difference between short-term disturbances, such as predation on the deer herd, and long-term changes in community structure. Further, Leopold recognized that the absence of a single keystone species may entirely modify the way an ecosystem functions.

When Leopold developed his land ethic, he used the concept of the ecological community, which incorporates "soils, waters, plants, and animals," and declared that "conservation is a state of harmony between men and the land."[10] Leopold essentially established an ethic for management where humans need to consider both the value and function of all members or parts of an ecosystem. This model has been very influential in contemporary restoration, where productivity may play second fiddle to other values such as "naturalness" and recovery of biotic diversity. Leopold emphasized the presence of all the original parts of a system, not just the harvestable white pines and deer. Further, he valued the soil and water for their own sake, not merely as abiotic factors necessary to plant growth.

Leopold was directly involved in the establishment of the University of Wisconsin–Madison Arboretum, which began experimental restoration of native plant communities during the 1930s. "The time has come," Leopold argued, "for science to busy itself with the earth itself. The first step is to reconstruct a sample of what we had to begin with."[11] As with his efforts in wilderness preservation, Leopold was looking back at the frontier and trying to protect or replicate what had not yet been plowed under. The early restoration projects at the arboretum emphasized the vanishing prairies, and coincidentally, after the first efforts failed to produce a viable native grassland, arboretum scientists began experimental management utilizing fire as a necessary disturbance. The successful establishment of the Curtis Prairie proved that fire was part of the "natural balance" or "natural cycle" and further convinced ecologists that maintaining all the parts of the ecosystem was necessary to maintaining the whole.

CONTEMPORARY PERSPECTIVES

The contemporary restorationist, particularly someone who works with wet-lands, prairies, or other native ecosystems, is likely to hold "naturalness" as a major goal, in terms of both ecosystem composition and function. A restoration might be considered successful if all the species originally present on the site have returned, if it has high diversity or the original diversity of species, or if natural disturbance cycles (such as natural fire regimes) have been reestablished. Further, there is a current concern for the inclusion of rare or unique elements, so the understory orchids, forgotten in the white pine plantings of the 1930s, might today receive a fair amount of managerial time during a restoration effort. Worry over the potential extinction of thousands of species worldwide has placed an extra emphasis on endangered species, and in some cases restoration efforts may actually be dominated by "recovery plans" for endangered flora and fauna. In federal land management there has been a shift from managing for the most productive, consumable, or, in the case of the National Park Service, "dramatic" elements of the system toward managing for the most limited, unique, or fragile elements.

Behind this philosophical orientation is a strong concept of "natural balance" and the necessity of keeping all the parts of a system, even if they look insignificant to us. Walter Westman, in a paper discussing potential ecological criteria for evaluating the success of a restoration project, has observed: "A common implicit goal of ecological restoration is to restore a self-sustaining, homeostatic system whose component species have a long coevolutionary history."[12] One could thus define an ecosystem once "sick" but now restored to "health" as: self-replicating or self-sustaining; characterized by or developing toward homeostasis (perhaps undergoing repeated disturbance but returning to a similar state); having biotic components that are interrelated and occur in established associations.

A restoration project typical of contemporary philosophy is the major effort made to restore not just the forest cover, but the actual topography of the Redwoods National Park during the late 1970s and early 1980s. Logging in the giant redwood stands had more than removed trees; it had also modified hydrology and initiated slope erosion. As well as attempting to establish new vegetation cover as quickly as possible, the National Park Service utilized heavy earth-moving equipment to obliterate roadbeds and reestablish the predistur-bance contour of the slopes. The park incorporated sites on serpentine bedrock that are very liable to soil erosion and landslides. The restoration project gave high priority to these serpentine grasslands (which are also known for their endemic flora), reconstructed the slopes, and reestablished native species. The project recognized, first, that logging-initiated disruption of hydrological cycles might encourage floods and higher than normal water levels on the streams, which in turn might harm the remaining unlogged redwoods.[13] Fur-ther, the logging roads were potential sources of ongoing erosion and drainage problems, as well as being potential long-term scars in the landscape. Although the National Park Service did not (and could not) attempt to bring the redwood forest immediately back to its former glory, they made a major effort to return the substrate to its prelogging condition and thereby to encourage homeostasis. The Great Smoky Mountains National Park, in contrast, made no attempt, after the heavy logging of certain watersheds in the 1920s and 1930s, to remove the skidder trails or accelerate the return of the cove forests.

Another example of contemporary restoration philosophy is the trend toward reestablishing predators in national parks. Although some of the species concerned are endangered, many are not. Cumberland Island National Seashore, for example, is in the process of reestablishing a bobcat population. The bobcat is neither endangered nor rare in the region. The species occurred on the island historically and is one of several predators extirpated by Euro-American occupation of the site. The public appears to accept the concept of restoring bobcats "just because they belong there." Managers, however, are concerned about intensive browsing of vegetation by native deer and the proliferation of nonnative wild hogs and armadillos. Thus the bobcat is a means of not just putting a predator, but also "predation," back into the island ecosystem.[14] The return of the eastern mountain lion, the wolf, and the black bear remain more controversial and technically problematic.

John Cairns says that "restoration means recreating both the structural and functional attributes of a damaged ecosystem."[15] Westman, after noting that structure and function cannot always be restored simultaneously, suggests monitoring structural characteristics and functional characteristics to determine restoration "performance."[16] He proposes evaluating structure by comparing species composition (or some measure of species importance) with the original species composition or with "regional baseline levels"; he suggests measuring function by using probabilistic (Markov) models to determine the likelihood of transition from one state to the next and monitoring the resilience of the ecosystem. The latter is rather like stress testing in humans. If the system can recover easily from perturbations, shows little deviation from natural successional processes, and is well damped (does not vary greatly from the expected degree of oscillation), the system is healthy.

LIMITS ON NATURAL RESTORATION

In reviewing contemporary trends in restoration, two important values repeatedly appear. First, current restoration practice tends to look to the past. It attempts to replicate previous conditions or to preserve disappearing ecosystems. Second, it places a high value on naturalness and the establishment of biotic communities that can survive without further human care. Often naturalness is interpreted as "natural balance." In many circumstances, these values are perfectly appropriate and one can only applaud the University of Wisconsin for the work it has done in preserving and restoring native American grasslands. Yet these values are also limiting. They create a dichotomy not only between "natural" and "human" but also between "natural" and "new." Our mental models and ideals may actually be constraining the ways in which we use ecological restoration techniques to solve environmental problems. Our concept of ecosystem health emphasizes "natural" homeostasis and past ecosystem states.

Holding the "natural past" as the ideal ignores a number of limitations that commonly affect restoration projects. Although Westman notes that "defining the historical condition of a habitat frequently is possible only in general terms," many attempts at determining restoration performance are based on poorly known previous system states.[17] The use of predictive models, even probabilistic models, must either be based on an accurate knowledge of the structure and function of an ecosystem prior to the restoration effort (and prior to the disturbance that is prompting the restoration), or it must be based on a general analysis of the structure and function of the desired ecosystem type. In the field, one is not always lucky enough to know what an area was like before major anthropogenic disturbance. Further, species associations tend to be rather plastic. The fact that a specific orchid was present before the critical perturbation does not mean that the species would have remained at the site for the next fifty years if that perturbation had not occurred.

Not only is it difficult to know what an ecosystem was like, it is also hard to know where it is headed, particularly in light of global change. In the example from Cape Hatteras cited earlier, the islands had already been heavily grazed by livestock before the artificial dune line was constructed. Therefore, the pre-dune line and pre-park state of the systems was not "natural" and we do not know exactly what vegetation would have been present if the islands had not been grazed. If cattle and ponies extirpated a rare plant species, we have no record of it. If we wished to remove the dune line and restore the vegetation, we cannot assume the shorelines will be static. We do not know with any certainty whether global climate change will cause a change in storm frequency or an increase or decrease in precipitation.

Further, many areas slated for restoration are no longer integrated with surrounding ecosystems in terms of their original landscape context. The area to be restored may only be part of a once far more extensive marsh, or it may be one of several high alpine areas in a mountain chain. The restored area may now be isolated from similar systems. Elements may be missing, and they may be difficult to replace. Large Predators, with the exception of the alligator and the recently reintroduced bobcat, are gone from Cumberland Island National Seashore, for example. One could bring in a couple of wolves or a panther or two, but this will not establish a viable population if there are no breeding, wild populations of wolves or panthers on the mainland or on the other adjoining islands.

Past human activities may have modified the geophysical environment to such an extent that certain previous residents of the native biota can no longer survive on the site. Disturbance regimes may also have been altered. The construction of a dam, for instance, changes flood frequency and intensity, as well as patterns of silt deposition on the floodplain. The presence of roads in an area may increase the occurrence of anthropogenic fires along the rights of way, while preventing small lightning-ignited blazes from crossing the highways. Even without direct human support and encouragement, nonnative species may have invaded an area and may be difficult to suppress or completely eliminate.

We often assume that "natural climax" ecosystems will be the most resilient, but this may also be a matter of scale. A patch of kudzu (*Pueraria lobata*), the fast-growing vine that often takes over roadsides and abandoned fields in the southeastern United States, is very resilient when disturbed (it is extremely difficult to eradicate), and the species inhibits native plant succession and prevents trees from reoccupying the site. Kudzu rarely penetrates large continuous areas of mature deciduous forest, yet in a fragmented landscape kudzu jungles often become one of the most stable features. Resilience is desirable in a restored ecosystem, but "most resilient" may not in turn mean "natural balance."

Contemporary restoration efforts are beset by a variety of scale and boundary problems (even though landscape and ecosystem boundaries may be difficult to define). The concept of "naturalness" may itself be susceptible to changes of scale. As Bryan Norton and colleagues suggest, all systems are, in the end, dynamic, and maintaining a reasonable degree of system integrity at the large-scale level requires maintaining a reasonable degree of system integrity at the landscape or small-scale level.[18]

Restorationists themselves are fully aware of these difficulties and recognize that the restored ecosystem may be anything but static. Grant Cottam, in fact, describes the long-term changes documented by a series of vegetation surveys in the restored prairies at the University of Wisconsin Arboretum and notes:

> Two characteristics are important: the first is that a certain amount of shifting in the distribution of community types does occur during the 25 years between the first and last survey, as introduced species find their way to optimum sites; the second, however, is that there is also a great deal of shifting that cannot be accounted for in this way. In fact, the various communities do not have static borders, but appear to change location with every survey in an amoeba-like movement that seems to be a response to the short-term climatic events of the years immediately preceding the survey.[19]

Restorationists have also been accepting compromise with completely "natural" restorations. One of the best examples of this is the move toward native "lawns" and plantings around developments as part of the landscape architect's repertoire. Native prairie species have been established around office buildings and suburban homes. The more adventurous efforts even incorporate burning of the native grasses, rather than mowing, to suppress shrubs and unwanted nonnative species.

FUTURE RELATIONSHIPS

Despite the progress made by more imaginative restorationists, our "natural past" model of restoration and ecosystem health still limits how and where restoration techniques are applied. We desire either a "natural ecosystem" or one that is productive or intensively managed and have little concept of anything in between. This means we either demand a national park or a cornfield. It is notable that in Europe over the centuries, seminatural woodlands and meadows evolved that were both productive and rich in native flora and fauna. English woodlands dating back to the Middle Ages and perhaps even to Celtic times often retain a diverse flora of understory forbs.[20] Hay meadows cut and fertilized on traditional rotations are often species-rich, as are many managed heath communities. Ecological reality confirms that seminatural communities and those maintained by continuing human interaction can help to preserve biotic diversity and other "natural values," particularly where the landscape is already intensively managed for human ends.[21]

We must take a careful look at how we evaluate human manipulation of systems relative to their health. We tend to view no manipulation as good and manipulation optimizing productivity as good and states in the middle as undesirable. Most of us recognize that cultures with long histories of interaction with local ecosystems often live "in balance" with those ecosystems. Rather than interpreting this as a healthy human/nature relationship, however, we often portray these cultures as representing "natural men"—that is, humans who have remained part of nature. Such situations are thus easily absorbed by the "natural past" model of health. This may also lead to a misunderstanding of how non-Western cultures have interacted with the landscape, and we may assume these cultures have been less liable to change than has actually been the case. An obvious example is the impact of the Native American agriculturist on New World ecosystems. Just as in Europe, new farming techniques were developed, agricultural areas expanded, and populations increased. There was never a magic point where humans found a perfect "balance" with the surrounding vegetation and wildlife. Climate change, depletion of game populations, and other factors may, in fact, have stressed or displaced Native American cultures throughout their occupation of the two continents. This suggests several conclusions:

- The degree of human manipulation of a "healthy" ecosystem depends on the landscape context. We might continue to consider constant human intervention undesirable in a national park, while accepting a moderate level of manipulation in woodlots surrounded by farm fields. We have to evaluate the impact of human manipulation at all ecosystem scales to fully discern "beneficial" and "unbeneficial" human interactions.
- Homeostasis is an unrealistic goal and restoration efforts should assume some change in species composition and abiotic factors through time.

Again, restoration should be placed in its landscape context. The biological integrity of a single site cannot be determined by a rigid list of necessary components, yet a large number of extinctions within a region or biogeographic province indicates that landscape change is occurring more quickly than the native biota can accommodate the disturbances.

- In some cases, new combinations of assemblages of species may be acceptable, or species may occupy new habitats. Although there are certain locations and ecosystem types where this may not be desirable, there are others where this strategy may be the only option.
- We need to understand how systems change—and then establish pragmatic goals concerning acceptable levels of change.

Among the dilemmas of natural area management, there are numerous situations where a broader view of either acceptable system change or the acceptable degree of human interaction might be desirable. In the southern Appalachians, for example, endangered rock outcrop plants are being trampled by rock climbers and scramblers. Some species, such as the southern Appalachian mountain avens (*Geum radiatum*), which grow on wide ledges, have probably lost entire populations to human ignorance. As the mountain avens is found on widely scattered cliff faces and rocky peaks, each population may have some genetic value in maintaining the species as a whole. As part of a restoration effort at Craggy Pinnacles on the Blue Ridge Parkway, North Carolina, greenhouse-raised mountain avens plants, from local genetic stock, were reestablished on disturbed rock ledges. (This and the following examples are from personal field experience and managerial contacts.)

Since the mountain avens population at Craggy Pinnacles is very limited in size, the suggestion was made that some of the artificially germinated plants be placed on man-made road cuts below the natural cliff faces. This is not the original habitat for the avens, nor is it a "natural" habitat. The road-cut plants, however, could serve as "genetic backup" should something happen to the population on the Pinnacles. Further, the plants on the road cuts would have a high-elevation environment, while any plants "stored" at a botanical garden would grow up in milder temperatures.

After careful evaluation of the microhabitats on the natural cliffs and on the road cuts, the National Park Service successfully established mountain avens on ledges created by blasting. Ironically, this portion of the Craggies project remains controversial because the Park Service does not wish to write an environmental impact statement for an artificially established rare species population each time they need to do maintenance work on the road shoulders and tunnels.[22] The U.S. Fish and Wildlife Service has wavered on whether an impact statement will be necessary. Yet road cuts could provide additional habitat for several other high-elevation outcrop species that are presently threatened or endangered, while colorful flowering plants, like the mountain avens, would greatly improve the appearance of bare rock faces. Moreover, road cuts are reasonably free of technical climbers and scramblers.

Someone interested in rare species protection might object at this point that establishing new populations, even if one uses local genetic stock or stock that cannot interbreed with other "natural" populations, invites destruction of existing endangered species habitat. If a careful legal distinction is made between the naturally established populations and those that are anthropogenic, and the latter are carefully established and managed, these difficulties will be minimized. We also must ask ourselves about the consequences of managing the mountain avens site by site, rather than as a series of populations in the southern Appalachian landscape. There may be two or more relevant scales for approaching the preservation of not just the mountain avens as a species but the genetic diversity contained within the various mountain avens populations.[23]

A second example is that of manatees using Georgia paper plant effluents which provide warm water and act as artificial warm springs. The manatees' use of the sites is two-edged because the paper plants pose certain threats to the manatees as well as providing a haven from the cold. The plant effluents, of course, may contain traces of toxins. And if the manatees stay around the effluents during the winter, they run the risk of being frozen to death if the effluent stops running or there is a sudden drop in temperature. Although they risk hypothermia in Georgia, manatees sometimes experience food shortages in Florida and the Georgia marshes provide a steady, if hard to reach, supply of saltmarsh hay (*Spartina alterniflora*). If we wish to protect manatees, then we should either try to stop them from using the effluents, and order them back to Florida, or else make the effluents as safe as possible for the manatees. "Safe" or "healthy," in this case, means designing an effluent as ecologically similar as possible to a natural spring, with the additional concern that the site be protected from boat traffic. Recent proposals for management of the effluent at one Georgia mill include developing a deep basin for the manatees, continuing warm-water flow at all times (particularly at low tide, when manatees are less likely to be feeding away from the effluent), and preventing entry by boats. This, then, is a new habitat on an "old natural" design.

A third example is that of the bobcat restoration and similar efforts to reestablish species on islands or in reserves of limited areas. If we decide we always must have a population that meets genetic viability criteria for minimum population size, then many small areas cannot support larger vertebrate predators. Larry Harris and others have suggested that establishment of corridors will relieve this problem, but this is not always possible.[24] Our "natural past" model inhibits us from accepting the fact that humans may have to intervene occasionally and manage the gene pool—perhaps by arranging a few "accidental" introductions of new blood. Bobcats can swim from the mainland to Cumberland Island and vice versa, but present coastal development patterns undoubtedly slow the rate of this exchange. Some genetic management may ultimately be necessary to prevent inbreeding depression on an island that can probably support only twenty-five to forty bobcats in the long run. Maintaining genetic "health" in this case may require human intervention.

A fourth example is the many Piedmont and Appalachian forests that have probably lost part of their understory herb species due to repeated cutting and other disturbances. We do not usually think about restoring the wildflowers on these sites, especially if they continue to be utilized for timber or they surround human suburbs. Yet, especially in the latter case, the restoration of the missing flowering species would add greatly to the beauty and biotic diversity of the stands. Further, the stands may be isolated from each other, and native forest floor species may have difficulty dispersing among widely separated sites. When the forests have regrown and the soils have recovered their litter layer, the climatic conditions within the stand may again be favorable for the still absent forbs. In this case, we must recognize that the return of the canopy does not mean the return of all native biota, and that with fragmentation of the surrounding landscape matrix, some of the more slow-growing species may be slow to reinvade without human assistance.

Another case concerning habitat loss and fragmentation is the destruction of the small meanders and the oxbow wetlands on Abrams Creek in Cades Cove, in Great Smoky Mountains National Park. The Soil Conservation Service suggested channelizing the stream, which runs through a historic district, to reduce erosion. The channelization resulted in little erosion control and seriously disturbed rare plant habitat along the banks and in the floodplain. A small wet meadow remained near the end of the cove, and several species of state concern were collected from this locality. Traditionally this meadow had been mowed. In recent years, however, mowing has been abandoned (the area is too wet for modem tractors) and shrubs have begun to displace forbs and grasses. Although mowing is a human activity, one could not say it was "unhealthy" for the site for it helped to maintain a high diversity of early successional and floodplain species, some of which had lost habitat during the channelization.

A last example takes us back to the artificial dune line at Cape Hatteras. Recently, the National Park Service has been experimenting with fire to temporarily control the shrubs encroaching on the road margins and wetland edges. The resulting plant communities are not those that would be found after overwash, nor are they those encouraged by the high, beach-grass-covered dune. The philosophical question then becomes: When one cannot suddenly remove the dune, because roads and developments will be more frequently flooded, is the pyric community acceptable as a substitute for the overwash community? One might argue, on the one hand, that the system will never be truly healthy until the natural overwash processes have been restored. Disaster is always looming just around the corner when natural coastal processes are disrupted. But the human coastal communities have not yet coped with the dilemma, and fire represents an easily managed disturbance that suppresses shrubs and results in native plant associations.

CONCLUSION

Our "natural past" model for determining the success of a restoration effort limits the ways in which we apply restoration techniques. It would be better, considering the number of threats to native species, to stratify and maintain "naturalness" and "homeostasis" as goals for certain sites while accepting some degree of "seminaturalness" and "human relationship" for others. We should also decouple "productivity" as a criterion from "unnatural" and assume that "seminatural" sites can maintain high productivity and high biotic diversity if humans manage them properly. Our present views of naturalness often ignore problems of scale, as well as possibilities for ecosystem management or restoration that will help to compensate for changes at both large and small scales. Ecosystem restoration is a relatively new field, and its applications are continually expanding. Our attachment to the "natural past" model of restoration may be causing us to miss good opportunities and to respond insufficiently to the ecosystem change and habitat fragmentation that is presently occurring worldwide.

NOTES

1. R. P. McIntosh, *The Background of Ecology: Concept and Theory* (Cambridge: Cambridge University Press, 1985), p. 81.

2. Records in park files indicate the deer herd was very small when the park was established in the 1930s. There may have been deer in locations other than The Hurricane, but sightings were rare. The U.S. National Park Service considered importing deer from Pisgah National Forest, where there was a greater density of native white-tails, but did not go through with the plan.

3. The red wolf has recently been slated for reintroduction in the Great Smoky Mountains National Park, but I doubt it was ever very common in the southern Appalachians. The eastern mountain lion may not have been completely extirpated at the time the park was designated, but no major attempt was made to establish its population status in the southern Appalachians in the 1930s and 1940s.

4. R. Dolan, P. J. Godbey, and W. E. Odum, "Man's Impact on the Outer Banks of North Carolina," *American Scientist* 61 (1973): 152–62; P. M. Schroeder, R. Dolan, and B. P. Hayden, "Vegetation Changes Associated with Barrier-Dune Construction on the Outer Banks of North Carolina," *Environmental Management* 1, no. 2 (1976): 105–14.

5. J. Muir, *My First Summer in the Sierra* (Boston: Houghton Mifflin, 1911).

6. J. Muir, *The Proposed Yosemite National Park—Treasures & Features* (Olympic Valley, Calif.: Outbooks, 1970), p. 56.

7. Ibid., p. 97.

8. A. Leopold, *A Sand County Almanac and Sketches Here and There* (London: Oxford University Press, 1949), p. 130–31.

9. Ibid., p. 132.

10. Ibid., p. 204.

11. W. R. Jordan, M. E. Gilpin, and J. D. Aber, "Restoration Ecology: Ecological Restoration as a Technique for Research," in *Restoration Ecology: A Synthetic Approach to Ecological Research* (Cambridge: Cambridge University Press, 1987), p. 12.

12. W. Westman, "Ecological Restoration Projects: Measuring Their Performance," *Environmental Professional* 13, no. 3 (1991) : 207–15.

13. J. Agee, "'Issues and Impacts of Redwood National Park Expansion," *Environmental Management* 4, no. 5 (1980): 407–23.

14. R. J. Warren, "Reintroduction of Bobcats on Cumberland Island, Georgia: A Biopolitical Lesson," *Transactions of the North American Wildlife and Natural Resources Conference* 55 (1990).

15. J. Cairns, "The Status of Theoretical and Applied Restoration Ecology," *Environmental Professional* 13, no. 3 (1991): 186–94.

16. Westman, "Ecological Restoration Projects," p. 186.

17. Ibid., 204.

18. B. G. Norton, R. E. Ulanowicz, and B. D. Haskell, *Scale and Environmental Policy Goals, A Report to the EPA* (Washington, D.C.: EPA, 1991).

19. G. Cottam, "Community Dynamics on an Artificial Prairie," in *Restoration Ecology*, p. 263.

20. G. F. Peterken, *Woodland Conservation and Management* (London: Chapman & Hall, 1981).

21. For a critique of the separation of the natural and the human, see J. B. Callicott, "The Wilderness Idea Revisited: The Sustainable Development Alternative," *Environmental Professional* 13, no. 3 (1991): 235–47.

22. Information sources for these restoration examples include Bart Johnson who is conduction the mountain avens restoration; Barbara Zoodsma, who is studying the manatees in Cumberland Sound; Robert Warren, who is supervising the bobcat restoration; and Albert Mier, who is working on herbaceous species diversity in old growth forests.

23. For a theoretical discussion of resolving scalar/hierarchical problems, see Norton, Ulanowicz, and Haskell, *Scale and Environmental Policy Goals*. For a discussion of the restoration of entire wilderness areas, see R. F. Noss, "Wilderness Recovery: Thinking Big in Restoration Ecology," *Environmental Professional* 13 (1991): 225–34.

24. L. Harris, "'Landscape Linkages: The Dispersal Corridor Approach to Wildlife Conservation," *Transactions of the North American Wildlife and Natural Resources Conference* 53 (1988): 595–607; L. Harris and P. B. Gallagher, "New Initiatives for Wildlife Conservation: The Need for Movement Corridors," in *Preserving Communities and Corridors* (Washington, D.C.: Defenders of Wildlife, 1989).

REFERENCES

Agee, J. "Issues and Impacts of Redwood National Park Expansion." *Environmental Management* 4, no. 5 (1980).

Cairns, J. "The Status of Theoretical and Applied Restoration Ecology." *Environmental Professional* 13, no. 3 (1991).

Callicott, J. B. "The Wilderness Idea Revisited: The Sustainable Development Alternative." *Environmental Professional* 13, no. 3 (1991).

Cottam, G. "Community Dynamics on an Artificial Prairie." In *Restoration Ecology: A Synthetic Approach to Ecological Research*, edited by W. R. Jordan, M. E. Gilpin, and J. D. Aber. Cambridge: Cambridge University Press, 1987.

Dolan, R., P. J. Godbey, and W. E. Odum. "Man's Impact on the Outer Banks of North Carolina." *American Scientist* 61 (1973).

Harris, L. "Landscape Linkages: The Dispersal Corridor Approach to Wildlife Conservation." *Transactions of the North American Wildlife and Natural Resources Conference* 53 (1988).

Harris, L., and P. B. Gallagher. "New Initiatives for Wildlife Conservation: The Need for Movement Corridors." In *Preserving Communities and Corridors*. Washington, D.C.: Defenders of Wildlife, 1989.

Jordan, W. R., M. E. Gilpin, and J. D. Aber. "Restoration Ecology: Ecological Restoration as a Technique for Research." In *Restoration Ecology: A Synthetic Approach to Ecological Research*. Cambridge: Cambridge University Press, 1987.

Leopold, A. *A Sand County Almanac and Sketches Here and There*. London: Oxford University Press, 1949.

McIntosh, R. P. *The Background of Ecology: Concept and Theory*. Cambridge: Cambridge University Press, 1985.

Muir, J. *My First Summer in the Sierra*. Boston: Houghton Mifflin, 1911.

————. *The Proposed Yosemite National Park—Treasures & Features*. Olympic Valley, Calif.: Outbooks, 1970.

Norton, B. G., R. E. Ulanowicz, and B. D. Haskell. *Scale and Environmental Policy Goals, A Report to the EPA*. Washington, D.C.: EPA, 1991.

Noss, R. F. "Wilderness Recovery: Thinking Big in Restoration Ecology." *Environmental Professional* 13, no. 3 (1991).

Peterkin, G. F. *Woodland Conservation and Management*. London: Chapman & Hall, 1981.

Schroeder, P. M., R. Dolan, and B. P. Hayden. "Vegetation Changes Associated with Barrier-Dune Construction on the Outer Banks of North Carolina." *Environmental Management* 1, no. 2 (1976).

Warren, R. J. "Reintroduction of Bobcats on Cumberland Island, Georgia: A Biopolitical Lesson." *Transactions of the North American Wildlife and Natural Resources Conference* 55 (1990).

Westman, W. "Ecological Restoration Projects: Measuring Their Performance." *Environmental Professional* 13, no. 3 (1991).

Part II
Fakes or Artifacts?

4

Faking Nature

Robert Elliot

I

onsider the following case. There is a proposal to mine beach sands for
rutile. Large areas of dune are to be cleared of vegetation and the dunes
themselves destroyed. It is agreed, by all parties concerned, that the dune area
has value quite apart from a utilitarian one. It is agreed, in other words, that it
would be a bad thing considered in itself for the dune area to be dramatically
altered. Acknowledging this the mining company expresses its willingness,
indeed its desire, to restore the dune area to its original condition after the
minerals have been extracted.[1] The company goes on to argue that any loss of
value is merely temporary and that full value will in fact be restored. In other
words they are claiming that the destruction of what has value is compensated
for by the later creation (recreation) of something of equal value. I shall call
this "the restoration thesis."

In the actual world many such proposals are made, not because of shared
conservationist principles, but as a way of undermining the arguments of conservationists. Such proposals are in fact effective in defeating environmentalist
protest. They are also notoriously ineffective in putting right, or indeed even
seeming to put right, the particular wrong that has been done to the environment. The sandmining case is just one of a number of similar cases involving
such things as open-cut mining, clear-felling of forests, river diversion, and
highway construction. Across a range of such cases some concession is made
by way of acknowledging the value of pieces of landscape, rivers, forests and so
forth, and a suggestion is made that this value can be restored once the environmentally disruptive process has been completed.

Imagine, contrary to fact, that restoration projects are largely successful,

Reprinted from Robert Elliot, "Faking Nature," *Inquiry* 25 (1982): 81–93.

that the environment is brought back to its original condition, and that even a close inspection will fail to reveal that the area has been mined, clear-felled, or whatever. If this is so then there is temptation to think that one particular environmentalist objection is defeated. The issue is by no means merely academic. I have already claimed that restoration promises do in fact carry weight against environmental arguments. Thus Mr. Doug Anthony, the Australian deputy prime minister, saw fit to suggest that sand-mining on Fraser Island could be resumed once "the community becomes more informed and more enlightened as to what reclamation work is being carried out by mining companies. . . ."[2] Or consider how the protests of environmentalists might be deflected in the light of the following report of environmental engineering in the United States.

> . . . about 2 km of creek 25 feet wide has been moved to accommodate a highway and in doing so engineers with the aid of landscape architects and biologists have rebuilt the creek to the same standard as before. Boulders, bends, irregularities and natural vegetation have all been designed into the new section. In addition. special log structures have been built to improve the habitat as part of a fish development program.[3]

Not surprisingly the claim that revegetation, rehabilitation, and the like restore value has been strongly contested. J. G. Mosley reports that:

> The Fraser Island Environmental Inquiry Commissioners did in fact face up to the question of the relevance of successful rehabilitation to the decision on whether to ban exports (of beach sand minerals) and were quite unequivocal in saying that if the aim was to protect a natural area such success was irrelevant. . . . The Inquiry said: ". . . even if, contrary to the overwhelming weight of evidence before the Commission, successful rehabilitation of the flora after mining is found to be ecologically possible on all mined sites on the Island . . . the overall impression of a wild, uncultivated island refuge will be destroyed forever by mining."[4]

I want to show both that there is a rational, coherent ethical system which supports decisive objections to the restoration thesis, and that that system is not lacking in normative appeal. The system I have in mind will make valuation depend, in part, on the presence of properties which cannot survive the disruption-restoration process. There is, however, one point that needs clarifying before discussion proceeds. Establishing that restoration projects, even if empirically successful, do not fully restore value does not by any means constitute a knock-down argument against some environmentally disruptive policy. The value that would be lost if such a policy were implemented may be just one value among many which conflict in this situation. Countervailing considerations may be decisive and the policy thereby shown to be the right one. If my argument turns out to be correct it will provide an extra, though by no means decisive, reason for adopting certain environmentalist policies. It will show that the resistance which environmentalists display in the face of restoration promises is not merely silly, or emotional, or irrational. This is important because so much of the debate assumes that settling the dispute about what is ecologically possible automatically settles the value question. The thrust of much of the discussion is that if restoration is shown to be possible, and economically feasible, then recalcitrant environmentalists are behaving irrationally, being merely obstinate, or being selfish.

There are indeed familiar ethical systems which will serve to explain what is wrong with the restoration thesis in a certain range of cases. Thus preference utilitarianism will support objections to some restoration proposal if that proposal fails to maximally satisfy preferences. Likewise classical utilitarianism will lend support to a conservationist stance provided that the restoration proposal fails to maximize happiness and pleasure. However, in both cases the support offered is contingent upon the way in which the preferences and utilities line up. And it is simply not clear that they line up in such a way that the conservationist position is even usually vindicated. While appeal to utilitarian considerations might be strategically useful in certain cases they do not reflect the underlying motivation of the conservationists. The conservationists seem committed to an account of what has value which allows that restoration proposals fail to compensate for environmental destruction despite the fact that such proposals would maximize utility. What, then, is this distinct source of value which motivates and underpins the stance taken by, among others, the Commissioners of the Fraser Island Environmental Inquiry?

II

It is instructive to list some reasons that might be given in support of the claim that something of value would be lost if a certain bit of the environment were destroyed. It may be that the area supports a diversity of plant and animal life, it may be that it is the habitat of some endangered species, it may be that it contains striking rock formations or particularly fine specimens of mountain ash. If it is only considerations such as these that contribute to the area's value then perhaps opposition to the environmentally disruptive project would be irrational provided certain firm guarantees were available; for instance that the mining company or timber company would carry out the restoration and that it would be successful. Presumably there are steps that could be taken to ensure the continuance of species diversity and the continued existence of the endangered species. Some of the other requirements might prove harder to meet, but in some sense or other it is possible to recreate the rock formations and to plant mountain ash that will turn out to be particularly fine specimens. If value consists of the presence of objects of these various kinds, independently of what explains their presence, then the restoration thesis would seem to hold. The environmentalist needs to appeal to some feature which cannot be replicated as a source of some part of a natural area's value.

Putting the point thus indicates the direction the environmentalist could take. He might suggest that an area is valuable, partly, because it is a natural area, one that has not been modified by human hand, one that is undeveloped, unspoiled, or even unsullied. This suggestion is in accordance with much environmentalist rhetoric, and something like it at least must be at the basis of resistance to restoration proposals. One way of teasing out the suggestion and giving it a normative basis is to take over a notion from aesthetics. Thus we might claim that what the environmental engineers are proposing is that we accept a fake or a forgery instead of the real thing. If the claim can be made good then perhaps an adequate response to restoration proposals is to point out that they merely fake nature: that they offer us something less than was taken away.[5] Certainly there is a weight of opinion to the effect that, in art at least, fakes lack a value possessed by the real thing.[6]

One way in which this argument might be nipped in the bud is by claiming that it is bound to exploit an ultimately unworkable distinction between what is natural and what is not. Admittedly the distinction between the natural and the nonnatural requires detailed working out. This is something I do not propose doing. However, I do think the distinction can be made good in a way sufficient to the present need. For present purposes I shall take it that "natural" means something like "unmodified by human activity." Obviously some areas will be more natural than others according to the degree to which they have been shaped by human hands. Indeed most rural landscapes will, on this view, count as nonnatural to a very high degree. Nor do I intend the natural/nonnatural distinction to exactly parallel some dependent moral evaluation; that is, I do not want to be taken as claiming that what is natural is good and what is nonnatural is not. The distinction between natural and nonnatural connects with valuation in a much more subtle way than that. This is something to which I shall presently return. My claim, then, is that restoration policies do not always fully restore value because part of the reason that we value bits of the environment is because they are natural to a high degree. It is time to consider some counterarguments.

An environmental engineer might urge that the exact similarity which holds between the original and the perfectly restored environment leaves no room for a value discrimination between them. He may urge that if they are *exactly* alike, down to the minutest detail (and let us imagine for the sake of argument that this is a technological possibility), then they must be *equally* valuable. The suggestion is that value-discriminations depend on there being intrinsic differences between the states of affairs evaluated. This begs the question against the environmentalist, since it simply discounts the possibility that events temporally and spatially outside the immediate landscape in question can serve as the basis of some valuation of it. It discounts the possibility that the manner of the landscape's genesis, for example, has a legitimate role in determining its value. Here are some examples which suggest that an object's origins do affect its value and our valuations of it.

Imagine that I have a piece of sculpture in my garden which is too fragile to be moved at all. For some reason it would suit the local council to lay sewage pipes just where the sculpture happens to be. The council engineer informs me of this and explains that my sculpture will have to go. However, I need not despair because he promises to replace it with an exactly similar artifact, one which, he assures me, not even the very best experts could tell was not the original. The example may be unlikely, but it does have some point. While I may concede that the replica would be better than nothing at all (and I may not even concede that), it is utterly improbable that I would accept it as full compensation for the original. Nor is my reluctance entirely explained by the monetary value of the original work. My reluctance springs from the fact that I value the original as an aesthetic object, as an object with a specific genesis and history.

Alternatively, imagine I have been promised a Vermeer for my birthday. The day arrives and I am given a painting which looks just like a Vermeer. I am understandably pleased. However, my pleasure does not last for long. I am told that the painting I am holding is not a Vermeer but instead an exact replica of one previously destroyed. Any attempt to allay my disappointment by insisting that there just is no difference between the replica and the original misses the mark completely. There is a difference and it is one which affects my perception, and consequent valuation, of the painting. The difference, of course, lies in the painting's genesis.

I shall offer one last example which perhaps bears even more closely on the environmental issue. I am given a rather beautiful, delicately constructed object. It is something I treasure and admire, something in which I find considerable aesthetic value. Everything is fine until I discover certain facts about its origin. I discover that it is carved out of the bone of someone killed especially for that purpose. This discovery affects me deeply and I cease to value the object in the way that I once did. I regard it as in some sense sullied, spoiled by the facts of its origin. The object itself has not changed but my perceptions of it have. I now know that it is not quite the kind of thing I thought it was, and that my prior valuation of it was mistaken. The discovery is like the discovery that a painting one believed to be an original is in fact a forgery. The discovery about the object's origin changes the valuation made of it, since it reveals that the object is not of the kind that I value.

What these examples suggest is that there is at least a prima facie case for partially explaining the value of objects in terms of their origins, in terms of the kinds of processes that brought them into being. It is easy to find evidence in the writings of people who have valued nature that things extrinsic to the present, immediate environment determine valuations of it. John Muir's remarks about Hetch Hetchy Valley are a case in point.[7] Muir regarded the valley as a place where he could have direct contact with primeval nature; he valued it not just because it was a place of great beauty, but because it was also a part of the world that had not been shaped by human hand. Muir's valuation was conditional upon certain facts about the valley's genesis; his valuation was of a literally natural object, of an object with a special kind of continuity with the past. The news that it was a carefully contrived elaborate *ecological* artifact would have transformed that valuation immediately and radically.

The appeal that many find in areas of wilderness, in natural forests and wild rivers, depends very much on the naturalness of such places. There may be similarities between the experience one has when confronted with the multifaceted complexity, the magnitude, the awesomeness of a very large city, and the experience one has walking through a rain forest. There may be similarities between the feeling one has listening to the roar of water over the spillway of a dam and the feeling one has listening to a similar roar as a wild river tumbles down rapids. Despite the similarities there are also differences. We value the forest and river in part because they are representative of the world outside our dominion, because their existence is independent of us. We may value the city and the dam because of what they represent of human achievement. Pointing out the differences is not necessarily to denigrate either. However, there will be cases where we rightly judge that it is better to have the natural object than it is to have the artifact.

It is appropriate to return to a point mentioned earlier concerning the relationship between the natural and the valuable. It will not do to argue that what is natural is necessarily of value. The environmentalist can comfortably concede this point. He is not claiming that all natural phenomena have value in virtue of being natural. Sickness and disease are natural in a straightforward sense and are certainly not good. Natural phenomena such as fires, hurricanes, and volcanic eruptions can totally alter landscapes, and alter them for the worse. All of this can be conceded. What the environmentalist wants to claim is that within certain constraints, the naturalness of a landscape is a reason for preserving it, a determinant of its value. Artificially transforming an utterly barren, ecologically bankrupt landscape into something richer and more subtle may be a good thing. That is a view quite compatible with the belief that replacing a rich natural environment with a rich artificial one is a bad thing. What the environmentalist insists on is that naturalness is one factor in determining the value of pieces of the environment. But that, as I have tried to suggest, is no news. The castle by the Scottish loch is a very different kind of object, value-wise, from the exact replica in the appropriately shaped environment of some Disneyland of the future. The barrenness of some Cycladic island would stand in a different, better perspective if it were not brought about by human intervention.

As I have glossed it, the environmentalist's complaint concerning restoration proposals is that nature is not replaceable without depreciation in one aspect of its value which has to do with its genesis, its history. Given this, an opponent might be tempted to argue that there is no longer any such thing as "natural" wilderness, since the preservation of those bits of it which remain is achievable only by deliberate policy. The idea is that by placing boundaries around national parks; by actively discouraging grazing, trail-biking, and the like; by prohibiting sandmining, we are turning the wilderness into an artifact, that in some negative or indirect way we are creating an environment. There is some truth in this suggestion. In fact we need to take notice of it if we do value wilderness, since positive policies are required to preserve it. But as an argument against my overall claim, it fails. What is significant about wilderness is its causal continuity with the past. This is something that is not destroyed by demarcating an area and declaring it a national park. There is a distinction between the "naturalness" of the wilderness itself and the means used to maintain and protect it. What remains within the park boundaries is, as it were, the real thing. The environmentalist may regret that such positive policy is required to preserve the wilderness against human, or even natural, assault.[8] However, the regret does not follow from the belief that what remains is of depreciated value. There is a significant difference between preventing damage and repairing damage once it is done. That is the difference that leaves room for an argument in favor of a preservation policy over and above a restoration policy.

There is another important issue which needs highlighting. It might be thought that naturalness only matters insofar as it is perceived. In other words, it might be thought that if the environmental engineer could perform the restoration quickly and secretly, then there would be no room for complaint. Of course, in one sense there would not be, since the knowledge which would motivate complaint would be missing. What this shows is that there can be loss of value without the loss being perceived. It allows room for valuations to be mistaken because of ignorance concerning relevant facts. Thus my Vermeer can be removed and secretly replaced with the perfect replica. I have lost something of value without knowing that I have. This is possible because it is not simply the states of mind engendered by looking at the painting, by gloatingly contemplating my possession of it, by giving myself over to aesthetic pleasure, and so on, which explain why it has value. It has value because of the kind of thing that it is, and one thing that it is is a painting executed by a man with certain intentions, at a certain stage of his artistic development, living in a certain aesthetic milieu. Similarly, it is not just those things which make me feel the joy that wilderness makes me feel that I value. That would be a reason for desiring such things, but that is a distinct consideration. I value the forest because it is of a specific kind, because there is a certain kind of causal history which explains its existence. Of course I can be deceived into thinking that a piece of landscape has that kind of history, has developed in the appropriate way. The success of the deception does not elevate the restored landscape to the level of the original, no more than the success of the deception in the previous example confers on the fake the value of a real Vermeer. What has value in both cases are objects which are of the kind that I value, not merely objects which I think are of that kind. This point, it should be noted, is appropriate independently of views concerning the subjectivity or objectivity of value.

An example might bring the point home. Imagine that John is someone who values wilderness. John may find himself in one of the following situations:

(1) He falls into the clutches of a utilitarian-minded supertechnologist. John's captor has erected a rather incredible device which he calls an experience machine. Once the electrodes are attached and the right buttons pressed one can be brought to experience anything whatso-

ever. John is plugged into the machine, and, since his captor knows full well John's love of wilderness, given an extended experience as of hiking through a spectacular wilderness. This is environmental engineering at its most extreme. Quite assuredly John is being shortchanged. John wants there to be wilderness and he wants to experience it. He wants the world to be a certain way and he wants to have experiences of a certain kind; veridical.

(2) John is abducted, blindfolded, and taken to a simulated, plastic wilderness area. When the blindfold is removed John is thrilled by what he sees around him: the tall gums, the wattles, the lichen on the rocks. At least that is what he thinks is there. We know better: We know that John is deceived, that he is once again being shortchanged. He has been presented with an environment which he thinks is of value but isn't. If he knew that the leaves through which the artificially generated breeze now stirred were synthetic he would be profoundly disappointed, perhaps even disgusted at what at best is a cruel joke.

(3) John is taken to a place which was once devastated by strip-mining. The forest which had stood there for some thousands of years had been felled and the earth torn up, and the animals either killed or driven from their habitat. Times have changed, however, and the area has been restored. Trees of the species which grew there before the devastation grow there again, and the animal species have returned. John knows nothing of this and thinks he is in pristine forest. Once again, he has been shortchanged, presented with less than what he values most.

In the same way that the plastic trees may be thought a (minimal) improvement on the experience machine, so too the real trees are an improvement on the plastic ones. In fact, in the third situation there is incomparably more of value than in the second, but there could be more. The forest, though real, is not genuinely what John wants it to be. If it were not the product of contrivance he would value it more. It is a product of contrivance. Even in the situation where the devastated area regenerates rather than is restored, it is possible to understand and sympathize with John's claim that the environment does not have the fullest possible value. Admittedly in this case there is not so much room for that claim, since the environment has regenerated of its own accord. Still, the regenerated environment does not have the right kind of continuity with the forest that stood there initially; that continuity has been interfered with by the earlier devastation. (In actual fact the regenerated forest is likely to be perceivably quite different to the kind of thing originally there.)

III

I have argued that the causal genesis of forests, rivers, lakes, and so on is important in establishing their value. I have also tried to give an indication of why this is. In the course of my argument I drew various analogies, implicit rather than explicit, between faking art and faking nature. This should not be taken to suggest, however, that the concepts of aesthetic evaluation and judgment are to be carried straight over to evaluations of, and judgments about, the natural environment. Indeed there is good reason to believe that this cannot be done. For one thing, an apparently integral part of aesthetic evaluation depends on viewing the aesthetic object as an intentional object, as an artifact, as something that is shaped by the purposes and designs of its author. Evaluating works of art involves explaining them, and judging them, in terms of their author's intentions; it involves placing them within the author's corpus of work; it involves locating them in some tradition and in some special milieu. Nature is not a work of art, though works of art (in some suitably broad sense) may look very much like natural objects.

None of this is to deny that certain concepts which are frequently deployed in aesthetic evaluation cannot usefully and legitimately be deployed in evaluations of the environment. We admire the intricacy and delicacy of coloring in paintings as we might admire the intricate and delicate shadings in a eucalyptus forest. We admire the solid grandeur of a building as we might admire the solidity and grandeur of a massive rock outcrop. And of course the ubiquitous notion of the beautiful has a purchase in environmental evaluations as it does in aesthetic evaluations. Even granted all this, there are various arguments which might be developed to drive a wedge between the two kinds of evaluation which would weaken the analogies between faking art and faking nature. One such argument turns on the claim that aesthetic evaluation has, as a central component, a judgmental factor concerning the author's intentions and the like, in the way that was sketched above.[9] The idea is that nature, like works of art, may elicit any of a range of emotional responses in viewers. We may be awed by a mountain, soothed by the sound of water over rocks, excited by the power of a waterfall, and so on. However, the judgmental element in aesthetic evaluation serves to differentiate it from environmental evaluation and serves to explain, or so the argument would go, exactly what it is about fakes and forgeries in art which discounts their value with respect to the original. The claim is that if there is no judgmental element in environmental evaluation, then there is no rational basis for preferring real to faked nature when the latter is a good replica. The argument can, I think, be met.

Meeting the argument does not require arguing that responses to nature count as aesthetic responses. I agree that they are not. Nevertheless there are analogies which go beyond emotional content, and which may persuade us to take more seriously the claim that faked nature is inferior. It is important to make the point that only in fanciful situations dreamt up by philosophers are there no detectable differences between fakes and originals, both in the case of artifacts and in the case of natural objects. By taking a realistic example where there are discernible, and possibly discernible, differences between the fake and the real thing, it is possible to bring out the judgmental element in responses to, and evaluations of, the environment. Right now I may not be able to tell a real Vermeer from a Van Meegeren, though I might learn to do so. By the same token I might not be able to tell apart a naturally evolved stand of mountain ash from one which has been planted, but might later acquire the ability to make the requisite judgment. Perhaps an anecdote is appropriate here. There is a particular stand of mountain ash that I had long admired. The trees were straight and tall, of uniform stature, neither densely packed nor too openspaced. I then discovered what would have been obvious to a more expert eye, namely that the stand of mountain ash had been planted to replace original forest which had been burnt out. This explained the uniformity in size, the density and so on: It also changed my attitude to that piece of landscape. The evaluation that I make now of that landscape is to a certain extent informed, the response is not merely emotive but cognitive as well. The evaluation is informed and directed by my beliefs about the forest, the type of forest it is, its condition as a member of that kind, its causal genesis, and so on. What is more, the judgmental element affects the emotive one. Knowing that the forest is not a naturally evolved forest causes me to feel differently about it: It causes me to perceive the forest differently and to assign it less value than naturally evolved forests.

Val Routley has eloquently reminded us that people who value wilderness do not do so merely because they like to soak up pretty scenery.[10] They see much more and value much more than this. What they do see, and what they value, is very much a function of the degree to which they understand the ecological mechanisms which maintain the landscape and which determine that it appears the way it does. Similarly, knowledge of art history, of painting techniques and the like, will inform aesthetic evaluations and alter aesthetic perceptions. Knowledge of this kind is capable of transforming a hitherto uninteresting landscape into one that is compelling. Holmes Rolston has discussed at length the way in which an understanding and appreciation of ecology generates new values.[11] He does not claim that ecology reveals values previously unnoticed, but rather that the understanding of the complexity, diversity, and integration of the natural world which ecology affords us opens up a new area of valuation. As the facts are uncovered, the values are generated. What the remarks of Routley and Rolston highlight is the judgmental factor which is present in environmental appraisal. Understanding and evaluation do go hand in hand; and the responses individuals have to forests, wild rivers, and the like are not merely raw, emotional responses.

IV

Not all forests are alike, not all rain forests are alike. There are countless possible discriminations that the informed observer may make. Comparative judgments between areas of the natural environment are possible with regard to ecological richness, stage of development, stability, peculiar local circumstance, and the like. Judgments of this kind will very often underlie hierarchical orderings of environments in terms of their intrinsic worth. Appeal to judgments of this kind will frequently strengthen the case for preserving some bit of the environment. Thus one strong argument against the Tasmanian Hydroelectricity Commission's proposal to dam the Lower Gordon River turns on the fact that it threatens the inundation of an exceedingly fine stand of Huon pine. If the stand of Huon pines could not justifiably be ranked so high on the appropriate ecological scale then the argument against the dam would be to that extent weakened.

One reason that a faked forest is not just as good as a naturally evolved forest is that there is always the possibility that the trained eye will tell the difference.[12] It takes some time to discriminate areas of Alpine plain which are naturally clear of snow gums from those that have been cleared. It takes some time to discriminate regrowth forest which has been logged from forest which has not been touched. These are discriminations which it is possible to make and which are made. Moreover, they are discriminations which affect valuations. The reasons why the "faked" forest counts for less, more often than not, than the real thing are similar to the reasons why faked works of art count for less than the real thing.

Origin is important as an integral part of the evaluation process. It is important because our beliefs about it determine the valuations we make. It is also important in that the discovery that something has an origin quite different to the origin we initially believe that it has can literally alter the way we perceive that thing.[13] The point concerning the possibility of detecting fakes is important in that it stresses just how much detail must be written into the claim that environmental engineers can replicate nature. Even if environmental engineering could achieve such exactitude, there is, I suggest, no compelling reasons for accepting the restoration thesis. It is worth stressing, though, that as a matter of strategy, environmentalists must argue the empirical inadequacy of restoration proposals. This is the strongest argument against restoration ploys, because it appeals to diverse value frameworks, and because such proposals are promises to deliver a specific good. Showing that the good won't be delivered is thus a useful move to make.

NOTES

1. In this case *full* restoration will be literally impossible because the minerals are not going to be replaced.

2. J. G. Mosley, "The Revegetation 'Debate': A Trap For Conservationists," *Australian Conservation Foundation Newsletter* 12, no. 8 (1980): 1.

3 Peter Dunk, "How New Engineering Can Work with the Environment," *Habitat Australia* 7, no. 5 (1979): 12.

4. See Mosley, "The Revegetation 'Debate,' " p. 1.

5. Offering something less is not, of course, always the same as offering nothing. If diversity of animal and plant life, stability of complex ecosystems, tall trees, and so on are things that we value in themselves, then certainly we are offered something. I am

not denying this, and I doubt that many would qualify their valuations of the above-mentioned items in a way that leaves the restored environment devoid of value. Environmentalists would count as of worth programs designed to render polluted rivers reinhabitable by fish species. The point is rather that they may, as I hope to show, rationally deem it less valuable than what was originally there.

6. See, e.g., Colin Radford, "Fakes," *Mind* 87, no. 345 (1978): 66–76; and Nelson Goodman, *Languages of Art* (New York: Bobbs-Merrill, 1968) pp. 99–122, though Radford and Goodman have different accounts of why genesis matters.

7. See chap. 10 of Roderick Nash, *Wilderness and the American Mind* (New Haven: Yale University Press, 1973).

8. For example, protecting the Great Barrier Reef from damage by the crown-of-thorns starfish.

9. See, e.g., Don Mannison, "A Prolegomenon to a Human Chauvinist Aesthetic," in *Environmental Philosophy*, ed. D. S. Mannison, M. A. McRobbie, and R. Routley, (Canberra: Research and School of Social Sciences, Australian National University. 1980), pp. 212–16.

10. Val Routley, "Critical Notice of Passmore's Man's Responsibility for Nature." *Australasian Journal of Philosophy* 53, no. 2 (1975): 171–85.

11. Holmes Rolston III, "Is There an Ecological Ethic?" *Ethics* 85, no. 2 (1975): 93–109.

12. For a discussion of this point with respect to art forgeries, see Goodman, *Languages of Art*, esp. pp. 103–12.

13. For an excellent discussion of this same point with respect to artifacts, see Radford, "Fakes," esp. pp. 73–76.

REFERENCES

Dunk, Peter. "How Engineering Can Work with the Environment." *Habitat Australia* 7, no. 5 (1979).

Goodman, Nelson. *Languages of Art*. New York: Bobbs-Merrill, 1968.

Mannison, Don. "A Prolegomenon to a Human Chauvanist Aesthetic." In *Environmental Philosophy*, edited by D. S. Mannison, M. A. McRobbie, and R. Routley. Canberra: Research School of Social Sciences, Australian National University, 1980.

Mosley, J. G. "The Revegetation 'Debate': A Trap for Conservationists." *Australian Conservation Foundation Newsletter* 12, no. 8 (1980).

Nash, Roderick. *Wilderness and the American Mind*. New Haven: Yale University Press, 1973.

Radford, Colin. "Fakes." *Mind* 87, no. 345 (1978).

Rolston, Holmes III. "Is There an Ecological Ethic?" *Ethics* 85, no. 2 (1975): 93–109.

Routley, Val. "Critical Notice of Passmore's *Man's Responsibility for Nature*." *Australasian Journal of Philosophy* 53, no. 2 (1975).

5

The Big Lie
Human Restoration of Nature
Eric Katz

> *The trail of the human serpent is thus over everything.*
> —William James, *Pragmatism*

I

begin with an empirical point, based on my own random observations: The idea that humanity can restore or repair the natural environment has begun to play an important part in decisions regarding environmental policy. We are urged to plant trees to reverse the "greenhouse effect." Real estate developers are obligated to restore previously damaged acreage in exchange for building permits.[1] The U.S. National Park Service spends $33 million to "rehabilitate" thirty-nine thousand acres of the Redwood Crock watershed.[2] And the U.S. Forest Service is criticized for its "plantation" mentality: It is harvesting trees from old-growth forests rather than "redesigning" forests according to the sustainable principles of nature. "Restoration forestry is the only true forestry," claims an environmentally conscious former employee of the Bureau of Land Management.[3]

These policies present the message that humanity should repair the damage that human intervention has caused the natural environment. The message is an optimistic one, for it implies that we recognize the harm we have caused in the natural environment and that we possess the means and will to correct these harms. These policies also make us feel good; the prospect of restoration relieves

Eric Katz, "The Big Lie: The Human Restoration of Nature." *Research in Philosophy and Technology* (1992). Reprinted by permission of JAI Press.

the guilt that we feel about the destruction of nature. The wounds we have inflicted on the natural world are not permanent; nature can be made "whole" again. Our natural resource base and foundation for survival can be saved by the appropriate policies of restoration, regeneration, and redesign.

It is also apparent that these ideas are not restricted to policymakers, environmentalists, or the general public—they have begun to pervade the normative principles of philosophers concerned with developing an adequate environmental ethic. Paul Taylor uses a concept of "restitutive justice" both as one of the basic rules of duty in his biocentric ethic and as a "priority principle" to resolve competing claims.[4] The basic idea of this rule is that human violators of nature will in some way repair or compensate injured natural entities and systems. Peter Wenz also endorses a principle of restitution as being essential to an adequate theory of environmental ethics; he then attacks Taylor's theory for not presenting a coherent principle.[5] The idea that humanity is morally responsible for reconstructing natural areas and entities—species, communities, ecosystems—thus becomes a central concern of an applied environmental ethic.

In this paper I question the environmentalists' concern for the restoration of nature and argue against the optimistic view that humanity has the obligation and ability to repair or reconstruct damaged natural systems. This conception of environmental policy and environmental ethics is based on a misperception of natural reality and a misguided understanding of the human place in the natural environment. On a simple level, it is the same kind of "technological fix" that has engendered the environmental crisis. Human science and technology will fix, repair, and improve natural processes. On a deeper level, it is an expression of an anthropocentric worldview, in which human interests shape and redesign a comfortable natural reality. A "restored" nature is an artifact created to meet human satisfactions and interests. Thus, on the most fundamental level, it is an unrecognized manifestation of the insidious dream of the human domination of nature. Once and for all, humanity will demonstrate its mastery of nature by "restoring" and repairing the degraded ecosystems of the biosphere. Cloaked in an environmental consciousness, human power will reign supreme.

II

It has been eight years since Robert Elliot published his sharp and accurate criticism of "the restoration thesis."[6] In an article entitled "Faking Nature," Elliot examined the moral objections to the practical environmental policy of restoring damaged natural systems, locations, landscapes. For the sake of argument, Elliot assumed that the restoration of a damaged area could be recreated perfectly, so that the area would appear in its original condition after the restoration was completed. He then argued that the perfect copy of the natural area would be of less value than the original, for the newly restored natural area would be analogous to an art forgery. Two points seem crucial to Elliot's argument. First, the value of objects can be explained "in terms of their origins, in terms of the kinds of processes that brought them into being."[7] We value an art work in part because of the fact that a particular artist, a human individual, created the work at a precise moment in historical time. Similarly, we value a natural area because of its "special kind of continuity with the past." But to understand the art work or the natural area in their historical contexts we require a special kind of insight or knowledge. Thus, the second crucial point of Elliot's argument is the coexistence of "understanding and evaluation." The art expert brings to the analysis and evaluation of a work of art a full range of information about the artist, the period, the intentions of the work, and so on. In a similar way, the evaluation of a natural area is informed by a detailed knowledge of ecological processes, a knowledge that can be learned as easily as the history of art.[8] To value the restored landscape as much as the original is thus a kind of ignorance; we are being fooled by the superficial similarities to the natural area, just as the ignorant art "appreciator" is fooled by the appearance of the art forgery.

Although Elliot's argument has had a profound effect on my own thinking about environmental issues, I believed that the problem he uses as a starting point is purely theoretical, almost fanciful.[9] After all, who would possibly believe that a land developer or a strip mining company would actually restore a natural area to its original state? Elliot himself claims that "the restoration thesis" is generally used "as a way of undermining the arguments of conservationists."[10] Thus it is with concern that I discover that serious environmentalist thinkers, as noted above, have argued for a position similar to Elliot's "restoration thesis." The restoration of a damaged nature is seen not only as a practical option for environmental policy but also as a moral obligation for right-thinking environmentalists. If we are to continue human projects which (unfortunately) impinge on the natural environment (it is claimed), then we must repair the damage. In a few short years a "sea-change" has occurred: What Elliot attacked as both a physical impossibility and a moral mistake is now advocated as proper environmental policy. Am I alone in thinking that something has gone wrong here?

Perhaps not enough people have read Elliot's arguments; neither Taylor nor Wenz, the principal advocates of restitutive environmental justice, list this article in their notes or bibliographies. Perhaps we need to reexamine the idea of recreating a natural landscape; in what sense is this action analogous to an art forgery? Perhaps we need to push beyond Elliot's analysis, to use his arguments as a starting point for a deeper investigation into the fundamental errors of restoration policy.

III

My initial reaction to the possibility of restoration policy is almost entirely visceral: I am outraged by the idea that a technologically created "nature" will be passed off as reality. The human presumption that we are capable of this technological fix demonstrates (once again) the arrogance with which humanity surveys the natural world. Whatever the problem may be, there will be a technological, mechanical, or scientific solution. Human engineering will modify the secrets of natural processes and effect a satisfactory result. Chemical fertilizers will increase food production; pesticides will control disease-carrying insects; hydroelectric dams will harness the power of our rivers. The familiar list goes on and on.

The relationship between this technological mindset and the environmental crisis has been amply demonstrated, and need not concern us here.[11] My interest is narrower. I want to focus on the creation of artifacts, for that is what technology does. The recreated natural environment that is the end result of a restoration project is nothing more than an artifact created for human use. The problem for an applied environmental ethic is the determination of the moral value of this artifact.

Recently, Michael Losonsky has pointed out how little we know about the nature, structure, and meaning of artifacts. "[C]ompared to the scientific study of nature, the scientific study of artifacts is in its infancy."[12] What is clear, of course, is that an artifact is not equivalent to a natural object; but the precise difference, or set of differences, is not readily apparent. Indeed, when we consider objects such as beaver dams, we are unsure if we are dealing with natural objects or artifacts. Fortunately, however, these kind of animal-created artifacts can be safely ignored in the present investigation. Nature restoration projects are obviously human. A human-built dam is clearly artifactual.

The concepts of function and purpose are central to an understanding of artifacts. Losonsky rejects the Aristotelian view that artifacts (as distinguished from natural objects) have no inner nature or hidden essence that can be discovered. Artifacts have a "nature" that is partially comprised of three features: "internal structure, purpose, and manner of use." This nature, in turn, explains why artifacts "have predictable lifespans during which they undergo regular and predictable changes."[13] The structure, function, and use of the artifacts determine to some extent the changes which they undergo. Clocks would not develop in a manner which prevented the measurement of time.

Natural objects lack the kind of purpose and function found in artifacts. As Andrew Brennan has argued, natural entities have no "intrinsic functions," as he calls them, for they were not the result of design. They were not created for a particular purpose; they have no set manner of use. Although we often speak as if natural individuals (for example, predators) have roles to play in ecosystemic well-being (the maintenance of optimum population levels), this kind of talk is either metaphorical or fallacious. No one created or designed the mountain lion as a regulator of the deer population.[14]

This is the key point. Natural individuals were not designed for a purpose. They lack intrinsic functions, making them different from human-created artifacts. Artifacts, I claim, are essentially anthropocentric. They are created for human use, human purpose—they serve a function for human life. Their existence is centered on human life. It would be impossible to imagine an artifact not designed to meet a human purpose. Without a foreseen use the object would not be created. This is completely different from the way natural entities and species evolve to fill ecological niches in the biosphere.

The doctrine of anthropocentrism is thus an essential element in understanding the meaning of artifacts. This conceptual relationship is not generally problematic, for most artifacts are human creations designed for use in human social and cultural contexts. But once we begin to redesign natural systems and processes, once we begin to create restored natural environments, we impose our anthropocentric purposes on areas that exist outside human society. We will construct so-called natural objects on the model of human desires, interests, and satisfactions. Depending on the adequacy of our technology, these restored and redesigned natural areas will appear more or less natural, but they will never be natural—they will be anthropocentrically designed human artifacts.

A disturbing example of this conceptual problem applied to environmental policy can be found in Chris Maser's *The Redesigned Forest*. Maser is a former research scientist for the United States Department of Interior Bureau of Land Management. His book attests to his deeply felt commitment to the policy of "sustainable" forestry, as opposed to the short-term expediency of present-day forestry practices. Maser argues for a forestry policy that "restores" the forest as it harvests it; we must be true foresters and not "plantation" managers.

Nonetheless, Maser's plans for "redesigning" forests reveal several problems about the concepts and values implicit in restoration policy. First, Maser consistently compares the human design of forests with Nature's design. The entire first chapter is a series of short sections comparing the two "designs." In the "Introduction," he writes, "[W]e are redesigning our forests from Nature's blueprint to humanity's blueprint."[15] But Nature, of course, does not have a blueprint, or a design. As a zoologist, Maser knows this; but his metaphorical talk is dangerous. It implies that we can discover the plan, the methods, the processes of nature, and mold them to our purposes.

Maser himself often writes as if he accepts that implication. The second problem with his argument is the comparison of nature to a mechanism that we do not fully understand. The crucial error we make in simplifying forest ecology—turning forests into plantations—is that we are assuming our design for the forest mechanism is better than Nature's. "Forests are not automobiles in which we can tailor artificially substituted parts for original parts."[16] How true. But Maser's argument against this substitution is empirical: "A forest cannot be 'rebuilt' and remain the same forest, but we could probably rebuild a forest similar to the original if we knew how. No one has ever done it. . . . [W]e do not have a parts catalog, or a maintenance manual. . . ."[17] The implication is that if we did have a catalog and manual, if nature were known as well as artifactual machines, then the restoration of forests would be morally and practically acceptable. This conclusion serves as Maser's chief argument for the preservation of old-growth and other unmanaged forests: "We have to maintain some original, unmanaged old-growth forest, mature forest, and young-growth forest as parts catalog, maintenance manual, and service department from which to learn to practice restoration forestry."[18] Is the forest-as-parts-catalog a better guiding metaphor than the forest-as-plantation?

This mechanistic conception of nature underlies, or explains, the third problem with Maser's argument. His goal for restoration forestry, his purpose in criticizing the short-term plantation mentality, is irredeemably anthropocentric. The problem with present-day forestry practices is that they are "exclusive of all other human values except production of fast-grown wood fiber."[19] It is the elimination of other human values and interests that concerns Maser. "We need to learn to see the forest as the factory that produces raw materials . . ." to meet our "common goal[:] . . . a sustainable forest for a sustainable industry for a sustainable environment for a sustainable human population."[20] Restoration forestry is necessary because it is the best method for achieving the human goods which we extract from nature. Our goal is to build a better "factory-forest," using the complex knowledge of forest ecology.

What is disturbing about Maser's position is that it comes from an environmentalist. Unlike Elliot's theoretical opponents of conservation, who wished to subvert the environmentalist position with the "restoration thesis," Maser advocates the human design of forests as a method of environmental protection and conservation for human use. His conclusion shows us the danger of using anthropocentric and mechanistic models of thought in the formulation of environmental policy. These models leave us with forests that are "factories" for the production of human commodities, spare-parts catalogs for the maintenance of the machine.

I began this section with a report of my visceral reaction to the technological recreation of natural environments. This reaction has now been explained and analyzed. Nature restoration projects are the creations of human technologies, and as such, are artifacts. But artifacts are essentially the constructs of an anthropocentric worldview. They are designed by humans for humans to satisfy human interests and needs. Artifactual restored nature is thus fundamentally different from natural objects and systems which exist without human design. It is not surprising, then, that we view restored nature with a value different from the original.

IV

To this point, my analysis has supported the argument and conclusions of Elliot's criticism of "the restoration thesis." But further reflection on the nature of artifacts, and the comparison of forests to well-run machines, makes me doubt the central analogy which serves as the foundation of his case. Can we compare an undisturbed natural environment to a work of art? Should we?

As noted in section II, Elliot uses the art/nature analogy to make two fundamental points about the process of evaluation: (1) the importance of a continuous causal history; and (2) the use of knowledge about this causal history to make appropriate judgments. A work of art or a natural entity which lacks a continuous causal history, as understood by the expert in the field, would be judged inferior. If the object is "passed off" as an original, with its causal history intact, then we would judge it to be a forgery or an instance of "faked" nature.

I do not deny that this is a powerful analogy. It demonstrates the crucial importance of causal history in the analysis of value. But the analogy should not be pushed too far, for the comparison suggests that we possess an understanding of art forgery that is now simply being applied to natural objects. I doubt that our understanding of art forgery is adequate for this task. L. B. Cebik argues that an analysis of forgery involves basic ontological questions about the meaning of art. Cebik claims that it is a mistake to focus exclusively on questions of value when analyzing art forgeries, for the practice of forgery raises fundamental issues about the status of art itself.[21]

According to Cebik, an analysis of forgeries demonstrates that our understanding of art is dominated by a limiting paradigm—"production by individuals." We focus almost exclusively on the individual identity of the artist as the determining factor in assessing authenticity. "Nowhere . . . is there room for paradigmatic art being fluid, unfinished, evolving, and continuous in its creation." Cebik has in mind a dynamic, communally based art, an everchanging neighborhood mural or music passed on for generations.[22] Another example would be classical ballet, a performance of which is a unique dynamic movement, different from every other performance of the same ballet.

These suggestions about a different paradigm of art show clearly, I think, what is wrong with the art/nature analogy as a useful analytical tool. Natural entities and systems are much more akin to the fluid evolving art of Cebik's alternative model than they are to the static, finished, individual artworks of the dominant paradigm. It is thus an error to use criteria of forgery and authenticity that derive from an individualistic, static conception of art for an evaluation of natural entities and systems. Natural entities and systems are nothing like static, finished objects of art. They are fluid, evolving systems which completely transcend the category of artist or creator. The perceived disvalue in restored natural objects does not derive from a misunderstanding over the identity of the creator of the objects. It derives instead from the misplaced category of "creator"—for natural objects do not have creators or designers as human artworks do. Once we realize that the natural entity we are viewing has been "restored" by a human artisan it ceases to be a natural object. It is not a forgery; it is an artifact.

We thus return to artifacts, and their essential anthropocentric nature. We cannot (and should not) think of natural objects as artifacts, for this imposes a human purpose or design on their very essence. As artifacts, they are evaluated by their success in meeting human interests and needs, not by their own intrinsic being. Using the art/nature analogy of forgery reinforces the impression that natural objects are similar to artifacts—art works—and that they can be evaluated using the same anthropocentric criteria. Natural entities have to be evaluated on their own terms, not as art works, machines, factories, or any other human-created artifact.

V

But what are the terms appropriate for the evaluation of natural objects? What criteria should be used? To answer this question we need to do more than differentiate natural objects from artifacts; we need to examine the essence or nature of natural objects. What does it mean to say that an entity is natural (and hence, not an artifact)? Is there a distinguishing mark or characteristic that determines the descriptive judgment? What makes an object natural, and why is the standard not met through the restoration process?

The simple answer to this question—a response I basically support—is that the natural is defined as being independent of the actions of humanity. Thus, Taylor advocates a principle of noninterference as a primary moral duty in his ethic of respect for nature. "[W]e put aside our personal likes and our human interests. . . . Our respect for nature means that we acknowledge the sufficiency of the natural world to sustain its own proper order throughout the whole domain of life."[23] The processes of the natural world that are free of human interference are the most natural.

There are two obvious problems with this first simple answer. First, there is the empirical point that the human effect on the environment is, by now, fairly pervasive. No part of the natural world lies untouched by our pollution and technology. In a sense, then, nothing natural truly exists (anymore). Second, there is the logical point that humans themselves are naturally evolved beings, and so all human actions would be "natural," regardless of the amount of technology used or the interference on nonhuman nature. The creation of artifacts is a natural human activity, and thus the distinction between artifact and natural object begins to blur.

These problems in the relationship of humanity to nature are not new. Mill raised similar objections to the idea of "nature" as a moral norm over a hundred years ago, and I need not review his arguments.[24] The answer to these problems is twofold. First, we admit that the concepts of "natural" and "artifactual" are not absolutes; they exist along a spectrum, where various gradations of both concepts can be discerned. The human effect on the natural world is pervasive, but there are differences in human actions that make a descriptive difference. A toxic waste dump is different from a compost heap of organic material. To claim that both are equally nonnatural would obscure important distinctions.

A second response is presented by Brennan.[25] Although a broad definition of "natural" denotes independence from human management or interference, a more useful notion (because it has implications for value theory and ethics) can be derived from the consideration of evolutionary adaptations. Our natural diet is the one we are adapted for, that is "in keeping with our nature." All human activity is not unnatural, only that activity which goes beyond our biological and evolutionary capacities. As an example, Brennan cites the procedure of "natural childbirth," that is, childbirth free of technological medical interventions. "Childbirth is an especially striking example of the wildness within us . . . where we can appreciate the natural at first hand. . . ." It is natural, free, and wild not because it is a nonhuman activity—after all, it is human childbirth—but because it is independent of a certain type of human activity, actions designed to control or to manipulate natural processes.

The "natural," then, is a term we use to designate objects and processes that exist as far as possible from human manipulation and control. Natural entities are autonomous in ways that human-created artifacts are not; as Taylor writes, "to be free to pursue the realization of one's good according to the laws of one's nature."[26] When we thus judge natural objects, and evaluate them more highly than artifacts, we are focusing on the extent of their independence from human domination. In this sense, then, human actions can also be judged to be natural—these are the human actions that exist as evolutionary adaptations, free of the control and alteration of technological processes.

If these reflections on the meaning of "natural" are plausible, then it should be clear why the restoration process fails to meet the criteria of naturalness. The attempt to redesign, recreate, and restore natural areas and objects is a radical intervention in natural processes. Although there is an obvious spectrum of possible restoration and redesign projects which differ in their value—Maser's redesigned sustainable forest is better than a tree plantation—all of these projects involve the manipulation and domination of natural areas. All of these projects involve the creation of artifactual natural realities, the imposition of anthropocentric interests on the processes and objects of nature. Nature is not permitted to be free, to pursue its own independent course of development.

The fundamental error is thus domination, the denial of freedom and autonomy. Anthropocentrism, the major concern of most environmental philosophers, is only one species of the more basic attack on the preeminent value of self-realization. From within the perspective of anthropocentrism, humanity believes it is justified in dominating and molding the nonhuman world to its own human purposes. But a policy of domination transcends the anthropocentric subversion of natural processes. A policy of domination subverts both nature and human existence; it denies both the cultural and natural realization of individual good, human and nonhuman. Liberation from all forms of domination is thus the chief goal of any ethical or political system.

It is difficult to awaken from the dream of domination. We are all impressed by the power and breadth of human technological achievements. Why is it not possible to extend this power further, until we control, manipulate, and dominate the entire natural universe? This is the illusion that the restoration of nature presents to us. But it is only an illusion. Once we dominate nature, once we restore and redesign nature for our own purposes, then we have destroyed nature—we have created an artifactual reality, in a sense, a false reality, which merely provides us the pleasant illusory appearance of the natural environment.

VI

As a concluding note, let me leave the realm of philosophical speculation and return to the world of practical environmental policy. Nothing I have said in this essay should be taken as an endorsement of actions that develop, exploit, or injure areas of the natural environment and leave them in a damaged state. I believe, for example, that Exxon should attempt to clean up and restore the Alaskan waterways and land that was harmed by its corporate negligence. The point of my argument here is that we must not misunderstand what we humans are doing when we attempt to restore or repair natural areas. We are not restoring nature; we are not making it whole and healthy again. Nature restoration is a compromise; it should not be a basic policy goal. It is a policy that makes the best of a bad situation; it cleans up our mess. We are putting a piece of furniture over the stain in the carpet, for it provides a better appearance. As a matter of policy, however, it would be much more significant to prevent the causes of the stains.

NOTES

1. In Islip Town, New York, real-estate developers have cited the New York State Department of Environmental Conservation policy of "no net loss" in proposing the restoration of parts of their property to a natural state, in exchange for permission to develop. A report in *Newsday* discusses a controversial case: "In hopes of gaining town-board approval, Blankman has promised to return a three-quarter-mile dirt road on his property to its natural habitat. . . ." Katti Gray, "Wetlands in the Eye of a Storm," Islip Special, *Newsday*, April 22, 1990, pp. 1, 5.

2. *Garbage: The Practical Journal for the Environment*, May/June 1990, rear cover.

3. Chris Maser, *The Redesigned Forest* (San Pedro: R. & E. Miles, 1988), p. 173. It is also interesting to note that there now exists a dissident group within the U.S. Forest Service called the Association of Forest Service Employees for Environmental Ethics (AFSEEE). They advocate a return to sustainable forestry.

4. Paul Taylor, *Respect for Nature: A Theory of Environmental Ethics* (Princeton: Princeton University Press, 1986), pp. 186–92, 304–306, and chapters 4 and 6 generally.

5. Peter S. Wenz, *Environmental Justice* (Albany: SUNY Press, 1988), pp. 287–91.

6. Robert Elliot, "Faking Nature," *Inquiry* 25 (1982): 81–93; reprinted in Donald Van De Veer and Christine Pierce, ed., *People, Penguins, and Plastic Trees: Basic Issues in Environmental Ethics* (Belmont: Wadsworth, 1986), pp. 142–50. All page citations are from the reprint.

7. Ibid., p. 145.

8. Ibid., p. 149.

9. Eric Katz, "Organism, Community, and the 'Substitution Problem,'" *Environmental Ethics* 7 (1985): 253–55.

10. Elliot, "Faking Nature," p. 142.

11. See, for example, Barry Commoner, *The Closing Circle* (New York: Knopf, 1971) and Arnold Pacey, *The Culture of Technology* (Cambridge: MIT Press, 1983).

12. Michael Losonsky, "The Nature of Artifacts," *Philosophy* 65 (1990): 88.

13. Ibid., p. 94.

14. Andrew Brennan, "The Moral Standing of Natural Objects," *Environmental Ethics* 6 (1984): 41–44.

15. Maser, *The Redesigned Forest*, p. xvii.

16. Ibid., pp. 176–77.

17. Ibid., pp. 88–89.

18. Ibid., p. 174.

19. Ibid., p. 94.

20. Ibid., pp. 148–49.

21. L. B. Cebik, "Forging Issues from Forged Art," *Southern Journal of Philosophy* 27 (1989): 331–46.

22. Ibid., p. 342.

23. Taylor, *Respect for Nature*, p. 177. The rule of noninterference is discussed on pp. 173–79.

24. J. S. Mill, "Nature," in *Three Essays on Religion* (London: n.p., 1874).

25. Andrew Brennan, *Thinking About Nature: An Investigation of Nature, Value, and Ecology* (Athens: University of Georgia Press, 1988), pp. 88–91.

26. Taylor, *Respect for Nature*, p. 174.

REFERENCES

Brennan, Andrew. "The Moral Standing of Natural Objects." *Environmental Ethics* 6 (1984).

———. *Thinking About Nature: An Investigation of Nature, Value, and Ecology.* Athens: University of Georgia Press, 1988.

Cebik, L. B. "Forging Issues from Forged Art." *Southern Journal of Philosophy* 27 (1989).

Commoner, Barry. *The Closing Circle.* New York: Knopf, 1971.

Elliot, Robert. "Faking Nature." *Inquiry* 25 (1982).

Garbage: The Practical Journal for the Environment. May/June 1990.

Gray, Katti. "Wetlands in the Eye of a Storm." Islip Special. *Newsday*, April 22, 1990.

Katz, Eric. "Organism, Community, and the 'Substitution Problem.'" *Environmental Ethics* 7 (1985).

Losonsky, Michael. "The Nature of Artifacts." *Philosophy* 65 (1990).

Maser, Chris. *The Redesigned Forest.* San Pedro: R. & E. Miles, 1998.

Mill, J. S. "Nature." In *Three Essays on Religion.* London: N.p., 1874.

Pacey, Arnold. *The Culture of Technology.* Cambridge: MIT Press, 1983.

Taylor, Paul. *Respect for Nature: A Theory of Environmental Ethics.* Princeton: Princeton University Press, 1986.

Van De Veer, Donald, and Christine Pierce, ed. *People, Penguins, and Plastic Trees: Basic Issues in Environmental Ethics.* Belmont: Wadsworth, 1986.

Wenz, Peter S. *Environmental Justice.* Albany: SUNY Press, 1988.

6

Restoration or Domination?
A Reply to Katz
Andrew Light

In this paper I will argue that Eric Katz has come to mistaken conclusions about the value and implications of ecological restoration. Katz's analysis of restoration has led him to take a deflationary stance at best, and a hostile stance at worst, to the practice of restoring damaged ecosystems. A more practically oriented philosophical contribution to discussions of our policies concerning ecological restoration is needed than has been provided by Katz and other environmental philosophers so far. A richer description of the ethical implications of restoration will identify a large part of its value in the revitalization of the human relationship with nature. Before reaching this conclusion, however, I will briefly consider a more practical framework for environmental philosophy as a whole, and then provide a detailed analysis of Katz's arguments against restoration.

PRAGMATISM AND ECOLOGICAL RESTORATION

Many environmental philosophers do not think of restoration ecology in a positive light. For example, influential thinkers such as Eric Katz, and to a lesser extent Robert Elliot, have argued forcefully that ecological restoration does not result in a restoration of nature, and that further, it may even create a disvalue in nature. But why? At present the focus in environmental philosophy is largely on the search for a description of the nonanthropocentric value of nature— that is, a description of the value of nature independent of human concerns and reasons for valuing nature. If the goal of environmental philosophy is to describe the non-human-centered value of nature, then it follows that if the value of nature is to be distinguishable from human appreciation of it then presumably nature cannot be the sort of thing that is dependent on human creation or manipulation. If nature were dependent on human creation then it would have an irreconcilable anthropocentric (or anthropogenic) component. So, if restorations are human creations, so the arguments of the philosophical critics go, then they cannot ever count as the sort of thing that contains natural value, nonanthropocentrically conceived, since humans cannot create the sorts of things that contain that sort of value.

Restorations are not natural on this view; they are, as Katz suggests, artifacts. To claim that environmental philosophers should be concerned with ecological restoration is therefore to commit a kind of category mistake: It is to ask that they talk about something that is not part of nature. But to label ecological restorations a philosophical category mistake is the best-case scenario for their assessment on this view. At worst, restorations represent the tyranny of humans over nature. Katz has put it most emphatically in arguing that "the practice of ecological restoration can only represent a misguided faith in the hegemony and infallibility of the human power to control the natural world."[1]

I have long disagreed with claims like this one. My previous answer to such positions has been to simply set aside these kinds of arguments and focus on other issues involving ecological restoration.[2] But I do not think it wise to ignore such arguments. Since Katz has explicitly rejected the idea that ecological restoration is an acceptable environmental practice, the restoration community as a whole may assume that environmental ethicists tend to be hostile to the idea of ecological restoration. As such, philosophers may be excluded from discussions concerning important public policy questions about ecological restoration.

Now, one may fairly wonder how environmental philosophers could make a contribution to questions of public policy even if they had an opportunity. I have argued elsewhere that if philosophers could help to articulate the normative foundations for environmental policies in a way that is translatable to the general public, then they will have made a contribution to the resolution of environmental problems commensurate with their talents. But making such a contribution may require doing environmental philosophy in some different ways. Specifically, it requires a more public philosophy, more focused on making the kind of argument that resonates with the moral intuitions which most people carry around with them on an everyday basis. Such intuitions usually cohere more with human-centered notions of value rather than comparatively abstract nonanthropocentric conceptions of natural value. If environmental philosophers are interested in trying to appeal to the existing intuitions of the public, they must be open to making ethical claims about the value of nature in anthropocentric terms, or at least must give up their tendency to cut humans out of the picture entirely.

I call the view that makes it plausible to appeal to human motivations in valuing nature *environmental pragmatism*. By this I simply mean the recognition that a responsible and complete environmental philosophy includes a public component with a clear policy emphasis.[3] It is certainly appropriate for philosophers to continue their search for a true and foundational nonanthropocentric description of the value of nature. But environmental philosophers would be remiss if they did not set aside that search at times and try to make other, perhaps more appealing, ethical arguments which may have an audience in an anthropocentric public. Environmental pragmatism, in my sense, is agnostic concerning the existence of nonanthropocentric natural value. Those embracing this view can either continue to pursue such a theory or they can take a more traditional pragmatist stance, denying the existence of such value.[4]

This approach modifies the philosophical contribution to questions about restoration ecology to positive effect. For pragmatists, restoration makes sense because on the whole it results in many advantages over mere preservation of ecosystems that have been substantially damaged by humans. As we will see in the last section of this chapter, some of those advantages have to do with the benefits of restoration to the human relationship with nature and not just benefits to nature itself. The philosopher may certainly have much to add to a full analysis of the relevant questions concerning the practice of ecological restoration. They may in fact be able to help us to rethink the very normative ground of restoration as a public environmental practice.

BENEVOLENT RESTORATIONS

Following intuitions like those just sketched, I have previously outlined some preliminary distinctions that paint a broader picture of the philosophical terrain up for grabs in restoration than that outlined by Katz and Elliot. Specifically, in response to Elliot's earlier critique of restoration I have tried to distinguish between two broad categories of ecological restoration that have differing moral implications.

Elliot begins his seminal article on restoration, "Faking Nature," with an identification of a particular kind of pernicious restoration—restoration that is used as a rationalization for the destruction of nature. On this claim, any harm done to nature by humans is ultimately reparable through restoration and so the harm should be discounted. Elliot calls this view the "restoration thesis" (it is later termed the "replacement thesis" in his more recent book). The restoration thesis states that "the destruction of what has value [in nature] is compensated for by the later creation (recreation) of something of equal value."[5] Elliot rejects the restoration thesis through an analogy based on the relationship between original and replicated works of art and nature. Just as we would not value a replication of a work of art as much as we would value the original, we wouldn't value a replicated bit of nature as much as we would the original thing.

In working through a possible answer to Elliot's criticisms of the value of restoration in this article I have proposed a distinction to help us think through the value of ecological restoration. My cue for this distinction comes from Elliot's intuitions that not all kinds of restoration are bad, or deceptive "fakes." While his recent book is explicit on this topic, even in his earlier article one can see Elliot working toward this conclusion: "Artificially transforming an utterly barren, ecologically bankrupt landscape into something richer and more subtle may be a good thing. That is a view quite compatible with the belief that replacing a rich natural environment with a rich artificial one is a bad thing."[6] Following Elliot's lead that some kinds of restoration may be beneficial I distinguish between two sorts of restorations: (1) malicious restorations, such as the kind described in the restoration thesis, and (2) benevolent restorations, or, those undertaken in order to remedy a past harm done to nature, though not offered as a justification for harming nature. Benevolent restorations, unlike malicious restorations, cannot serve as justifications for the conditions which would warrant their engagement. While Elliot doubts that restored nature can ever have the same value as original nature, I believe he would accept this distinction today.

If this distinction holds, then we can claim that Elliot's original target was not all of restoration, but only a particular kind of restoration, namely, malicious restorations. It is certainly not the case, for example, that the prairie restorations undertaken at the University of Wisconsin Arboretum or as part of the Chicago Wilderness project (the Nature Conservancy–led restoration of the Oak Savannah in the forest preserves surrounding Chicago) are offered as excuses or rationales for the destruction of nature. The restorations involved in mountaintop mining projects in rural West Virginia, however, are clearly examples of malicious restorations. Mountaintop mining—where tops of mountains are destroyed and dumped into adjacent valleys—is in part rationalized through a requirement that the damaged streambeds in the adjacent valleys be restored. The presumed ability to restore these streambeds is used as a justification for allowing mountaintop mining, counting this practice as a clear instantiation of Elliot's restoration thesis. The upshot, however, of this malicious-benevolent distinction is that one may be able to grant much of Elliot's claim that restored nature is not original nature while still not denying that there is some kind of positive value to the act of ecological restoration in many cases. Even if benevolent restorations are not restorations of original nature, and hence more akin to art forgeries rather than original works of art, they still contain some kind of positive content.

The opening of the possibility of benevolent restorations does much to clear away ground for a positive philosophical contribution to questions of restoration. Katz, however, unlike Elliot, denies the positive value of any kind of restoration. For him, as was evidenced in the quote above, all restorations "can only" be malicious because they all represent evidence of human arrogance or hubris toward nature. But surprisingly, even though Katz draws on Elliot's work in formulating his own position, he seems to ignore the fact that Elliot's original description of the restoration thesis was primarily directed against particular kinds of restorations. In his earliest and most famous article on restoration, "The Big Lie: Human Restoration of Nature," Katz expresses surprise to see environmental thinkers (such as forester Chris Maser) advocating "a position similar to Elliot's 'restoration thesis.'" This position, as Katz interprets it, is that "restoration of damaged nature is seen not only as a practical option for environmental policy but also as a moral obligation for right-thinking environmentalists." But Maser's position is not the restoration thesis as Elliot defines it. Katz never does show that Maser, or any other restoration advocate that he analyzes, actually argues for restoration as a rationale for destruction of nature. If that is the case, then what is wrong with restoration on Katz's view?

KATZ AGAINST RESTORATION

As Katz describes it, there are actually two separable questions to put to advocates of restoration: (1) Do we have an obligation to try to restore damaged nature? and (2) Do we have the ability to restore damaged nature? Katz argues quite forcefully that we do not have the ability to restore nature because what we actually create in ecological restorations are humanly produced artifacts and not nature, nonanthropocentrically conceived. Based on this claim he assumes that the first question—whether we have an obligation to try to restore nature—is moot. Katz's logic is simple: We do not have an obligation to do what we can't in principle do.

But even if we were to grant Katz the argument that it is impossible to restore nature, in the sense that Katz understands nature, it might still be the case that we have moral obligations to restore nature. How could this be true? There are a number of reasons, which I will raise below, but for now consider that what we are really restoring with restoration is not necessarily nature itself, but some kind of relationship with nature (whether actually there in the restoration, adjacent to it, or as a more abstract idea). But before fully explicating this position we need to first better understand Katz's arguments.

There are five separable, but often overlapping, arguments in Katz's work on restoration against both the suggestion that we can restore nature and against the practice of trying to restore nature. They are listed below in order of how they arise in Katz's work, accompanied with an example of supporting evidence from Katz's various papers on restoration.

KR1. The Duplicitous Argument

"I am outraged by the idea that a technologically created 'nature' will be passed off as reality."[8]

KR2. The Arrogance (or "Hubris") Argument

"The human presumption that we are capable of this technological fix demonstrates (once again) the arrogance with which humanity surveys the natural world."[9]

KR3. The Artifact Argument

"The re-created natural environment that is the end result of a restoration project is nothing more than an artifact created for human use."[10]

KR4. The Domination Argument

"The attempt to redesign, recreate and restore natural areas and objects is a radical intervention in natural processes. Although there is an obvious spectrum of possible restoration[s] . . . all of these projects involve the manipulation and domination of natural areas. All of these projects involve the creation of artifactual realities, the imposition of anthropocentric interests on the processes and objects of value. Nature is not permitted to be free, to pursue its own independent course of development."[11]

KR5. The Replacement Argument

"If a restored environment is an adequate replacement for the previously existing natural environment [which of course for Katz it can never be], then humans can use, degrade, destroy, and replace natural entities and habitats with no moral consequence whatsoever. The value in the original natural entity does not require preservation."[12]

Here, I will focus on KR4, the domination argument, which is perhaps the argument that comes up the most throughout all of Katz's restoration papers. I will argue that the rest of Katz's arguments can be conceded as long as KR4 can be independently answered.

KR 1–3 and 5 can be ignored in rejecting Katz's position so long as we are prepared to concede for now one important premise to all of his arguments. This is Katz's ontological assumption (a claim concerning the nature or essence of a thing) that humans and nature can be meaningfully separated, thus grounding the argument that restored nature is an artifact, a part of human culture, rather than a part of nature. As Katz has admitted in an as yet unpublished public forum on his work, he is a nature-culture dualist.[13] If one rejects this overall ontological and metaphysical view about the separation of humans from nature, then one may reject most of Katz's objections to restoration.

I will accept here, even though I disagree with it, the underlying assumption by Katz that restored nature does not reproduce nature; that is to say, it does not reproduce whatever value Katz wishes to attribute to nature. But even if I grant this point that restored nature is not really nature, KR4 is still false because it is arguably the case that restoration does not "dominate" nature in any coherent sense but often instead helps nature to be "free" of just the sort of domination that Katz is worried about. The reasoning here is straightforward enough. If I can show that restorations are valuable for nature, even if I concede that they do not recreate nature, then the various motivations for restoration will distinguish whether a restoration is duplicitous (KR1) or arrogant (KR2). A benevolent restoration, for example, would not risk KR1 or 2 because in principle it is not trying to fool anyone nor is it necessarily arrogant. Further, and more simply, conceding Katz's ontological claim about the distinction between nature and culture eliminates the significance of KR3, since we no longer care that what is created may or may not be an artifact, as well as KR5, since we have given up hope that a restoration could ever actually serve as a replacement for "real" nature. (Notice, too, that KR5 is only a problem if one wishes to defend malicious restorations, which I doubt any environmentalist is willing to do.)

Now back to the domination argument. KR4 is a claim that could hold even for a view that conceded Katz's nature-culture distinction. The reason for Katz would be that even a failed attempt to duplicate natural value—or create something akin to nature while conceding that in principle "real" nature can never be restored by humans—could still count as an instance of "domination" as Katz has described it. An attempt at restoration, on Katz's logic, would still prohibit nature from ever being able to pursue its own development. The reason is that for Katz, restoration always is a substitute for whatever would have occurred at a particular site absent human interference. The idea is that even if humans can produce a valuable landscape of some sort on a denuded acreage, this act of production is still an instance of domination over the alternative of a natural evolution of this same acreage even if a significant natural change would take ten times as long as the human induced change and would be arguably less valuable for the species making use of it. Still, there are a number of arguments that one can muster against KR4 (I will provide four) and still play largely within Katz's biggest and most contentious assumption about the ontological status of restored nature.

First, we can imagine cases where nature cannot pursue its own interests (however one wishes to understand this sense of nature having interests) because of something we have done to it which must be rectified by restoration. For example, many instances of restoration are limited to bioactivation of soil which has become contaminated by one form or another of hazardous industrial waste. If restoration necessarily prohibits nature from being "free" as KR4 maintains, then how do we reconcile the relative freedom that bioactivation makes possible with this claim? Restoration need not determine exactly what grows in a certain place, but may in fact simply be the act of allowing nature to again pursue its own interests rather than shackling it to perpetual human-induced trauma. In many cases of restoration this point can be driven home further when we see how anthropogenically damaged land (or soil) can be uniquely put at risk of invasion by anthropogenically introduced exotic plants. South African ice plant, an exotic in southern California which destroys the soil it is introduced onto, is highly opportunistic and can easily spread onto degraded land, thus ensuring that native plants will not be able to reestablish themselves. I highlight here this contentious native-exotic distinction because

I suspect that given Katz's strong nature-culture distinction he would necessarily have to prefer a landscape of native plants over a landscape of exotics where the existence of the exotics is a result of an act of human (cultural) interference in nature. If the original nature at such a site were never put at risk of invasion by exotics introduced by humans, then we can be relatively sure that those exotics would not have made inroads onto the site. Allowing nature to pursue its own interests, given prior anthropogenic interference, thus involves at least as strong a claim to protect it from further anthropogenic risk through restoration practices as the case Katz makes for leaving it alone.

Second, going back to a point made earlier, even if we do agree with Katz that restorations only produce artifacts, can't it still be the case that the harm we cause to nature requires us to engage in what we would have to term, following Katz, "attempted restorations"? It simply does not follow from the premise that something is more natural when it is relatively free of human interference that we should conclude that therefore we must always avoid interfering with nature. It is a classic premise of holism in environmental ethics (the theory that obligations to the nonhuman natural world are to whole ecosystems and not to individual entities, which makes it often opposed to the sort of views advocated by animal rights advocates) that some interference is warranted when we are the cause of an imbalance in nature: e.g., hunting of white-tailed deer is thought to be permissible under holism since humans have caused that species' population explosion. If such interventions as hunting are permissible as an aid to help to "rectify the balance of nature" then why are there not comparable cases with the use of restoration as an aid for the: "original," "real" nature? We can even imagine that such cases would be less controversial than holist defenses of hunting.

It turns out in fact that there are good cases where restoration, even if it results in the production of an artifact, does not lead to the domination described by Katz. Imagine the case where the restoration project is one which will restore a corridor between two wilderness preserves. If there is positive natural value in the two preserves that is threatened because wildlife is not allowed to move freely between them, then restoration projects which would restore a corridor (such as removing roads, for example) would actually not only be morally permissible but possibly ethically required depending on one's views of the value of the nature in the preserves. This is not restoration as a "second best" to preservation, or a distraction away from preservation, it is restoration as an integral and critical part of the maintenance of natural value. So, even if we agree with Katz that humans cannot really restore nature, it does not follow that they ought not to engage in restoration projects which actually repair the damage caused by past domination rather than furthering that domination.

Given objections like the two discussed so far, it is important to try to get a better handle on exactly what sort of damage is caused by domination in the sense described by Katz. It turns out that the worst damage to nature for Katz is domination which prevents the "self-realization" of nature: The fundamental error is thus domination, the denial of freedom and autonomy.

Anthropocentrism, the major concern of most environmental philosophers, is only one species of the more basic attack on the preeminent value of self-realization. From within the perspective of anthropocentrism, humanity believes it is justified in dominating and molding the nonhuman world to its own human purposes.[14] Thus, the problem with restoration is that it restricts natural self-realization by forcing nature onto a path that we would find more appealing.

Third, with this clarification, we can further object to Katz that his sense of restoration confuses restoration with mitigation, for example, the practice of creating new wetlands where none had existed before in order to make up for the loss of an original wetland elsewhere. The force of the charge of domination is that we mold nature to fit our "own human purposes." But with restoration as a practice the point of most scientific disputes over it is precisely that anything does not go. While there is always some variability in what can be restored at a particular site (what period, after all, do we restore to?), we cannot restore a landscape just any way we wish and still have a good restoration in scientific terms. We are also bound in the context of restoration, as was mentioned before, of restoring to some preexisting state even if we are unsure which particularly historical state we ought to restore to. If that is the case, then the broadly construed historical and scientific boundaries of restoration limit the purposes to which we can put a restoration. If Katz objects that when we restore a denuded bit of land we are at least making something that fits our need of having more attractive "natural" surroundings—an argument that Katz often makes—we can reply that because of the constraints that are on restoration, as opposed to mitigation, the fact that we find a restored landscape appealing is only contingently true. It can clearly be the case (and there are plenty of empirical examples) that what we must restore to is not the preferred landscape of most people. The Chicago Wilderness project is in fact in a lot of trouble over exactly these kinds of worries. Many people see this project as involving the destruction of aesthetically pleasing forests in order to restore the original oak savannas. But philosophically, because a restored landscape can never necessarily be tied only to our own desires (since our desires are not historically and scientifically determined in the same way as the parameters of a restoration) then those desires cannot actually be the direct cause of any restriction on the self-realization of nature.[15]

Finally, we must wonder at this value of self-realization. Setting aside the inherent philosophical problems with understanding what this claim to self-realization means in the case of nature, one has to wonder how we could know what natural self-realization would be in any particular case and why we would totally divorce a human role in helping to make it happen if we could discern it. In an analogous case involving two humans, we do not say that a human right to (or value of) self-realization is abrogated when a criminal who harms someone is forced to pay restitution. Even if the restitution is forced against the will of the victim, and even if the compensation in principle can never make up for the harm done, we would not say that somehow the victim's self-realization has been restricted by the act of restitution by the criminal. Again, there seems to be no clear argument here for why the moral obligation to try to restore has been diminished by Katz's arguments that we do not have the ability to really restore nature or pass off an artifact as nature.

RESTORING ENVIRONMENTAL PHILOSOPHY

If I am justified in setting aside the rest of Katz's arguments (KR 1–3 and 5) by accepting his claim that humans really cannot restore "real" nature, then what sort of conclusions could we draw about the role of philosophy in sorting out the normative issues involved in restoration? As it turns out, Katz gives us an insight in figuring out the next step.

After explaining the harm we do to nature in the domination we visit upon it through acts of restoration, Katz briefly assesses the harm that we do to ourselves through such actions. But a policy of domination transcends the anthropocentric subversion of natural processes.

A policy of domination subverts both nature and human existence; it denies both the cultural and natural realization of individual good, human and nonhuman. Liberation from all forms of domination is thus the chief goal of any ethical or political system.[16] Though not very clearly explained by Katz, this intuition represents a crucial point for proceeding further. In addition to connecting environmental philosophy to larger projects of social liberation, Katz here opens the door to a consideration of the consequences of restoration on humans and human communities. As such, Katz allows an implicit assertion that there is a value involved in restoration that must be evaluated other than the value of the objects that are produced by restoration.

But the problem with drawing this conclusion is that this passage is also perhaps the most cryptic in all of Katz's work on restoration. What does Katz mean by this claim? How exactly does restoration deny the realization of an individual human or cultural good? This claim can only be made understandable by assuming that there is some kind of cultural value connected to nature which is risked through the act of domination or otherwise causing harm to nature. But what is this value?

I think that the value that Katz is alluding to here, though which he never explores seriously, somehow describes the value of that part of human culture that is connected to external, nonhuman nature. This is not simply a suggestion that we humans are part of nature (for the implication here is that we cause a disvalue to ourselves and to nature by acting on nature in some way, thus confirming Katz's nature-culture distinction) but rather that we have a relationship with nature which exists on a moral as well as physical terrain in such a way that our actions toward nature can reciprocally harm us. If this is the view implicit in this claim then it is still consistent with much of the rest of Katz's larger views about the value of nature. We have a relationship with nature even if we are separable from it. Without fully explicating the content of that relationship it seems that Katz is right in assuming that somehow the way in which we act toward nature morally implicates us in a particular way. In the same sense, when we morally mistreat another human we not only harm them but harm ourselves (by diminishing our character, by implicating ourselves in evil, however you want to put it).

Now if this assumption is correct, and if there is anything to the arguments I have put forward so far that there can be some kind of positive value to our interaction with nature, then doing right by nature will have the same reciprocal effect of morally implicating us in a positive value as occurs when we do right by other persons. Perhaps Katz would agree. Where Katz would disagree is with the suggestion I would add to this that there is some part of many kinds of restoration (if not most kinds) that contain positive value. Aside from the other suggestions I have already made concerning the possible positive content of restoration, one can also consider that the relationship with nature that is implied in Katz's view has a moral content in itself that is not reducible to the value of fulfilling this relationship's concomitant obligations. The relationship between humans and nature imbues restoration with a positive value even if it cannot replicate natural value in its products. But understanding this point will require some explanation.

Consider that if I have a reciprocal relationship with another human (where I do right by them and they do right by me) then, to generalize Katz's account, there is a moral content to both of our actions which implicates each of us as persons. Each of us is a better person morally because of the way we interact with each other in the relationship. But the relationship itself, or rather just the fact of the existence of the relationship, also has a moral content of its own (or what we would call a "normative content," meaning that the relationship can be assessed as being in a better or worse state) which is independent of the fulfillment of any obligations. If this point of the possible separation between the value of a relationship and the value of the fulfillment of obligations does not follow intuitively, imagine the case where two people act according to duty toward each other without building a substantive normative relationship between them. Consider the following example: I have a brother to whom I am not terribly close. While I always act according to duty to him— I never knowingly do harm to him and I even extend special family obligations to him—I do not have a substantive relationship with him which in itself has a normative content. Thus, if I do not speak to him for a year, nothing is lost (indeed, neither of us feel a loss) because there is no relationship there to maintain or that requires maintenance for normative reasons. But if my brother needed a kidney transplant, I would give him my kidney unhesitatingly out of a sense of obligation something I would not feel obliged to do for non-family members—even though I still do not feel intimately comfortable around him in the same way that I do with my closest friends. Our relationship as persons—that sense of intimate affection and care for another person that I have experienced with other people—has no positive value for me. (It isn't necessarily a disvalue, only it is a sense of indifference, a lack of closeness.) So, I can have interaction with another person, even interaction which involves substantial components of obligation and duty (and in Katz's terms I will never put myself in a position to dominate that other person) but still not have a relationship with them that involves any kind of positive value, or which has normative standards of maintenance.

I do not think that I have any obligation to have a relationship in this sense with my brother. I in fact do not, even though my mother would like it if I did. But if I did have a relationship with my brother in this sense, then it would have a value above and beyond the moral interaction that I have with him now (the obligations that I have to him that can be iterated) that aids in a determination of our moral character. If we had a relationship with normative content there would be a positive or negative value that could be assessed if I lost touch with my brother or ceased to care about his welfare. (I could very well claim that it would be better for me to have such a relationship with him, but this would require a further argument.)

Consider further that if I wanted to rectify or create anew a substantive normative relationship with my brother, like the relationship I have with several close friends, how would I do it? One thing that I could do would be to engage in activities with him. The same sorts of activities (let us call them "material interactions") that I do with my friends now. I might work with him to put up a fence, or help him plant his garden. I might begin to talk over my personal and professional problems with him. I might go on a long journey with him that demanded some kind of mutual reliance, such as white water rafting or visiting a foreign city where neither of us spoke the native language. In short, though there are of course no guarantees, I could begin to have some kind of material relationship with him as a prelude to having some kind of substantive normative relationship with him. Many factors might mitigate the success of such a project. For one thing, the distance between the two of us—he lives in our hometown of Atlanta and I live in upstate New York. So, if I was really serious about this project of building a relationship between us, that had value independent of the value of the fulfillment of our mutual obligations to each other which already exist, I'd have to come up with ways to bridge these interfering factors. Importantly though, I couldn't form a substantive normative relationship with him merely by respecting his right of self-realization and autonomy as a person, I would have to somehow become actively involved with him.

Now, when we compare the case of the estranged brother to that of nature, many parallels arise. We know that we can fulfill obligations to nature in terms of respecting its autonomy and self-realization as a subject (in Katz's terms) without ever forming a substantive normative relationship with it. Assuming also that there is a kind of relationship with nature possible on Katz's scheme (for this is in part what we harm when we dominate nature) it is fair to say that a relationship consisting in positive normative value with nature is compatible with Katz's overall view of the human-nature relationship. Because he says so little about what our positive relationship to nature could be, he is in no position to restrict it a priori. We also know that, as in the case of the estranged brother, we need some kind of material bridge to create a relationship with nature in order to see that relationship come about.

How to build that bridge? Suggesting ways to overcome the gap between humans and nature (without necessarily disvaluing it) seems in part to be the restored role of environmental philosophy in questions of ecological restoration. Certainly, as in the case of my brother, distance is a problem. Numerous environmental professionals have emphasized the importance of being in nature in order to care for nature. Also, acts of preservation are important in order for there to be nature to have a relationship with. But what about restoration? Can restoration help engender such a positive normative relationship with nature? It seems clear to me that it can. When we engage in acts of benevolent restoration we are bound by nature in the same sense that we are obligated to respect what it once was attempting to realize before we interfered with it. In Katz's terms, we are attempting to respect it as an autonomous subject. But we are also bound to nature in the act of restoring. In addition to the ample sociological and anthropological evidence on the positive value with nature that is engendered in benevolent restoration, we can say that restoration restores the human connection to nature by restoring that part of culture that has historically contained a connection to nature. While it would take further argument to prove, I believe that this is the kind of relationship that is a necessary condition for encouraging people to choose to preserve the natural system and landscapes around them rather than trade them offer short term monetary gains garnered by development. If I am in a normative relationship with the land around me (whether it is "real" nature or not) I am less likely to allow it to be harmed further.[18]

We can even look to Katz for help in completing this pragmatic task. We don't want restorations that try to pass themselves offer the real thing when they are really "fakes" (KR1) or are pursued through arrogance (KR2), nor are we interested in those that are offered as justifications for replacing or destroying nature (KR5). Nor would we want our human relationships to exhibit those properties, either. But even given the legacy of inhuman treatment of each other, we know that it is possible to restore human relationships that do not resemble KR1, 2, or 5. There is, however, one possible worry to attend to in KR3, the artifact argument. While earlier I had said that the importance of KR1 is diminished by granting Katz's nature-culture distinction, there is a way that it can still cause us problems in grounding attempts at restoration in the positive value of strengthening the human-nature relationship.

Katz may object to my relationship argument that if we allow his claim that what has been restored is not really nature then what we are restoring is not a cultural relationship with nature but, in a sense, only extending the artifactual material culture of humans. At best, all we can have with restoration is a relationship with artifacts, not nature. Maybe he will allow that we improve relations with each other through cooperative acts of restoration, but this is not the same as a restoration of a relationship with nature itself.

But it should be clear by now that Katz would be mistaken to make such an objection for several reasons stemming in part from my earlier remarks. First, even if we admit that restored nature is an artifact and not real nature, restored nature can also serve as a conduit for real nature to free itself from the shackles we have previously placed upon it. Restoration can allow nature to engage in its own autonomous restitution. Of the different sorts of restoration projects which I have sketched above, many amount to aids to nature rather than creations of new nature.

Second, even if restoration is the production of an artifact, these artifacts do bear a striking resemblance to the real thing. This is not to say that restorations can be good enough to fool us (KR1). Rather, it is simply to point out that an opportunity to interact with the flora and fauna of the sort most common in benevolent restorations will have the effect of increasing the bonds of care that people will have with nonrestored nature. If a denuded and abandoned lot in the middle of an inner-city ghetto is restored by local residents who have never been outside of their city, then it will give them a better appreciation of the fragility and complexity of the natural processes of nature itself should they encounter them. The fact that restorationists are engaged in a technological processes does not necessarily mean that their practices do not serve the broader purpose of restoring a relationship with nature. Just as starting some form of mediated communication with my brother (like e-mail or regular phone calls) does not restore a fully healthy communicative relationship with him that could be found through face-to-face conversation, it still helps me to get used to the idea of some form of immediate and substantive communication.

And finally, if Katz persists in his worry that the act of restoration reifies domination by reaffirming our power over nature through the creation of artifacts, we can say that exactly the opposite is likely the case (at least in the case of benevolent restorations) where the goal is restoring the culture of nature if not nature itself. Restorationists get firsthand (rather than anecdotal and textbook) exposure to the actual consequences of human domination of nature. A better understanding of the problems of bioactivating soil, for example, gives us a better idea of the complexity of the harm we have caused to natural processes. Knowing that harm can be empowering in a much healthier way than Katz seems willing to admit in that it can empower us to know more precisely why we should object to the kinds of activities that can cause that harm to nature in the first place.[19]

It seems clear that benevolent restorations are valuable because they help us to restore our relationship with nature, by restoring what could be termed our culture of nature. This is true even if Katz is correct that restored nature has the ontological property of an artifact. Restoration is an obligation exercised in the interests of forming a positive community with nature, and thus is well within the boundaries of a constructive, pragmatic environmental philosophy.[20]

NOTES

1. Eric Katz, "The Problem of Ecological Restoration," *Environmental Ethics* 18 (1996): 222, my emphasis.

2. See Andrew Light and Eric Higgs, "The Politics of Ecological Restoration," *Environmental Ethics* 18 (1996): 22–24.

3. See for example, Andrew Light, "Environmental Pragmatism as Philosophy or Metaphilosophy," in *Environmental Pragmatism*, ed. Andrew Light and Eric Katz (London: Routledge, 1996), pp. 325–38; "Compatibilism in Political Ecology," in *Environmental Pragmatism*, pp. 161–84; and "Callicott and Naess on Pluralism," *Inquiry* 39 (1996): 23–94.

4. See for example, Kelly Parker, "Pragmatism and Environmental Thought," in *Environmental Pragmatism*, pp. 21–37.

5. Robert Elliot, "Faking Nature," in *Environmental Ethics* (Oxford: Oxford University Press, 1995), p. 76. The replacement thesis is explicated in Robert Elliot, *Faking Nature* (London: Routledge, 1997).

6. Elliot, "Faking Nature," p. 82. Elliot strengthens the more charitable view of restoration in his more recent book.

7. Eric Katz, *Nature as Subject: Human Obligation and Natural Community* (Lanham, Md.: Rowman & Littlefield Publishers, 1997), p. 96. Katz has four main papers on restoration: "The Big Lie: Human Restoration of Nature," "The Call of the Wild: The Struggle Against Domination and the Technological Fix of Nature," "Artifacts and Functions: A Note on the Value of Nature," and "Imperialism and Environmentalism." All of these papers are collected in the book just cited. It is the versions of these papers as they appear in this volume that I have drawn on for this chapter.

8. Katz, *Nature as Subject*, p. 97. Originally in "The Big Lie"(as are KR2–KR4). KR 1 is restated later in "The Call of the Wild": ". . . what makes value in the artifactually restored natural environment questionable is its ostensible claim to be the original." (Ibid., p. 114)

9. Ibid., p. 97.

10. Ibid. KR3 is most thoroughly elaborated later in "Artifacts and Functions."

11. Ibid., p. 105. The domination argument is repeated in "The Call of the Wild" (ibid., p. 115) with the addition of an imported quote from Eugene Hargrove: Domination "reduces [nature's] ability to be creative." The argument is also repeated in "Artifacts and Functions" and further specified in "Imperialism and Environmentalism." As far as I can tell though, the argument for domination is not really expanded on in this last paper, except that imperialism is deemed wrong because it makes nature into an artifact (KR3).

12. Ibid., p. 113. Originally in "The Call of the Wild," and repeated in "Imperialism and Environmentalism." (Ibid., p. 139)

13. The forum mentioned here is the same as the one referenced in n. 1.

14. Ibid, p. 105.

15. Bill Throop has pointed out to me that choosing any historical point of reference for a restoration could count as domination on Katz's view. My only response at this time is that we can imagine cases where the good for biodiversity done by restoration would outweigh such worries and significantly, what counts as the good for biodiversity at a particular site is usually historically grounded. So, history is at least mutually constraining here: it holds us and nature to a range of historical influences simultaneously.

16. Ibid., p. 105.

17. On a broader scale, just as there can be a town full of decent, law abiding citizens, they may not constitute a moral community in any significant sense.

18. It is also the case that restoration will only be one out of a large collection of practices available for adaptive management. Indeed, there could even be cases where something akin to mitigation (albeit a benevolent kind) would be justified rather than restoration if a claim to sustaining some form of natural value warranted it. In a project to clean up an abandoned mine site, for example, we can imagine a case where restoring the site to a landscape that was there before would not be the best choice and that instead some other sustainable landscape which would help to preserve an endangered species now in the area would be more appropriate. But overall, environmentalists must accept human interaction with nature as an acceptable practice in order to begin the ethical assessment of any case of environmental management. I am indebted to Anne Chapman for pressing me to clarify this point.

19. Katz can legitimately respond here that there seems to be no unique reason why people couldn't get these kinds of experiences that generate a closer relationship with nature out of some other kinds of activities. Why couldn't we just use this sort of argument to encourage more acts of preservation, or simply walking though nature, etc. Such an objection would however miss a crucial point. Even if it can be proved that we can get these kinds of positive experiences with nature in forms other than acts of restoration (and I see no reason why we couldn't) this does not diminish the case being built here: that restoration does not necessarily result in the domination of nature. The goal of my argument here is not to provide a unique value that restoration provides that no other environmental practice provides, but only to reject the claim that there is no kind of positive value that restoration can contribute to nature in some sense. So, an objection by Katz of this sort would miss the target of our substantive disagreement. Additionally, one could also argue that (1) restoration does in fact produce some unique values in our relationship with nature, and that (2) even if non-unique in itself, restoration helps to improve other sorts of unique values in nature. A case for (2) could be made, for example, by appeal to Allen Carlson's work on the importance of scientific understanding for appreciating the aesthetic value of nature. (See Allen Carlson, "Nature, Aesthetic Appreciation, and Knowledge," *Journal of Aesthetics and Art Criticism* 53 [1995]: 393–400.) Arguably, our experiences as restorationists give us some of the kinds of understandings of the workings of natural processes required for aesthetic appreciation on Carlson's account. Importantly, this understanding is a transitive property: it not only gives us an ability to aesthetically appreciate the nature we are trying to restore, but also the nature we are not trying to restore. Restoration thus could provide a unique avenue into the aesthetic appreciation of all of nature, restored or not. The main point however should not be lost: Restoration is an important component in a mosaic of efforts to revive the culture of nature. Absent any reason to believe that it has other disastrous effects it seems warranted within a prescribed context even if it is not a cure-all.

20. This paper is a shortened version of my "Ecological Restoration and the Culture of Nature: A Pragmatic Perspective," in *Restoring Nature: Perspectives from the Social Sciences and Humanities*, ed. Paul Gobster and Bruce Hall (Washington, D.C.: Island Press, 2000). Presentations of the paper were made at a plenary session of the 1998 International Symposium on Society and Resource Management at the University of Missouri, as the keynote address of the Eastern Pennsylvania Philosophy Association annual meeting, Bloomsburg University, November 1998, and at Georgia State Univer-

sity, SUNY Binghamton, and Lancaster University (UK). I have benefited much from the discussions at all of these occasions and especially from the helpful comments provided by Cari Dzuris, Cheryl Foster, Warwick Fox, Paul Gobster, Leslie Heywood, Bruce Hull, Bryan Norton, George Rainbolt, William Throop, and Christopher Wellman.

REFERENCES

Carlson, Allen. "Nature, Aesthetic Appreciation, and Knowledge." *Journal of Aesthetics and Art Criticism* 53 (1995).

Elliot, Robert. "Faking Nature." In *Environmental Ethics*. Oxford: Oxford University Press, 1995.

———. *Faking Nature*. London: Routledge, 1997.

Katz, Eric. "The Problem of Ecological Restoration." *Environmental Ethics* 18 (1996).

Light, Andrew. "Callicott and Naess on Pluralism." *Inquiry* 39 (1996).

———. "Compatibilism in Political Ecology." In *Environmental Pragmatism*, edited by Andrew Light and Eric Katz. London: Routledge, 1996.

———. "Environmental Pragmatism as Philosophy or Metaphilosophy." In *Environmental Pragmatism*, edited by Andrew Light and Eric Katz. London: Routledge, 1996.

———. "Ecological Restoration and the Culture of Nature: A Pragmatic Perspective." In *Restoring Nature: Perspectives from the Social Sciences and Humanities*, edited by Paul Gobster and Bruce Hall. Washington, D.C.: Island Press, 2000.

Light, Andrew, and Eric Higgs. "The Politics of Ecological Restoration." *Environmental Ethics* 18 (1996).

Parker, Kelly. "Pragmatism and Environmental Thought." In *Environmental Pragmatism*, edited by Andrew Light and Eric Katz. London: Routledge, 1996.

Katz, Eric. *Nature as Subject: Human Obligation and Natural Community*. Lanham, Md.: Rowman & Littlefield Publishers, 1997.

7

Rehabilitating Nature and Making Nature Habitable

Robin Attfield

C an nature be reconstituted, recreated, or rehabilitated? And would the goal of doing so be a desirable one? There again, is wild nature intrinsically valuable, or are parks, gardens, and farms sometimes preferable or of greater value? This cluster of questions arises from recent debates about preservation, restoration, wilderness, and sustainable development. In discussing them I hope to throw some light on both the concept and the value of nature, and in due course on the attitudes which people should have toward it, the policies which should guide their practice, and thus on the proper role of humanity with regard to the natural world.

To begin with, we need a clear sense of "nature," and thus to turn to John Stuart Mill's celebrated essay on that subject.[1] Now when the possibility of nature being restored is at issue, "nature" cannot be used in Mill's first sense, "all which is the powers and properties of all things." For in this sense there is no possibility of nature being destroyed or damaged, let alone reconstructed. Mill's second sense of "nature," rather, is the relevant one: "what takes place without . . . the voluntary and intentional agency of man [sic]." Nature (in this sense) can obviously be modified by human activity. Moreover a difficulty already emerges about the possibility of restoring it: How can anything be restored by human agency the essence of which is to be independent of human agency? This is a question to which we shall return.

Meanwhile it is apposite here to remark that Mill argues against the desir-

Robin Attfield, "Rehabilitating Nature and Making Nature Habitable," in *Philosophy and the Natural Environment*, ed. R. Attfield and A. Belsey (Cambridge: Cambridge University Press, 1994). Reprinted by permission of Cambridge University Press.

ability of imitating nature (in this sense), holding that civilization has made progress precisely through turning its back on this policy, and that nature is not an exemplar fit to be followed. His case is, indeed, well made. It may further be noted that his own understanding of the tendency of humanity to value nature is that this tendency arises from the vastness of natural forces; but the astonishment and awe which are thus inspired are said to be prone to "intrude into matters with which they ought to have no concern."[2] They are, in particular, no guide for ethics or conduct.

This essay was composed during the 1850s, before Darwin's theory of evolution was published. Thus, conservationist as he was, Mill was in no position to appreciate the evolutionary systems and networks which are among the modern bases for the appreciation of nature. Yet more than this is missing from his account of responses to nature. He grasped the terror-inspiring vastness of natural forces, and to this he ascribed their sublimity; but he seems to have omitted the sense of nature's otherness or strangeness, and the importance that this has in renewing both wonder and perspective. Nor does he mention another aspect of nature's strangeness, its inexhaustible diversity; while little is said, beyond the passage about sublimity, about natural beauty. Since so much that he says about nature is convincing, it is worth drawing attention from the start both to his omissions and to these further grounds for valuing nature.

But this does not show that whatever is natural is invariably valuable. Robert Elliot, whose views on attempts at the restoration of nature will shortly be discussed, recognizes this at the outset of his essay "Faking Nature"; treating "natural" as meaning (approximately) "unmodified by human activity,"[3] he gives sickness and disease as examples of natural phenomena which are not good, and mentions how fires, hurricanes, and volcanic eruptions can alter landscapes for the worse. He does claim, however, that "within certain constraints, the naturalness of a landscape is a reason for preserving it, a determinant of its value." One constraint which he supplies is this: "Artificially transforming an utterly barren, ecologically bankrupt landscape into something richer and more subtle may be a good thing." Here the naturalness of the landscape is not regarded as a sufficient reason for preserving it. Nevertheless, he argues, the natural origin or genesis of a feature or landscape is always a factor which contributes to its value;[4] and to this conclusion I shall be returning.

A rather stronger position about the value of nature is taken by Eric Katz.[5] Katz basically defines "natural" as "being independent of the actions of humanity," and less basically as "objects and processes that exist as far as possible from human manipulation and control."[6] The key characteristic of natural individuals is that they "were not designed for a purpose," but "evolve to fill ecological niches in the biosphere," unlike artifacts, which Katz represents as created for human purposes, and thus "essentially anthropocentric."[7] Further, "natural entities are autonomous in ways that human-created artifacts are not"; thus "when we . . . judge natural objects, and evaluate them more highly than artifacts, we are focussing on the extent of their independence from human domination."[8] For the preeminent value is self-realization, and that is what natural entities, being autonomous, are free to pursue.[9] Katz, like Elliot, uses his metaphysical and axiological claims about nature to argue against attempts to restore damage caused by human interventions.

For his part Elliot maintains that if a reconstituted natural setting is qualitatively indistinguishable from other natural settings or from its own earlier condition, its value is less because it is a "fake," lacking the right kind of origin. Just as the value of works of art depends on their having the right sort of provenance, so, too, the value of apparently wild and natural settings depends in part on their being genuinely so, and having originated through natural processes and not through artifice.[10] Elliot adds that it is wise for conservationists to argue in addition the inadequacy of the restorations which developers promise;[11] but he believes that in protesting that even the best of restorations lacks the value had by what is to be restored simply because it is a fake they already have a rational case.[12]

To this case, Katz and Richard Sylvan, conservationists both, reply that actual deception is rarely in question, and thus that little is achieved by representing restoring as faking or restorations as fakes.[13] While this reply is apposite, Sylvan finds merit all the same in Elliot's arguments in favor of the significance of an item's origins and history for its value, taking the view that this is where the strength of his case really lies, and not in the faking analogy.[14]

Now certainly the symbolic and aesthetic value of an item can depend in part on its origins and history; but this approach puts the value of natural items with the right kind of origins in much the same position as that of cultural artifacts such as vases or paintings, despite the manifest differences between art appreciation and nature appreciation, differences which Elliot well recognizes and expresses.[15] And plausibly the value of such items is what Frankena calls "inherent value";[16] it depends ultimately on the actual or potential appreciation of valuers, rather than supplying grounds for preservation independent of psychological states of valuers in the way that intrinsic or independent value is held to do. Certainly this appreciation is itself sometimes dependent on the valued item having the right kind of origin or history, and that is an independent characteristic of the item in question, as Elliot points out.[17] But this does not serve to make the case for its preservation (and thus for its nonreplacement) any stronger than the like case for the preservation of cultural artifacts. Indeed unless it has further grounds, its strength is surely proportionate to the number of humans susceptible to the right kind of appreciation.

While for Elliot restorations of nature are possible but of inferior value, for Katz they are impossible. Restorations are artifacts, which are invariably anthropocentric; whereas nature is without design, is capable of self-realization and is precisely not an artifact. Most of this, however, is open to challenge. For the moment I set on one side the reply that most areas of the earth, however apparently natural, have in fact been influenced by human activity, and thus would have to be seen by purists as artifacts. Further replies concern restorations of nature specifically, and are raised by Sylvan. Thus restorations of nature are largely achieved "by nature doing its own thing" (what used to be called *natura naturans*), and are not the products of human making or human creation. Humans weed them or remove rubbish, but their contribution amounts to helping along a natural process of healing. Thus Katz has illicitly extended the meaning of "artifact" to restorations, which, unsatisfactory as they standardly are, should still not be regarded as artifacts.[18]

Sylvan here adds that the point of restorations is not invariably human pleasure or human use, and is often "the welfare and persistence of other creatures and natural features," or alternatively the enrichment or enhancement of an area's value. Thus restorations, albeit designed by humans, need not have a shallow or "anthropocentric" motivation, and need not conflict with the natural development of natural creatures. Even if artifacts were essentially anthropocentric, which they are not, this would still not apply to restorations. Sylvan does not discuss Katz's contentious claim that the preeminent value is self-realization, but does not need to do so to make the point that the case for restorations is liable to concern whether there is an increase in value, as there sometimes is, and not a false metaphysical account of their essence. He gives the example of an ecosystem which has been impoverished by "creaming," and which is restored by reintroducing the creamed species from elsewhere; here value is clearly enhanced.[19]

Sylvan goes on to recognize the many problems facing attempts at rehabilitation of a natural setting. Besides obvious practical obstacles there are problems deriving from lack of information and also from lack of suitable technology. Yet "technology-assisted restoration nonetheless has a point and place." The modest role envisaged here for technology is in complete contrast to belief in "universal technological repair and . . . total rehabilitation," or in there being a technological fix for each and every ecological problem, something against which Katz is right to protest.[20] Even former wildernesses can sometimes be restored, by closing off the roads which enter them.[21] Rehabilitation is thus possible, and sometimes admissible and worthwhile. For societies (as opposed to individuals) able to put this into effect it can actually be obligatory, just as it is obligatory to reduce the erosion of substantially natural environments. But there is nothing glamorous about it; it is the cleaning up of some of the appalling mess around us, and resembles, as much as anything, "housework in a slum."[22] This does, however, show that "Letting Be" (what Hargrove calls "therapeutic nihilism"[23]) is frequently inappropriate, at least for disturbed areas.[24]

While I consider that Sylvan's critique, as just presented, can largely be accepted, it raises certain problems of both metaphysics and ethics which call for further investigation. In particular it recalls the metaphysical problem mentioned above when Mill's second sense of "nature" was introduced: How can anything be restored by human agency the essence of which is to be independent of human agency? Indeed it further raises the whole question of the role of humanity vis-à-vis nature, and the related ethical questions of the principles by which conduct and policy should be guided with respect to an environment mostly already heavily affected by previous use, in circumstances when pressing human needs require its further use for as long as the future can be foreseen.

To tackle the metaphysical problem first, there certainly is a paradox concerning human agency restoring what is essentially independent of human agency. But it should also be noted that there is no question of this where nature is undamaged and wilderness untrammeled. Intervention could certainly be required to prevent disturbance (and on occasion could be justifiable), but this would not be restoration. Only where disruption has already taken place, as, however, is the case in most of the areas of Britain recognized as "ancient forest," is restoration or rehabilitation possible; and what is sometimes possible is reversing the damage and returning an area to a condition closely resembling its erstwhile condition in which evolutionary processes proceed independent of further human agency. Sylvan's example of returning creamed species could be a case in point. Although Elliot's historical requirement for nature to have its full aesthetic value is not satisfied, and the area cannot be regarded as in all respects wild, there could in theory be the same blend of creatures each living in accordance with its own nature, and jointly forming a system just like the pristine one which preceded human intervention. Although the outcome is, broadly, what human agency intended, it is still equivalent to what unimpeded nature would have produced. Besides, if there is intrinsic value in the fulfillment of the capacities of the various natural creatures, each in accordance with its own nature, as I have argued elsewhere, then there is present the same intrinsic value as there would have been if humanity had never intervened. Further, if the area was ever to regain this condition, nothing but the intervention of an intentional agency could bring this about. Indeed the paradox is perhaps no stronger than that involved when the agency and interventions of parents bring about the possibility of autonomy for their children as they grow to adulthood; though here autonomy is of course initiated rather than restored.

The deliberate restoration of nature (to something like the condition of wilderness) is thus a possibility. So is the preservation of nature, where intervention prevents the natural course of events being disturbed. Yet the difficulties, including those mentioned by Katz and Sylvan, will often make this more a theoretical than a practical possibility. Katz objects that even if there were a plan in a natural system, we could not know it;[25] while we might in theory know how to rectify the *status quo ante*, without knowing the full story of how this particular ecosystem works we are most unlikely to, or to act in a manner precisely proportioned to what we should need to know. And so on. Yet it would still be possible (as Sylvan says) to enrich the area and increase its value; and where the enrichment was considerable, this might be regarded as rehabilitation, even if it would not technically be restoration. For the outcome could still (at least in theory) be an area in which, without further human intervention, evolutionary processes produced ever new communities of thriving wild creatures, much more than was possible up to the time of intervention, and this would surely count as rehabilitation if anything ever would. Whether a particular act of rehabilitation is justified would, however, often turn on further factors, such as whether value could be enhanced in an alternative way, or whether the proposed rehabilitation was a ploy proposed to offset environmentalist criticism of a destructive development like strip-mining which the proposers intend to carry out first.

Indeed not too much can be derived from these possibilities about the role of humanity vis-à-vis nature; for humanity has many obligations besides wilderness preservation, restoration and rehabilitation, if indeed these are obligations. The suggestion that they are not, together with several related issues of ethics and policy, has recently been debated by J. Baird Callicott and Holmes Rolston;[26] a brief account of this debate is now in place, before the outstanding metaphysical, ethical and policy issues are further tackled.

Callicott ascribes to Aldo Leopold support not only for preserving wild sanctuaries but also for the view that human activity sometimes enhances ecosystems.[27] He proceeds to question the viability of wilderness preservation, and then to criticize the very concept of wilderness as unnecessarily dualistic, and objectionably ethnocentric and static.[28] Conservation, he suggests, should rather be blended with sustainable development, economic development being at the same time reconceived in the light of ecology, with (for example) reintroduced native ungulates both sustaining New World ecosystems and being ranched to feed humans there.[29]

Rolston for his part ably defends the concept of wilderness. The concepts of nature and culture are fundamentally distinct (as indeed has effectively been shown also in the passages concerning Mill, Elliot and Katz), and the concept of wilderness preservation need not be ethnocentric, and does not ignore temporal change.[30] There are values intrinsic to wild nature, which thus ought to be preserved both for its own sake and for the good of humanity; wilderness advocates recognize values which do not depend on human valuations, but which humans nevertheless ought and need to affirm.[31] Rolston accepts the importance of sustainable development within the realms of culture and cultivation, but rejects the possibility of wilderness management and that of humans improving wild nature as contradictions in terms.[32] He also regards as inadequate Callicott's anthropogenic value theory, which makes values ultimately dependent on human valuations.[33]

As will already be apparent, there is no alternative but to recognize the conceptual case for the impossibility of managing or enhancing areas of pure wilderness. Yet rather little of the earth's surface amounts to pure wilderness, and in Europe virtually none. There is a strong case for preserving such areas as there are for the sake of the creatures within them, because of the needs of human science and because of the value to humans of the availability of what is wild and wholly other; and this applies both to untouched wilderness and to wilderness (or semiwilderness) only lightly affected by humanity, as by the primitive technology of forest peoples—as long as these people are not excluded from their own forests. But it is at least equally important to reflect on how best to treat the remaining areas of the earth which have ceased to be wilderness, but remain significantly wild, and a vital contrast to the frenetic life of cities and motorways. As has been seen, the possibilities of enhancing, rehabilitating, and even restoring such areas certainly can arise. Indeed, conservationists cannot afford to reject the enhanced value of restored wilderness, despite what Rolston calls its "different historical genesis."[34] While there is, as Rolston (in line here with Elliot) says, "a radical change of value type,"[35] the deficiency (I have suggested) concerns one particular kind of aesthetic value, while much which is of intrinsic value remains, together with the restored intactness of ancient ecosystems.

Next, to be fair to Callicott, his idea of wilderness management should not be ruled out entirely, despite the contradiction which it generates where the express aim is wilderness preservation, and despite the strong ethical case for preserving wilderness untrammeled. Callicott writes of management with a view to the vital part which wilderness can play in biological conservation, by which he could easily mean "species conservation"; and if a species whose original habitat has ceased to be viable can only be preserved (or can best be preserved) by its introduction into a wilderness (which its introduction would admittedly modify), the implicit clash of values confronting decision makers would not seem to produce a clear-cut case every time against introduction. But this minor rehabilitation of the case for wilderness management does not make and should not be taken as a case for the management of wildernesses in general, which, as Callicott acknowledges, might "artificialize" any wilderness to which it is applied.[36]

This discussion of restoring wilderness and of managing wilderness does, however, serve to bring to light the way Rolston sometimes overstates his case. Rolston writes that it is a "fallacy to think that a nature allegedly improved by humans is any more real nature at all," and goes on to claim that "the values intrinsic to wilderness cannot, on pain of both logical and empirical contradiction, be 'improved' by deliberate human management, because deliberation is the antithesis of wildness."[37] This is the passage which leads up to the claim that wilderness management is a contradiction in terms. Though the context concerns wilderness, the claim here about nature happens to imply both that areas like parks and gardens, designed and intentionally improved by humans for the sake of beauty and its aesthetic enjoyment, contain neither natural creatures nor natural processes, and also that the species modified for agriculture have ceased to have natural capacities and propensities, and thus a good natural to their kind. Yet natural goods can in fact persist far away from wilderness; and this is just as well for the citizens of modern urban and rural areas alike, for the creatures they cultivate and for the ethics of the treatment of those creatures.

Relatedly, the values intrinsic to wilderness include the intrinsic value of the flourishing of the creatures which originate there, the value of intact ecosystems, and the value of the human appreciation of wildness, of otherness, and of living systems which originate from evolution alone and lack any human modification. But only some of these values are distinctive of pure wilderness. While restored wilderness lacks only the last-mentioned value (living systems originating from evolution alone), the intrinsic value of the flourishing of natural creatures occurs wherever they are to be found throughout the earth, and not only in wilderness. While this does not of itself affect Rolston's point about wilderness management, it does show that the value of wilderness does not only consist in its wildness; indeed it suggests that it does not principally consist in this. And if so, the wildness of wilderness might not be a conclusive ethical reason against proposals to manage it; indeed much that is wild ought to be managed more than it is, including certain philosophical theories (but I am not referring here to Rolston's). In any case, some of the values originating in wilderness are transferable out of the wild without ceasing to be natural, when, as Rolston goes on to remark, humans rebuild the natural world they inherit. And this, too, is important, as the appreciation of nature, and to a limited extent of its otherness and even of its wildness, can be significantly available even in places like Europe, where wilderness has virtually ceased to exist, and in Third World settings, where, as Callicott points out, most landscapes have long been inhabited by *Homo sapiens* as well as by other species.[38]

These considerations are not without their importance when, as I shortly shall, we turn to the role of humanity vis-à-vis nature. The importance of sustainable development is recognized both by Callicott, who regards it as the main route to conservation, and by Rolston, who reasonably enough requires that there be some wilderness preservation independently of it, but who implies too great an absence of the natural within the sphere of human culture and cultivation. Sylvan too recognizes that sustainable development may have much merit, but rapidly adds that it is "not nature *enhancing* but rather purports to limit further rot and decline," that it is less benign than nature rehabilitation, and that it and its subtypes, sustainable forestry and sustainable agriculture, are typical of a shallow (i.e., anthropocentric) rather than a deep value theory.[39] While his context concerns nature restoration, these remarks still gravely underestimate the values which sustainable development can uphold and which often motivate its advocates.

To take the last point first, sustainable development is aimed at satisfying future as well as present needs, and not only human needs at that. For sustainability involves the preservation of ecological systems. As Callicott puts it: "We conservationists . . . may hope realistically that in the future, ecological, as well as technological feasibility may be taken into account in designing new and redesigning old ways of humans living with the land."[40] This well conveys the approach of enlightened human self-interest; but the Brundtland Report, the deservedly influential text which continues to inspire the advocacy of sustainable development, is clear that ecological systems are also to be preserved for the sake of nonhuman species and of their own intrinsic value, and proceeds to urge a considerable amount of wilderness preservation alongside its advocacy of sustainable production. To cite a relevant passage: "The case for the conservation of nature should rest not only with development goals. It is part of our moral obligation to other living beings and future generations."[41]

Thus, while sustainable development is not specifically focused on nature *restoration*, it is not, essentially or centrally, an anthropocentric or shallow policy; indeed the pursuit of sustainability is, to say the least, compatible with the restoration of forests, and may sometimes require it. Thus Rolston too is adrift when he declares that "sustainable development is, let's face it, irremediably anthropocentric";[42] it should, however, be acknowledged that he endorses much that Callicott says in its favor, including the apparently non-anthropocentric remark "Human economic activities should at least be compatible with the ecological health of the environments in which they occur."[43] Callicott in fact goes further, advocating (under the banner of sustainable development) "economic activity that positively enhances ecosystemic health";[44] there is, as has already been seen, no contradiction in this, and conservationists can and should welcome this suggestion for a wide range of ecologically impoverished environments.

Sustainable development has the further merit that it takes seriously people's obligations to satisfy human needs both in the present and into the indefinite future. Since the development thus facilitated of essential human capacities has intrinsic value, as also has the flourishing of nonhuman creatures (or so I have argued elsewhere[45]), a policy which promotes or sustains both these tendencies yields greater value and enriches the world much more than a policy (such as the restoration of wilderness) with only one of these outcomes. This does not show that the entire surface of the planet should be devoted to processes of sustainable development, not least because this would undermine numerous nonhuman species;[46] but it does suggest that there is in general a stronger obligation to support and implement sustainable development than there is to enhance the value of natural areas.

Not too much more can be said here about priorities, but what has just been said has important implications. Thus, whether an area should be restored, or even first mined or felled and then restored, depends not only on the value implications for nonhuman nature, as the general tone of Sylvan's remarks suggests, but, as Elliot says, on the whole range of relevant ethical considerations, and thus on the overall balance of values at issue,[47] for all that Sylvan takes him to task for saying so.[48] The ethical verdict may thus not always come out as conservationists would wish; but that is no reason for regarding the value theory which makes this possible as shallow. (It might be shallow in another sense if it did not underwrite protests against exploitation and injustice; but it does.)

Thus the role of human beings is not only that of preservers of nature, not even when the role of restorers is added to that of preservers. Besides the role of rehabilitating nature, people have the role of making nature habitable, and sustainably so—habitable for human beings of the present and the future and also for those nonhuman creatures which they rear or cultivate as part of their civilization or their culture—without at the same time undermining those whose wildness and otherness they need or whose flourishing is of value in itself. Unsustainable processes of agriculture, forestry, and industry can seldom contribute to this, except where they are needed as initial investment to inaugurate genuinely sustainable processes. Among sustainable processes, those which are globally sustainable are preferable to those which are only sustainable in some regions at the expense of others; likewise those which take into account the full range of values are preferable to those with any kind of discriminatory tendency. The suggestion that humanity should cultivate the earth and through skills and crafts make it habitable (though not for humanity alone) is an ancient one, put forward originally by such church fathers as Basil, Gregory, Augustine, and others as work which fulfills the purpose of the creator.[49] and it is none the worse for that. That humanity has this role (whether with or without these theological overtones) is also a key part of my present conclusion, without negating the conclusion that the proper role of humanity also includes preservation and rehabilitation.

This is not the place to discuss in depth whether the particular strategies urged by Callicott are the best way to fulfill these roles. His proposals for the ranching of ungulates in their original habitats has much to commend it, but may perhaps pay too little regard to the interests of the ungulates themselves. His proposals that designated wilderness areas serve as *"refugia"* for the less tolerant or the less easily tolerated species[50] are trenchantly criticized by Rolston,[51] as are his attempts to represent human activities in general as natural; yet the idea of *refugia* may have a point in some cases in connection with species preservation, especially "for species not tolerant of or tolerated by people."[52] And his remarks about the symbiotic relations of the Kayapo Indians of the Amazon and their rainforest reveal an apparent paradigm of sustainability there, and strengthen the belief that designs for nature reserves can and should (where it is viable) "require planners to take account of and integrate local peoples culturally and economically," as United Nations policy apparently already enjoins.[53]

But all this would come to very little if Callicott's or similar accounts of the nature of value and the status of value language were granted; accordingly a brief mention of metaethics is finally in place. As Rolston reminds us, Callicott maintains that "intrinsic value ultimately depends upon human valuers"[54] and that "value is, as it were, projected onto natural objects or events by the subjective feelings of observers."[55] Thus nothing would be of value unless valued by humans (or other valuers) in at least some possible world. Partially similar conclusions are maintained by Sylvan, whose "nonobjectivism" is as much intended to deny the independence of value from valuers as to deny that it is a quality of valuers, that is, to reject both objectivism (both naive and sophisticated) and subjectivism, too.[56] Thus Sylvan too implies that there would be no value if there never were any valuers. Meanwhile Elliot, without relativizing value to valuers, still represents it as always relative to a valuational framework; and while any given framework offers interpersonal reasons ultimately there are apparently no reasons for preferring one valuational framework to another.[57]

Thus, in some ways it is here that Rolston makes his most trenchant and possibly most important contribution to the debate, maintaining that Callicott's is a truncated theory of value, making wild nature valueless without humans, and that on the contrary wild nature is of value and would still be valuable even in the complete absence of valuers and their valuations.[58] There can be little doubt that he is committed to saying much the same about the theories of Sylvan, and perhaps to a corresponding response to the valuational subjectivism of Elliot, too. While Rolston does not here expound the meaning of "value" in this objectivist sense, there would seem to be no problem about it meaning "supplying interpersonal reasons for being fostered, promoted or preserved," as I have suggested elsewhere.[59] Indeed, with Rolston, I maintain that intrinsic value of this kind attaches to the flourishing of living creatures, and would still so attach even in the absence of all valuers both actual and possible; and also that such valuational frameworks as would preclude this value are objectively inferior to those which do not. But this is not a point which can be further elaborated or defended here, especially as it has received detailed treatment elsewhere, both from Rolston and myself.[60]

Rolston suggests that Callicott's truncated value theory accounts for his truncated account of biodiversity preservation.[61] There must indeed be at least a risk that a metaethics which effectively undermines any ethics, whatever its content, reduces the likelihood of a defensible ethics being adhered to, not least in matters of preservation, though, as I have argued, some of Callicott's latest views, such as his advocacy of sustainable development, are eminently defensible. Yet it remains importantly true that sound and stable environmental policies are liable to require not only stable foundations by way of a sound value theory and ethics, but the underpinning of an appropriately robust metaphysics and metaethics, too.

NOTES

1. John Stuart Mill, "Nature," in *Three Essays on Religion* (New York: Greenwood Press, 1969), pp. 3–65.
2. Ibid., pp. 26 f.
3. Robert Elliot, "Faking Nature," *Inquiry* 25 (1982): 84.
4. Ibid., p. 87.
5. Eric Katz, "The Big Lie: Human Restoration of Nature,'" *Research in Philosophy and Technology* 12 (1992): 231–41.
6. Ibid., pp. 238 f.
7. Ibid., p. 235.
8. Ibid., p. 239.
9. Ibid., pp. 239 f .
10. Elliot, "Faking Nature," pp. 87–89.
11. Ibid., p. 92.
12. Ibid., pp. 83, 92.
13. Katz, "The Big Lie," pp. 237 f.; Richard Sylvan, "Mucking with Nature," unpublished paper, pp. 11–13.

14. Sylvan, "Mucking with Nature," p. 13.

15. Elliot, "Faking Nature," pp. 81–93.

16. William K. Frankena, "Ethics and the Environment," in *Ethics and Problems of the 21st Century*, ed. Kenneth E. Goodpaster and Kenneth M. Sayre (Notre Dame and London: University of Notre Dame Press, 1979).

17. Elliot, "Faking Nature," pp. 87 f.

18. Sylvan, "Mucking with Nature," pp. 22f.

19. Ibid., p. 23.

20. Ibid., p. 26.

21. Ibid., p. 27.

22. Ibid., p. 28.

23. Eugene C. Hargrove, *Foundations of Environmental Ethics* (Englewood Cliffs, N.J.: Prentice-Hall, 1989), pp. 160 f.

24. Sylvan, "Mucking with Nature," p. 290.

25. Katz, "The Big Lie," p. 236.

26. J. Baird Callicott, "The Wilderness Idea Revisited: The Sustainable Development Alternative," *Environmental Professional* 13 (1991): 235–47; Holmes Rolston III, "The Wilderness Idea Reaffirmed," *Environmental Professional* 13 (1991): 370–77.

27. Callicott, "The Wilderness Idea Revisited," pp. 235–38.

28. Ibid., pp. 238–42.

29. Ibid., pp. 239, 242–45.

30. Rolston, "The Wilderness Idea Reaffirmed," pp. 370 f, 373–75.

31. Ibid., pp. 371, 375.

32. Ibid., pp. 371 f.

33. Ibid., pp. 370, 376.

34. Ibid., p. 372.

35. Ibid.

36. Callicott, "The Wilderness Idea Revisited," pp. 239.

37. Rolston, "The Wilderness Idea Reaffirmed," pp. 371.

38. Callicott, "The Wilderness Idea Revisited," pp. 242.

39. Sylvan, "Mucking with Nature," p. 28.

40. Callicott, "The Wilderness Idea Revisited," p. 236.

41. World Commission on Environment and Development, *Our Common Future* (The Brundtland Report) (Oxford: Oxford University Press, 1987), p. 57.

42. Rolston, "The Wilderness Idea Reaffirmed," p. 376.

43. Ibid., pp. 370, 375; there he quotes Callicott, "The Wilderness Idea Revisited," p. 239.

44. Callicott, "The Wilderness Idea Revisited," p. 243.

45. Robin Attfield, *A Theory of Value and Obligation* (London: Croom Helm, 1987), chaps. 2–5.

46. Eric Katz, "The Call of the Wild," *Environmental Ethics* 14 (1992) : 265–73.

47. Elliot, "Faking Nature," pp. 82 f.

48. Sylvan, "Mucking with Nature," pp. 9 f.

49. Clarence J. Glacken, *Traces on the Rhodian Shore: Nature and Culture in Western Thought from Ancient Times to the End of the Eighteenth Century* (Berkeley and London: University of California Press, 1967), pp. 298–301; for some counterpart modern views, see Mark C. Cowell, "Ecological Restoration and Environmental Ethics," *Environmental Ethics* 15 (1993): 19–32.

50. Callicott, "The Wilderness Idea Revisited," pp. 236, 237 f., 240.

51. Rolston, "The Wilderness Idea Reaffirmed," pp. 373 f., 376 f.

52. Callicott, "The Wilderness Idea Revisited," p. 236.

53. Ibid., p. 239.

54. J. Baird Callicott, "Non-Anthropocentric Value Theory and Environmental Ethics," *American Philosophical Quarterly* 21 (1984): 305; cited by Rolston, "The Wilderness Idea Reaffirmed," p. 376.

55. J. Baird Callicott, "On the Intrinsic Value of Nonhuman Species," in *The Preservation of Species*, ed. Bryan G. Norton (Princeton: Princeton University Press, 1986), p. 156.

56. Richard Routley and Val Routley, "Human Chauvinism and Environmental Ethics," in *Environmental Philosophy*, ed. Don Mannison, Michael McRobbie, and Richard Routley (Canberra: Research School of Social Sciences, Australian National University, 1980), pp. 154–57.

57. Robert Elliot, "Meta-Ethics and Environmental Ethics," *Metaphilosophy* 16 (1985): 103–17.

58. Rolston, "The Wilderness Idea Reaffirmed," p. 376.

59. Robin Attfield, *The Ethics of Environmental Concern*, 2d ed. (Athens, Ga., and London: University of Georgia Press, 1991), P. xiii.

60. For further discussion of these matters, see Attfield, *A Theory of Value and Obligation*, chaps. 10–12. Rolston's own case against Callicott's metaethics is more fully expressed at Holmes Rolston III, *Environmental Ethics: Duties to and Values in the Natural World* (Philadelphia: Temple University Press, 1988), pp. 112–17.

61. Rolston, "The Wilderness Idea Reaffirmed," p. 376.

REFERENCES

Attfield, Robin. *A Theory of Value and Obligation*. London: Croom Helm, 1987.

———. *The Ethics of Environmental Concern*. 2d ed. Athens, Ga., and London: University of Georgia Press, 1991.

Callicott, J. Baird. "Non-Anthropocentric Value Theory and Environmental Ethics." *American Philosophical Quarterly* 21 (1984).

———. "On the Intrinsic Value of Nonhuman Species." In *The Preservation of Species*, edited by Bryan G. Norton. Princeton: Princeton University Press, 1986.

———."The Wilderness Idea Revisited: The Sustainable Development Alternative." *Environmental Professional* 13 (1991).

Cowell, Mark C. "Ecological Restoration and Environmental Ethics." *Environmental Ethics* 15 (1993).

Elliot, Robert. "Faking Nature." *Inquiry* 25 (1982).

———. "Meta-Ethics and Environmental Ethics." *Metaphilosophy* 16 (1985).

Frankena, William K. "Ethics and the Environment." In *Ethics and Problems of the 21st Century*, edited by Kenneth E. Goodpaster and Kenneth M. Sayre. Notre Dame and London: University of Notre Dame Press, 1979.

Glacken, Clarence J. *Traces on the Rhodian Shore: Nature and Culture in Western Thought from Ancient Times to the End of the Eighteenth Century*. Berkeley and London: University of California Press, 1967.

Hargrove, Eugene C. *Foundations of Environmental Ethics*. Englewood Cliffs, N.J.: Prentice-Hall, 1989.

Katz, Eric. "The Big Lie: Human Restoration of Nature." *Research in Philosophy and Technology* 12 (1992).

———. "The Call of the Wild." *Environmental Ethics* 14 (1992).

Mill, John Stuart. "Nature." in *Three Essays on Religion*. New York: Greenwood Press, 1969.

Rolston, Holmes III. *Environmental Ethics: Duties to and Values in the Natural World*. Philadelphia: Temple University Press, 1988.

———. "The Wilderness Idea Reaffirmed." *Environmental Professional* 13 (1991).

Routley, Richard, and Val Routley. "Human Chauvanism and Environmental Ethics." In *Environmental Philosophy*, edited by Don Mannison, Michael McRobbie, and Richard Routley. Canberra: Research School of Social Sciences, Australian National University, 1980.

Sylvan, Richard. "Mucking with Nature." Unpublished paper.

World Commission on Environment and Development. *Our Common Future* (The Brundtland Report). Oxford: Oxford University Press, 1987.

8

Restoration

Holmes Rolston III

Where human interference has degraded ecosystems, what about restoring them? In legislation such as the Water Quality Act of 1965 and the Clean Water Act of 1987, we intend that once-polluted systems, when the toxins are removed, will be rejuvenated and return to health. Often, if we cease the interruption, natural systems will be self-healing; but, especially if systems have been pushed far from their equilibriums, or if species have been exterminated or soils lost, the damage may require managed repair. We may need clean up and fix up. One goal of the Endangered Species Act is recovery of the endangered populations; U.S. Fish and Wildlife officials are instructed to form a recovery plan. As just noted, there are only scraps of native prairie remaining in the U.S. Midwest and people have become concerned to restore prairie.[1]

All this commendable activity poses some philosophical puzzles.[2] These arise from the various senses of what is natural, as they affect natural value. In the first sense, everything that humans do deliberately, being a cultural activity, interrupts spontaneous nature and is in that sense therefore unnatural. But what if humans come in and deliberately repair a degraded prairie? That is a cultural activity; there are work crews organized by the Society for Ecological Restoration. They sketch ground plans for what they will put where; they work at it, often long and hard. Then there it is: behold, a prairie! As good as new. Or is it? A prairie is a phenomenon of spontaneous nature, but this restored prairie? *People* built it. Perhaps it is an artifact, in which case it cannot be wild nature. Hence, a rebuilt prairie is a contradiction in terms. There it is: a faked prairie!

Lest you shake your head at how philosophers, arguing about words, can

From Holmes Rolston III, *Conserving Natural Value* (New York: Columbia Unviersity Press, 1994), pp. 88–93. Reprinted by permission of Columbia University Press.

produce a puzzle anywhere they please, and are only causing trouble, casting doubt on a perfectly commendable activity, we hasten to point out that this matter has considerable relevance. As soon as you accept, uncritically, this rebuilt prairie as the real thing, having all the values of the original, there will arrive a delegation from the mining company, who want to mine the coal under the last remnant of real prairie that *does* exist. If you object that there is little prairie left, and refuse to license the mine, they will reply that they will, after mining, put the prairie back like it was. Almost every development project that disrupts natural systems, in order to get a permit, has to meet certain legal restoration criteria. Often, if one area is destroyed, such as a fishing stream or a wetland, there will be a requirement for mitigation, met when they create another fishing stream or wetland somewhere else or put nature back when they finish.

Unfortunately, restorations are seldom as good as the original. The diversity of species may not be there, nor the complexity of ecosystemic interrelations. So the restored ecosystem will lack integrity. Once, I was deciding where to hike, looking at trails on either side of the road below Independence Pass near Aspen, Colorado. Reading the trail signs, I found that one trail headed into an old-growth forest; the other headed into a forest that had been replanted about a half a century before, after logging. Instantly, I knew which trail I wanted to take. Recent studies in Appalachian forests have found that, though the dominant trees may come back, the forest undercover is only about one-third as rich as it was before, even where there are some efforts at restoration.[3] I look for rare mosses, and I had considerable doubt that the Forest Service restoration team had replanted any undiscovered species of rare mosses! Still, I was glad that the forest had been replanted, even though I chose to hike in the pristine one. So the first point to make is that restorations, although valuable, are not as valuable as pristine nature, because they are simply not as rich.[4]

But more value is at stake, and this turns on a philosophical rather than a technical point. Even if the restoration were 100 percent, what then? Eric Katz calls restorations "the Big Lie!"[5] Robert Elliot complains, "Faked nature!"[6] This is because the historical genesis of the system has been interrupted, and, even though both Katz and Elliot approve of restorations, they insist that the value of even a perfect restoration is always in principle something less than the value of pristine nature, since it is not the handiwork of nature but of humans, who have cleverly restored it. The proper response to make in a restored forest is not, "How marvelous a work of nature! Nature is superb! just look at those mosses festooning the trees." Rather, we exclaim, "What clever landscape architects. Superb job of restoration! Why, I would never have known. Just look at the moss festooning those trees; it looks like it's been there for centuries. They really fooled me!" Even a perfectly restored nature isn't the genuine article; it can only be an artifact. The imitation, however accurate, is not authentic nature.

To work our way out of these troubles, notice that there are all kinds and degrees of restoration. At the one extreme, if a forest has been clear-cut, or strip-mined, there is nothing there; the landscape is blitzed, so any new forest is a complete replacement, a replica. This would be like replicating the *Niña*, one of Christopher Columbus's ships. The replica is made from scratch and has no historical continuity at all with the original. This is not really restoration at all, but replication. On the other end of the spectrum, if the forest has been cut by selection of a few trees here and there, and new trees replanted to substitute for these, there is restoration.

A restoration is the original, once damaged and now restored. A replica is a new creation, without causal continuity to the old one. While replicas can exist simultaneously with originals, restorations obviously cannot. We do speak—loosely—of the new forest being a restoration, whether it was rebuilt from scratch, or simply facilitated by replanting removed trees, with much of the forest continuing uninterrupted. But, speaking more carefully, replicas are replacements, while restorations continue much of the historical continuity. Restoration of a famous painting, such as da Vinci's *The Last Supper*, is not making a replica and passing it off as the original. By the same token, restoration of a famous natural area, such as Thoreau's Walden Pond, ought to be a careful and respectful rehabilitation. The result is nature *restored*, not nature *faked*.

The comparison with an artwork is somewhat misleading, however, because in nature we restore by rehabilitating. The painting, which is an artifact, does not heal itself when restored; it is a passive object. Strictly speaking, one does not rehabilitate paintings. But nature, as a community of living beings and processes, may, once we put the parts back in place, heal itself. Revegetating after strip-mining cannot properly be called rehabilitation either, because there is in fact nothing left to rehabilitate. But one can rehabilitate a prairie that has been not too badly overgrazed. Overgrazing allows many introduced weeds to outcompete the natives; perhaps all one has to do is pull the weeds and let nature do the rest; that is undoing as much as doing. Overgrazing allows some native plants to outcompete other natives, those that once reproduced in the shade of the taller grasses. So perhaps, after the taller grasses return, one will have to dig some holes, put in some seeds that have been gathered from elsewhere, cover them up, go home, and let nature do the rest. Maybe all that is needed is to just put the seeds in the weed holes to aid in rehabilitation. In the restoration of art, there can be no analog to this self-healing.[7]

The naturalness returns. The restoration ceases to be an artifact. In the days before high-tech medicine, many physicians who were congratulated on their cures used to say, modestly, "Really, I just treated you, and nature healed you." When a doctor sets a broken arm, he just holds the pieces in place with a splint and nature does the rest. He is not really to be congratulated for his skills at creating arms. He arranges for the cure to happen naturally. One does not complain, thereafter, that he has an artificial limb. Likewise with restoration: It is more like being a midwife than being an artist or engineer. You arrange the raw materials back on site, and place them where they can do their thing.

The point is that restorations do not fake so much as facilitate nature, help it along, mostly by undoing the damage that humans have introduced, and then letting nature do for itself. As the restoration is completed, the wild processes take over. The sun shines, the rains fall, the forest grows. Birds arrive on their own and build their nests. Hawks and owls catch rodents. Perhaps you return some otters, locally extinct, and put them back in the rivers. But, after a few generations, the otters do not know they were once reintroduced, they behave instinctively as they are genetically programmed to do. They catch muskrats as they can; population dynamics is restored and natural selection takes over. The adapted fits survive in their niches.

Succession resumes. In due course, lightning will strike and wildfire burn the forest again, after which it will regenerate itself. Even a new species could evolve. If such things happened decades, centuries, millennia after some thoughtful humans had once facilitated a restoration, it would seem odd to label all these events as artifacts, lies, fakes. Perhaps the best way to think of it is that the naturalness of a restored area is time bound. Any restoration is an artifact at the moment that it is deliberately arranged, but it gradually ceases to be so as spontaneous nature returns—but if, and only if, humans back off and let nature take its course.

Nevertheless, the unbroken historical continuity in natural systems is important to humans. That, after restoration, we back off to let nature take its course proves that we wish that the course of nature had never been broken on the landscape we now conserve. We are glad to have broken arms healed; we would just as soon never have broken arms. Though the spontaneity of natural systems might all return, the historical discontinuity can never he repaired. In that respect, the restored area does suffer permanent loss of natural value. Natural systems, like human beings, are not replaceable in their historical identity and particularity. They are characteristically idiographic and deliver their values in historical process, diminished in value if interrupted. Restoring does not restore this interruption. If one is appreciating the present spontaneity of wild nature—the plant or animal in its *ecology*—that can be returned, and will, after complete restoration, be present undiminished. But if one is appreciating the *evolutionary history*—the plant or animal in its historical lineage—even though the genetics may be back in place, there still interrupted wildness. The forest is no longer virgin, no longer pristine, and, in a sense, it is less "real."

"Restore" connotes the idea of putting something back as it was earlier. However, we need to be clear what this something is and what it is not. We are not resetting the forest to what it was a century ago. That suggests going backward in time, and is simply impossible. We cannot replace the past. We are only capable today of putting back in place products of nature (i.e., seeds, seedlings, nutrients, species, soils, clean waters), and, with this, encourage the reappearance of what we are really putting back: natural processes. Restoration cannot be a backward-looking activity, though, to be sure, one does have to look to uninterrupted systems to discover what was once there. In fact, restoration must be a forward-looking event to rehabilitate for the future.

We cannot go back in history and undo the undoing we humans once did.

We cannot go back to yesterday as though we could restore pre-Columbian America. We ought not do so even if we could, because culture is a good thing on the American landscape and that would diminish value. But we have erred in our excess, in our ignorance, in our insensitivity, in our haste, in our greed; we have lost natural value. Facing up to that loss, often we do want to restore ecosystemic integrity and health. The sin, however, once committed, is done forever. The only recourse is restitution, and such restitution is both possible and desirable.

Sometimes we will restore for pragmatic reasons, since we have often found that the degradation of ecosystems harms us people as well. Sometimes this will be an altruistic restoration, putting it back for the sake of the wild others who may re-reside there. Such restoration is restitution, a moral word. We make restitution where we ought not to have destroyed values. This includes natural values as surely as cultural ones. Restoration as restitution, moreover, is going to increase our human sense of identity with nature; we are going to appreciate the biotic community we have studied and helped to restore. We will be more careful elsewhere about our harmony with the natural systems that we will continue to disturb. That sense of identity and harmony is not inauthentic at all. It is the fundamental imperative of conserving natural value.

NOTES

1. William R. Jordan III, " Ecological Restoration and the Reintegration of Ecological Systems," in *Bioscience—Society*, ed. D. J. Roy, B. E. Wynne, and R. W. Old (San Francisco: John Wiley and Sons, 1991), pp. 151–62; William R. Jordan III, Michael E. Gilpin, and John D. Aber, ed., *Restoration Ecology: A Synthetic Approach to Ecological Research* (New York: Cambridge University Press, 1987).

2. Mark C. Cowell, "Ecological Restoration and Environmental Ethics," *Environmental Ethics* 15 (1993): 19–32.

3. David Cameron Duffy and Albert J. Meier, "Do Appalachian Herbaceous Understories Ever Recover from Clearcutting?" *Conservation Biology* 6 (1992): 196–201.

4. Walter E. Westman, "Ecological Restoration Projects: Measuring Their Performance," *Environmental Professional* 13 (1991): 207–15; Leslie Roberts, "Wetlands Trading is a Loser's Game, Say Ecologists," *Science* 260 (1993): 1890–92.

5. Eric Katz, "The Big Lie: Human Restoration of Nature," *Research in Philosophy and Technology* 12 (1992): 231–41.

6. Robert Elliot, "Faking Nature," *Inquiry* 25 (1982): 81–93.

7. Alastair S. Gunn, "The Restoration of Species and Natural Environments," *Environmental Ethics* 13 (1991): 291–310.

REFERENCES

Cowell, Mark C. "Ecological Restoration and Environmental Ethics." *Environmental Ethics* 15 (1993).

Duffy, David Cameron, and Albert J. Meier. "Do Appalachian Herbaceous Understories Ever Recover from Clearcutting?" *Conservation Biology* 6 (1992).

Elliot, Robert. "Faking Nature." *Inquiry* 25 (1982).

Gunn, Alastair S. "The Restoration of Species and Natural Environments." *Environmental Ethics* 13 (1991).

Jordan, William R. III. "Ecological Restoration and the Reintegration of Ecological Systems." In *Bioscience—Society*, edited by D. J. Roy, B. E. Wynne, and R. W. Old. San Francisco: John Wiley and Sons, 1991.

Jordan, William R. III, Michael E. Gilpin, and John D. Aber, ed. *Restoration Ecology: A Synthetic Approach to Ecological Research*. New York: Cambridge University Press, 1987.

Katz, Eric. "The Big Lie: Human Restoration of Nature." *Research in Philosophy and Technology* 12 (1992).

Roberts, Leslie. "Wetlands Trading is a Loser's Game, Say Ecologists." *Science* 260 (1993).

Westman, Walter E. "Ecological Restoration Projects: Measuring Their Performance." *Environmental Professional* 13 (1991).

Part III
Ends and Means

9

Carving Up the Woods
Savanna Restoration in Northeastern Illinois
Jon Mendelson, Stephen P. Aultz,
and Judith Dolan Mendelson

In this paper we raise concerns about the direction of management in natural areas, particularly management strategies whose stated goal is the restoration of savanna communities in northeastern Illinois. Our principal example is the Nature Conservancy's Palos/Sag Project in Cook County, Illinois, specifically the work occurring in Cap Sauers Holding, a dedicated Illinois Nature Preserve owned by the Forest Preserve District of Cook County.

We begin with some thoughts about the relationship between nature and humans, for it is against this background that the value of restorations must ultimately be judged. Natural systems are always in a process of becoming. The essence of nature lies not in the organization we perceive, but in the creative act itself. The creativity of nature, however, is not preceded by a plan or idea comparable to a blueprint or design. Instead, in the words of the philosopher Eugene Hargrove,[1] nature creates her works indifferently. What we perceive as organization in nature—species, communities, ecosystems—arises through the interactions of organisms with one another and with their physical environment. These interactions have no overarching purpose, nor do they result in an inevitable pattern. Henry Gleason recognizes this in his summary of an idea that has influenced several generations of ecologists:

> There is the birth of my theory on the plant association. All the glamour has disappeared. Far from being an organism, an association is merely the fortuitous juxtaposition of plants. What plants? Those that can live together under the physical environment and under their interlocking spheres of influence and which are already located within migrating distance.[2]

Jon Mendelson, Stephen P. Aultz, and Judith Dolan Mendelson, "Carving Up the Woods: Savanna Restoration in Northeastern Illinois," *Restoration and Management Notes* 10 (1992): 127–31. Reprinted by permission of the University of Wisconsin Press.

Yet it is these "fortuitous juxtapositions," endlessly varied, never duplicatable, these products of creative indifference, that make the natural world so fascinating.

Restorations are inherently different from these products of natural creativity. In a restoration, some set of ideas about how nature should look or how nature should behave precedes and dictates management strategies. The result must inevitably reflect human ideas, perceptions, and values. Restorations are forever subject to the limitations of our understanding and to the imposition of our values. We see this increasingly in the destruction of species deemed, for one reason or another, "unsuitable" to a particular restoration.

Subject inevitably to these constraints, all restoration plans and projects should be carefully evaluated against the alternative of letting natural processes continue, whatever their direction, without human interference. This is especially important when human conceptions are imposed on areas where the vast majority of species present are indigenous, and where ecosystem processes are intact. It is in such areas that we have the unique opportunity to watch the panorama of successional change unfold naturally.

SAVANNA

The particular idea that has influenced the savanna restoration movement is the concept that "savanna" is a distinct community characterized by a unique flora,[3] and, by implication, that plant communities in general are definable realities. We believe this to be no longer a supportable assumption about the organization of nature. The postulated uniqueness of the savanna flora, as Roger Anderson has recently suggested, is an illusion.[4] It represents a failure to grasp Gleason's individualistic concept of species behavior and, at best, is a misreading of the work of Curtis, Whittaker, and others who have shown convincingly that the vegetation of a region forms a series of continua—unbroken sequences of species whose abundances change in a regular way along environmental gradients. "Savanna" is no more than a name applied to an arbitrarily defined segment of a particular continuum. It represents an ecotone of uncertain width and uncertain stability lying between grassland and forest. What portion of the continuum is defined as savanna depends on the definer; it is not inherent in the vegetation.

Seen in this light, the management activities so popular today lose some of their romance. They are not so much noble attempts to restore a unique savanna community as they are increasingly destructive efforts to shove existing assemblages of species in one direction or another along a vegetational continuum. In practice, the direction is always the same. The attempts at restoration we have seen have all been perpetrated on species assemblages lying on the forested end of the continuum, and the shove, accomplished with fire, saws, and poison, is always in the xeric direction.

The reasons for this are not hard to fathom: People have historically chosen woodlands for preservation. Because such areas constitute the bulk of natural land now in public ownership they have become more vulnerable to the manipulations of resource managers. On the other hand, areas once thinly wooded with a prairielike understory are much less available. They have largely been cleared and cultivated, and are now increasingly being developed. Almost all are in private ownership. This is indeed tragic, no less so than the destruction of the prairies themselves. It does not, however, justify the expediency of managing northeastern Illinois woodlands, great portions of which occupy landscapes which suggest long-term forest occupancy, and which certainly lack a savannalike character today, as if they were savannas.

An example of this kind of restoration can be seen in the area of Cap Sauers Holding (CSH), a six-hundred-hectare (fifteen-hundred-acre) dedicated Illinois Nature Preserve in Cook County located on the south side of the Sag Valley.[5] The CSH Preserve itself is designated as a first-priority restoration site in the Nature Conservancy's Palos/Sag Project.[6] It is currently being heavily managed to give it a savannalike appearance, even though in topography and soils (to say nothing of the existing vegetation itself), it is a landscape clearly favoring the establishment of closed woodland. For example, CSH occupies the south wall of the Sag Valley, a broad, north-facing slope. North-facing slopes, typically cooler and more moist than other slope aspects, encourage the growth of trees. This slope, moreover, is well dissected, a rather extensive ravine system having grown up the valley wall. In northeastern Illinois, woodlands have everywhere developed under the protection of dissected land forms.

If one considers the soils of the area, the inappropriateness of the CSH project becomes even more apparent. Virtually the entire management area is occupied by Morley silt loam,[7] perhaps the most characteristic woodland soil of northeastern Illinois. Morley is a widespread soil. In southeastern Wisconsin, where it is also found, Morley develops under southern mesic forest,[8] a portion of the woodland continuum dominated by sugar maple (*Acer saccharum*), basswood (*Tilia americana*), slippery elm (*Ulmus rubra*), red oak (*Quercus rubra*), and other true forest species.[9] These same species are also associated with Morley soils in Illinois, particularly on its steeper phases (Morley E and F). The gentler phases (Morley B and C), together with a related soil, Blount silt loam, support woodlands with greater proportions of oak.

This configuration of vegetation, topography, and soils is hardly unique to CSH. Dissected north-facing slopes throughout northeastern Illinois harbor forests and forest soils. Good examples may be found in northeastern Will County. Here, large patches of forest, including Thorn Creek Woods and the woodlands of the Plum Valley, among others, have developed in conjunction with stream systems cutting into north-facing slopes—in this case, the inner slopes of the Valparaiso Morainic system. None of these woodlands is an isolated prairie grove; none, a "savanna in the tough." They are true forests. Like CSH, they occupy landscapes that are the most mesic in the region and, like CSH, they represent poor candidates for the renovations envisioned. Choosing areas with this configuration of landscape elements for savanna restoration suggests not simply the expediency of their availability, but a failure of perception as well.

There is an additional point to be made. The dissected landscapes which have been chosen for restoration are not frozen in time. Rather, as Cowles pointed out long ago, they represent the most dynamic elements in the still youthful and evolving northeastern Illinois area.[10] The headward growth of stream systems is sufficiently rapid that discernable topographic modifications may occur within the life-span of a typical forest tree. A commonly observed example of this process is a ravine channel which, having first undercut the roots of a living tree, has subsequently grown many meters in an upstream direction. Thus these ravine systems, which everywhere support the most mesic components of the forest, are themselves growing, altering the landscape to encourage further the spread of forest trees. As managers try, therefore, to develop an environment conducive to a prairielike understory by destroying the existing vegetation, the continued dissection of these landscapes is shifting the competitive balance in the opposite direction.

Given these difficulties, we wonder why managers have paid so little attention to soils, their arrangement in the landscape, and the meaning of that arrangement with respect to vegetational patterns. Soils, we believe, serve as the best indication of the prior extent of all vegetation types in the region. Soils that supported savannalike vegetation, for example, are widespread in northeastern Illinois. Two of the common savanna soils are Beecher and Markham silt loams. These soils have A horizons of thickness and color intermediate between the thin, pale Morley A horizon and the thick, dark horizons of true prairie mollisols. Beecher and Markham are indeed found in the CSH area, but they lie to the south of the Sag Valley, on rolling, undissected morainic upland.[11] In northeastern Will County exactly the same pattern is found but on a larger scale. Morley soils occupy the broad north-facing morainic slopes. Beecher and Markham dominate an extensive area to the south, the rolling, undissected uplands of successive morainic crests.[12]

In this part of Will County, as in northeastern Illinois generally, these savanna lands have been badly disturbed; natural vegetation is largely gone and little has been preserved. Nevertheless, by virtue of topography and soil they are our savanna landscapes. They should be the focus of restorationists. Of course, restoration here would require techniques much different from those currently employed. Rather than the wholesale destruction that we observe in the woods today, a creative, nurturing approach would be required: growing a savanna rather than carving one out.

TECHNIQUES

At Cap Sauers Holding (CSH), and we suspect at other sites, managers have chosen inappropriate landscapes to restore to savanna and open woodlands. These choices force them to use inappropriate techniques to accomplish their goals. Further, it seems to us that managers at CSH are struggling to define these goals. We visited CSH on four separate occasions in the fall and winter of

1991, alone and in the company of the Nature Conservancy stewards. They discussed interchangeably both restoring savanna on the site, and opening up the woodlands to increase oak reproduction and to encourage spring wildflowers. We heard and saw the results of confused purpose being imposed upon the wrong landscape with inappropriate techniques.

We were shown ravines in CSH where managers burn up north-facing slopes. Since the prevailing winds in the region are from the southwest, it is unlikely that north-facing slopes in our region burned with great frequency. As a result, they were probably forested at the time of European settlement. Further, we have seen steep-sided ravines and bottomland woods where managers have cut out native shrubs and saplings along with alien shrubs prior to burning. These areas are moist, sheltered habitats that historically would have burned infrequently, if at all. Beneath the closed woodland canopy of these "restored" sites we find no native shrubs, virtually no saplings or seedling of forest trees, and no savanna flora. Thus, these inappropriately chosen sites, with their relatively closed canopy and their artificially opened understory, resemble no natural community that we are familiar with.

We visited sites where white ash (*Fraxinus americana*), basswood, black cherry (*Prunus serotiria*), hawthorn (*Crataegus* spp.), dogwood (*Cornus* spp.), and northern arrowwood (*Viburnum rafinesquianum*)—all native to northeastern Illinois woodlands—have been selectively cut and burned. This is done on the assumption that these natives are "weeds" in their own community and that their presence retards oak reproduction. We think such actions not only are based on questionable value judgments, but show an incomplete understanding of woodland ecology as well. White ash, for example, seeds abundantly and can frequently appear to be taking over an area. However, it is our observation that ash has a low survival rate. Thus, in spite of its apparent early dominance, ash is eventually replaced by other species.

Basswood, which we have seen girdled because it appears "out of place" in upland settings, actually has a bimodal distribution.[13] It frequently grows in poorly drained patches in otherwise xeric areas. Neither of these species represents a threat to the oaks or to the forest fabric. Their crime lies only in failing to fit human preconceptions of how particular pieces of nature should appear.

We observed woodland knolls that have been burned with such intensity and frequency that the young oaks are killed and canopy oaks are severely damaged. If the goal of such a fire regime is to encourage oak reproduction, such a policy is at best misguided. If the purpose is to shove an existing assemblage of plants toward savanna, the cost is too great.

The effects of fire run along a continuum from no damage at all to actual sterilization of the upper soil horizons. Natural fires typically burn in a mosaic pattern, with anywhere from 0 to 100 percent of a given area being burned.[14] The systematic burning of small areas within larger communities by managers has the effect of increasing fire intensity and coverage. This process is exacerbated by the practice of waiting for the best conditions in order to get a "good burn." It is our opinion that nature does not operate in such a nonrandom manner. If the purpose of burning oak woodlands is to enhance oak reproduction, then these intense fires at frequent intervals do not seem appropriate. High-intensity fires may mimic prairie fires, but woodlands, with their increased shade and corresponding soil moisture would burn less often and less intensely than prairie. Yet under current management strategies many of our woodlands are burned each year.

In many cases, when cutting and burning do not bring the desired savanna physiognomy in the desired time frame, managers then use what we consider to be increasingly intrusive techniques. The use of poison is the prime example. It is ironic that managers have turned to the use of toxic chemicals, while the rest of us have become increasingly concerned about chemicals contaminating land, food, and water supplies. Even if managers are trained in the careful application of these chemicals, we believe they should never be used in our few remaining natural areas.

It is interesting to note that the major thrust of savanna/open woodlands restoration in northeastern Illinois comes from prairie managers. This has led to the wholesale importation of prairie techniques into woodlands without an understanding of ecosystem processes in these communities. For example, a prairie burn removes a large percentage of aboveground biomass, all of which regrows the following year. Cutting and burning in a woodland destroys aboveground biomass as well, but replacement of this pool of organic matter, and the habitat it represents, takes many years. The accumulation of biomass is such a lengthy process that woodlands need to be viewed over decades, not months, seasons, or years. Moreover, these same techniques—frequent fire and cutting—serve both to expose the forest floor and to reduce the stabilizing network of living roots. The results are accelerated erosion rates in dynamic landscapes which already favor tree growth. With increased stream dissection comes the inevitable march of forest, a potential outcome that only highlights the inappropriate use of prairie restoration strategies in many woodland settings.

FIRE HISTORY

We believe that the role of fire in northeastern Illinois woodlands has been incompletely analyzed. Fire is perhaps the principal tool employed by restorationists, and its use is routinely justified as the reintroduction of a much-needed natural process. We do not question that fire can indeed influence these woodlands, or that it has done so in the past. Nor do we doubt that if fire frequency has been substantially reduced, this, too, would affect woodland structure. Our concerns lie with the actual results of fire suppression in today's woodlands and its relationship to other disturbance factors.

To approach this question we must look to recent forest history. Northeastern Illinois woodlands have had a short but intense relationship with Euro-American settlers. Not only did these woodlands suffer changes in fire regime upon settlement, but they experienced for the first time in their postglacial history extensive cutting and systematic grazing as well. Thus fire reduction was only one of several interrelated disturbance elements.

We believe that the major effect of fire reduction was largely limited to the period immediately following settlement. During this time, decreased fire frequency, together with cutting substantial portions of the presettlement canopy, allowed for increased seedling survival and the release of previously suppressed young individuals. In Thorn Creek Woods, an area with which we are most familiar, this reproductive surge continued for roughly forty years from about 1840 to 1880.[15] The legacy of this period is trees that are now 110 to 150 years old. These trees today dominate the canopy of Thorn Creek Woods and other northeastern Illinois woodlands as well. We emphasize that these dominant canopy trees are the product of early fire suppression and cutting, and are almost exclusively of postsettlement origin.

In Thorn Creek Woods, as in other regional woodlands, trees roughly between fifty and one hundred years old are rare. This suggests that during the period between 1880 and 1940, relatively few individuals successfully entered the population. We attribute this lengthy reproductive gap not to fire suppression, but to another disturbance factor: the pervasive and long-term effect of grazing livestock in these woods, with its attendant increases in soil compaction, and the cropping of newly emerged woody plants.

Tree reproduction in Thorn Creek Woods began again in the late 1930s and early 1940s, dates which coincide well with the decline of farming in the area. These post-1930 trees and shrubs, which today form the understory of the woods, are the product of a period well separated in time from that which produced the generation of canopy trees. Their presence cannot be considered a proximate outcome of fire suppression. By the time this group of woody plants had made its appearance, fires had long been stopped. Instead, the understory represents the response of woodland to the cessation of grazing. Stands of young oaks, thickets of hawthorn, even places where aliens have gained a foothold—in fact, the whole vegetational mosaic—is much more understandable in terms of local differences in grazing intensity than by invoking the generality of regionwide fire suppression.

We believe this historical pattern is common to most northeastern Illinois woodlands, allowing for some variation in the timing and intensity of various disturbances. If this is the case, what conclusions do we draw? First, we do not consider the existing shrub-sapling layer to be an unnatural assemblage in need of alteration or removal. On the contrary, it represents a healthy, vigorous recovery from disturbance, a recovery that should be allowed to continue unhindered. Second, we believe the rationale for the manipulation of the understory—"savanna restoration"—is itself flawed. Destroying the understory will not recreate savanna. The canopy of these woodlands is not composed of open-grown presettlement trees. It is composed largely of forest grown postsettlement trees. No amount of alteration of the shrub-sapling layer can give a savanna aspect to this canopy. As we have pointed out earlier, the results are landscapes of obvious artificiality.

DISCUSSION

All these efforts in northeastern Illinois to restore savanna have been done without any agreed-upon definition of what a savanna is. Each state in the Midwest has a different definition for savanna ranging from 40 percent to 100 percent canopy cover.[16] Packard has tried to compile a list of indicator species, but this list seems to ignore Gleason's concept of fortuitous plant assemblages and seems to rely almost entirely on historic observations and very little scientific data.[17] As Nuzzo has stated, historic descriptions of savanna vegetation are not necessarily accurate and may only have accented the "pretty."[18] Also, descriptive words such as "oak opening," "oak barrens," and so on, are not universally accepted by anyone.

This leaves savanna advocates with little evidence of savanna composition and encourages speculation on a savanna archetype with special plant assemblages. Further, it leads to spurious arguments for restoring savanna based on false assumptions. Therefore, it seems to us that it is time to accept savanna as an ecotone composed of a variety of plant assemblages.

Any idea behind savanna restoration is only a human approximation of reality and precedes the creative act. The end product is not the limitless creativity of nature, but a form of landscape architecture limited by the imagination of the manager. In the long run, current forest management practices prohibit the woods from becoming what it would be. Gone are the conditions of presettlement woodlands. Restoration of the presettlement forest is an impossibility. What value is it to choose a single moment in time as the aim of a restoration effort? As Noss has shown, in the larger paleoecological perspective each point in time represents a "transient association of species, each responding individualistically to long-term change."[19] Insistence on a preferred archetype is merely placing nature in a historical role and relegating its existence to that of an artifact, encased behind museum walls.

We have many things to gain by limiting current restoration practices. We can study nature reclaiming and reshaping the forest. We can gain in the realization that nature is becoming; that its creative force is active today and not just a thing of the past. The forest that our modern resource managers are viewing is the forest that is reclaiming itself. Cutting and burning our woodlands prevents nature from doing what it does best: evolving.

Calvin DeWitt reflects on managing nature by letting it be.[20] As a result of his experience of living near a natural area, he now questions the "corrective actions" of restorationists. Might not the timescale of our efforts be too limiting? After all, what is the life-span of humans when compared to an evolving forest? Or, might it be our own inability to leave things alone that pushes us into opinions of what a natural area should be? Whatever it is, it is led by a genuine misunderstanding of nature. As John Fowles says:

> . . . nature is unlike art in terms of its product—what we in general know it
> by. The difference is that it is not only created, an external object with a his-

tory, and so belonging to a past; but also creating in the present, as we experience it. As we watch, it is so to speak rewriting, reformulating, repainting, rephotographing itself. It refuses to stay fixed and fossilized in the past, as both the scientist and the artist feel it somehow ought to; and both will generally try to impose this fossilization on it.[21]

ACKNOWLEDGMENTS

We thank Mary and Wally McCarthy, former stewards at Cap Sauers, who graciously showed us the restoration sites. Their deep affection for CSH was evident throughout. We also thank Dennis Nyberg of UICC and Marcy DeMauro-Roth of the Will County Forest Preserve District for stimulating discussions that hopefully clarified thoughts on all sides.

NOTES

1. E. C. Hargrove, *Foundations of Environmental Ethics* (Englewood Cliffs, N.J.: Prentice-Hall, 1989).

2. H. A. Gleason, "Delving Into the History of American Ecology," *Bulletin of the Ecological Society of America* 56, no. 4 (1952): 7–10.

3. S. Packard, "Just A Few Oddball Species: Restoration and the Rediscovery of the Tallgrass Savanna," *Restoration and Management Notes* 6, no. 1 (1988): 13–22.

4. R. C. Anderson, "Savanna Concepts Revisited," *Bioscience* 41, no. 6 (1991): 37.

5. United States Geologic Survey, Sag Bridge Quadrangle, Ill.—Cook County, 1963, 137N, R12E, principally sec. 19, 20.

6. K. S. King and S. L. Zoars, "Natural Areas Inventory and Management Recommendations, Palos and Sag Valley Divisions." Forest Preserve District of Cook County, Illinois, 1990.

7. USDA Soil Conservation Service, Soil Survey of DuPage and part of Cook County, Illinois, 1979, Map 91.

8. F. D. Hole, *Soils of Wisconsin* (Madison: University of Wisconsin Press, 1976), pp. 157–58.

9. J. Curtis, *The Vegetation of Wisconsin* (Madison: University of Wisconsin Press, 1959), p. 104.

10. H. C. Cowles, "The Physiographic Ecology of Chicago and Vicinity," *Botanical Gazette* 31, no. 2 (1901): pp. 73–108; 31, no. 3: 145–82.

11. USDA Soil Conservation Service, Soil Survey, Maps 91 and 96.

12. University of Illinois Agricultural Experiment Station, Will County Soils, Soil Report 80, 1962, Southeast Sheet.

13. Curtis, *Vegetation of Wisconsin*, pp. 100–101.

14. National Park Service, "The Greater Yellowstone Fires of 1988: Questions and Answers." Background notes on the 1988 Yellowstone Fires, 1990.

15. U.S.G.S., Sag Bridge Quadrangle, T34N, R13E, sec. 1, 2, 11, 12; J. Mendelson, "Age-Size Relationships among the Trees of Thorn Creek Woods," unpublished.

16. V. A. Nuzzo, "Extent and Status of Midwest Oak Savanna: Pre-settlement and 1985," *Natural Areas Journal* 6, no. 1 (1986): 6–36.

17. Packard, "Just a Few Oddball Species," pp. 13–22.

18. Nuzzo, "Extent and Status of Midwest Oak Savanna," pp. 6–36.

19. R. F. Noss, "On Characterizing Pre-settlement Vegetation: How and Why," *Natural Area Journal* 5, no. 1 (1985): 5–17.

20. C. DeWitt, "Let It Be," *Restoration and Management Notes* 7, no. 2 (1989): 80–81.

21. John Fowles, *The Tree* (Boston: Little, Brown Company, 1979).

REFERENCES

Anderson, R. C. "Savanna Concepts Revisited." *Bioscience* 41, no. 6 (1991).

Cowles, H. C. "The Physiographic Ecology of Chicago and Vicinity." *Botanical Gazette* 31, nos. 2 and 3 (1901).

Curtis, J. *The Vegetation of Wisconsin*. Madison: University of Wisconsin Press, 1959.

DeWitt, C. "Let It Be." *Restoration and Management Notes* 7, no. 2 (1989).

Fowles, J. *The Tree*. Boston: Little, Brown & Co., 1979.

Gleason, H. A. "Delving into the History of American Ecology (1952)." *Bulletin of the Ecological Society of America* 56, no. 4 (1975).

Hargrove, E. C. *Foundations of Environmental Ethics*. Englewood Cliffs, N.J.: Prentice-Hall, 1989.

Hole, F. D. *Soils of Wisconsin*. Madison: University of Wisconsin Press, 1976.

King, K. S., and S. L. Zoars. "Natural Areas Inventory and Management Recommendations, Palos and Sag Valley Divisions." Forest Preserve District of Cook County, Illinois, 1990.

Mendelson, J. "Age-Size Relationships among the Trees of Thorn Creek Woods." Unpublished.

National Park Service. "The Greater Yellowstone Fires of 1988: Questions and Answers." Background Notes on the 1988 Yellowstone Fires, 1990.

Noss, R. F. "On Characterizing Pre-settlement Vegetation: How and Why." *Natural Areas Journal* 5, no. 1 (1985).

Nuzzo, V. A. "Extent and Status of Midwest Oak Savanna: Pre-settlement and 1985." *Natural Areas Journal* 6, no. 1 (1986).

Packard, S. "Just a Few Oddball Species: Restoration and the Rediscovery of the Tallgrass Savanna." *Restoration and Management Notes* 6, no. 1 (1988).

University of Illinois Agricultural Experiment Station. Will County Soils. Soil Report 80, 1962.

United States Geologic Survey. Sag Bridge Quadrangle, Ill.–Cook County. 7.5 Minute series, 1963.

U.S.D.A. Soil Conservation Service. Soil Survey of DuPage and Part of Cook County, Illinois, 1979.

10

Restoring Oak Ecosystems

Steve Packard

Two recent articles in these pages have offered stimulating critiques of the savanna restoration efforts by myself and others in northeastern Illinois. Eric Katz focused on whether this restoration produced "nature" or a degraded "artifact."[1] Jon Mendelson, Stephen P. Aultz, and Judith Dolan Mendelson challenged certain specific management practices at one preserve and questioned aspects of restoration management as it is now widely practiced in northeastern Illinois and elsewhere.[2]

Conservation biology, natural areas management, and restoration ecology are emerging disciplines that have been generating new definitions, information, understandings, goals, and values. In various ways our critics challenge all of these, some explicitly and some implicitly. New ideas, of course, are not necessarily right. Conservationists feel an urgency to act before it is too late, but ideas born of haste may be particularly suspect. I will try to use the opportunity afforded by these criticisms to explore some of the thinking behind recent initiatives of the Nature Conservancy and other conservation organizations that have attracted this criticism.

Many of the arguments these authors bring forward are logical within the framework of conservation ethics and scientific thinking that have prevailed over much of the twentieth century. I suspect that most people, even most people involved in conservation and science, would initially agree with the concepts and values that our critics express. But the experience of many managers has gradually convinced us that those ideas are fundamentally inadequate. They haven't worked in practice. Ideas about nature that are deeply ingrained in our culture are coming into conflict with new directions in the science and practice of nature conservation. While as yet there is no real consensus among

Steve Packard, "Restoring Oak Ecosystems," *Restoration and Management Notes* 11 (1993): 5–16. Reprinted by permission of the University of Wisconsin Press.

conservationists on which new concepts and values should replace the old, there is at least sufficient clarity about what has gone wrong and how to do better that many of us in conservation agencies have substantially changed the way we do our work. I think we in the Midwest have bumped up against the traditional thinking particularly hard because in savanna restoration we have a particularly knotty challenge on our hands. Oak ecosystems generally and oak savannas in particular have been the exception that tested the rule.

To start, let me try to summarize elements of the earlier conventional wisdom as expressed by Mendelson, Katz, and others:

- Nature is best defined as "animals and plants unaffected by people."
- Biodiversity thrives if we just leave nature alone.
- When brush or weeds overrun a preserve, that is "natural succession."
- The savanna is not a natural community in its own right but is an ecotone between two true communities.

I will try to untangle some of these interrelated ideas by analyzing how they have been applied to the Midwestern tallgrass savanna. In the process I'll do my best to describe how the working consensus among conservationists has begun to change.

WHAT IS NATURE?

Five million people in the City of Chicago and three million more in the suburbs populate Cook County, Illinois. Most of rural Illinois, fencerow to fencerow, is farmland. But 67,000 acres (36,800 hectares)—fully 10 percent—of Cook County is "forest preserves." The farsighted 1913 charter of the Forest Preserve District of Cook County requires that the district "preserve, protect, restore, and restock said lands in their natural state and condition as near as may be." Excellent language. But what does "natural state" mean?

The Nature Conservancy and nature preserve agencies in Illinois and neighboring states have no formal definitions of the word "nature." For decades conservationists have used the word more or less as in definition five in my *Random House College Dictionary*: "plants, animals, geographical features, etc., or the places where these exist largely free of human influence."

But what does "largely free" mean? There once was no doubt that the principal job of nature conservation was to resist the relentless proliferation of the ever more heavy-handed influence of humans. The inspiringly noncompromising "Rules for Management of Illinois Nature Preserves" is essentially a long list of the most likely meddlings to which misguided managers might subject the preserves, each accompanied by a prohibition of it.[3] The idea of nature, as the absence of the effects of people, had been codified.

In 1964 and 1965, twelve nature preserves were dedicated in Illinois under the new statute, which subsequently served as an inspiration for similar state statutes across the country. Of these twelve preserves, ten, including Cap Sauers Holding, which Mendelson and his colleagues discuss in their article, were owned by the Forest Preserve District of Cook County. Some of these areas were known to support rare species and unusually "high-quality" natural communities. Others, like Cap Sauers, which at 1520 acres (608 hectares) acres was by far the largest, consisted of ordinary former farmsteads. Its fields and woodlots were expected to return to a state of nature through natural succession. Cap Sauers would become ever more truly nature by being left alone—that was the theory.

No one paid much attention to this nature preserve for the next two decades. The plants and animals of its prairielike openings were gradually being shaded out by bushes and young trees. Oak groves grew dense underbrush, beneath which sprouting acorns found too little light and died. Old oaks were not being replaced by young oaks. Hundreds of acres of former prairie and open oak woodlands, which over a century and a half earlier had become plowed field or pasture, now grew up into impenetrable thickets of buckthorn, hawthorn, and similar aggressive species, both native and exotic.

The thinking had been that, left alone, Cap Sauers would become more "natural." Wasn't that how we defined nature—wild plants and animals with a minimum of human influence? In those terms, of course, the project was a success: Cap Sauers had been protected from obvious human influences. But another aspect of our understanding of nature was that it was biologically diverse; rare native species should thrive there. Is this what, in time, Cap Sauers would protect?

Botanical nature in the Midwest was made much clearer by John Curtis's *The Vegetation of Wisconsin*.[4] Curtis defined, described, and quantified plant communities and was highly and deservedly influential throughout the Midwest and beyond. When in the mid-1970s the Illinois Natural Areas Inventory set nature preservation priorities for the state, it drew heavily on the work of Curtis. The inventory identified 670 "natural areas" with high-quality plant communities in Illinois, but it found no significant natural feature at Cap Sauers. This preserve and some of those other early ones were found to support neither rare species nor high-quality ecological communities as described by Curtis. They were considered an embarrassment to the Nature Preserves system.

During the 1980s, the new *Journal of the Natural Areas Association* provided a forum for John Humke of the Nature Conservancy and John Schwegman of the Illinois Department of Conservation to debate whether the term "natural area" was becoming obsolete.[5] But of course the real question was: What is a natural area—or what is nature? The Illinois conservationists had defined nature in largely negative terms, as the absence of human influence. Thus the biologists who conducted the inventory rejected out of hand sites that had been disturbed by people in any way, unless the biota was judged to have recovered. Inventory director John White trained his biologists to look for certain species when they evaluated sites—not because these species were important in themselves—but because they were indicators of a lack of disturbance.

Meanwhile, Nature Conservancy scientists under the leadership of Robert Jenkins were developing different ideas about how to define, identify, and evaluate nature. Jenkins focused principally on rare species, discrete elements that readily lent themselves to computerized conservation priority setting.

Here, then, were what seem like two profoundly different approaches to nature. The debate over them flared and then died down—in part because the Conservancy's rare species so often depended on the "natural areas" that were thought to thrive in the absence of people. Despite the philosophical difference, in practice both the rare species and the high-quality communities were sought out for conservation by all involved. In defining nature for conservation purposes perhaps the two concepts—lack of human interference and presence of native species diversity—would turn out to be functionally equivalent. But the experience of on-the-ground preserve managers would prove otherwise. In the July 1982 issue of the *Natural Areas Journal*, Susan Bratton sounded a clarion call with her article "The Effects of Exotic Plant and Animal Species on Nature Preserves." The subsequent and continuing deluge of articles about alien species, fire management, problems of predator/prey imbalance, and the like soon made it clear that although the greatest overall threat to biodiversity is habitat destruction by people, the principal threat to the nature in nature preserves is not human disturbance. The threat to nature there consists of processes that we once called natural.

During the 1980s, the Conservancy began to recognize the need for strong "stewardship" (i.e., management) teams for every chapter. State natural areas programs began to fight as hard for stewardship staff as they did for land acquisition. In earlier years there had been consensus that land acquisition must be the first priority. But in time we began to see the natural features of certain preserves (acquired at great cost) succumb so utterly to alien invaders that the species we thought we had protected in those preserves died out.

It had become apparent that the "nature" we wanted to conserve needed a new definition. Many people just stopped talking about nature and replaced the term with "biodiversity" or "presettlement ecological community." But I believe that we have become wiser about nature and that we ought recognize a definition that reflects the way conservationists actually use the word.

How critical to such a definition is the presence or absence of humans? In most parts of the world, certainly in Illinois, the human species has played an important role in the landscape for thousands of years. Native people, through hunting, gathering, and burning, were as much a part of nature here as were the beaver, buffalo, bear, and bumblebee. The fact that people helped make or perpetuate these prairies didn't mean that prairies weren't nature. When my dictionary defined nature as ". . . largely free of human influence," they had it pretty close to right, but for this definition to work for conservation, the word "largely" needs to be understood with some sophistication. Consider "largely" to mean "essentially"—in other words, the influence was neither so great nor so rapid that essential processes were destroyed. Seen in this way, it is the communities of species that have gradually shifted their relationships and their positions on the landscape over millennia in response to all sorts of influences—human and nonhuman—that are nature. The "presettlement" Native American–inhabited landscape of Illinois was nature. In fact, as we will see, the loss of people from a natural system in which we have played an essential role can be as destructive to the functioning and survival of that community as the loss of a key predator, pollinator, herbivore, or any other key species.

This understanding needs to be worked into a clear definition of the word nature as used by conservationists. There are other definitions of nature, of course. The community of microorganisms in the bowels of a healthy person, the stars, flirting teenagers, the successional processes of an abandoned city lot, are all nature by one legitimate definition or another. So is everything else—as in Random House definition number six: "the universe, with all its phenomena."

But the nature that needs preserving, the nature of natural areas inventories and natural heritage programs, is better defined as *complex assemblages of species as they have evolved in their environments over the ages*. Whether people have played a role in this evolution is not key. If people—or anything else—change the environment sufficiently rapidly so that substantial numbers of species die instead of evolve, then what we have is degradation (or "development") rather than nature. Using this specialized biodiversity definition, regardless of whether *Homo sapiens* is or is not present, if nothing causes changes so rapid as to eliminate species from any long-evolved community, this is nature. In fact, if people intervene and go to great lengths to restore the conditions of relative stability which allow the continued existence and evolution of those ancient lineages and interdependencies, the result is still nature.

NATURAL SUCCESSION VS. ARTIFICIAL SUCCESSION

Our critics find the direction of natural areas management and restoration to be increasingly intrusive, limiting, and destructive. Responding to the concern of some conservationists that maples are replacing the oaks in many of our preserves (and in the process eliminating most of the plant and animal species of the open oak woodland), Mendelson and his colleagues counsel us to avail ourselves of this "unique opportunity to watch the panorama of successional change unfold naturally."

But there are many kinds of succession, just as there are many definitions of nature. When ditches are dug to drain a marsh, a successional process begins. In time, succession will produce an entirely different community. The process may be an interesting one for a scientist to study. But, particularly if that marsh was the last of its type, or if it harbored a number of endangered wetland species, it is easy to understand why conservationists might consider a successional process that killed them to be unnatural.

If grazing animals are spared predation and thus reach population levels dramatically higher than a given plant community is evolutionarily equipped to support, a successional process begins. Whether the animals are cows in a fenced prairie, sheep on an oceanic islet, or deer spared predation by wolf extirpation and a hunting ban, the process is similar. Certain species increase, some temporarily. Others decrease or disappear at various rates. An Illinois prairie under heavy grazing by fenced cattle can lose most of its original animal species in just a year or two. In a decade or two even the plants will consist almost entirely of the few now-ubiquitous, mostly Eurasian species adapted to life in pastures. The species of plants and animals best adapted to intensive grazing will have won out. This is succession. It is not, however, driven by "natural" forces in the sense that conservation biologists use the word. The result of this kind of succession is a degradation—a loss of natural diversity. This process is not natural succession; it might better be referred to as artificial succession. The system continues to evolve. But it has lost thousands to millions of years of evolved prairie richness.

Such artificial succession is what occurs when fire is removed from a fire-adapted system that has evolved over eons; a process of degradation begins that in many ways parallels what happened to the ditched marsh and the overgrazed prairie. In the case of the highly fire-dependent tallgrass savanna, this loss of biodiversity was so rapid that most of the original plant and animal species were gone from a typical site within twenty years of fire suppression, judging from the accounts of eyewitnesses like John Muir.

In Midwestern oak woodlands the erosion of species takes longer, but the results are much the same.[6] John Curtis eloquently described how this process proceeds with a stand of white and black oak in Wisconsin:

> Due to complete fire protection afforded the stand in the last 50 years, the mesic trees began to spread out, basswood going first and farthest, followed by an almost solid wall of young sugar maples . . . shade from the maples brought about the death of the typical oak forest understory . . . the first effect was on reproduction, with flower and fruit production greatly reduced. As the period of exposure to low light lengthened, the oak plants gradually died out altogether, although some of them persisted for decades in a weak, entirely vegetative condition.[7]

Botanists today are studying this phenomenon in some detail. Gerould Wilhelm, for example, has analyzed the character of the herbaceous species lost when oak woodlands are not burned.[8] What happens is not what the classical theory of succession would lead us to expect. We do not see the replacement of relatively weedy species by species associated with more advanced successional communities, but in fact, the reverse. It is often highly conservative species that drop out and relatively needy species that move in. Thus, the process is distinctly one of artificial succession. The natural community is degrading as a result of the removal of one of its natural processes—fire.

Studies by Panzer, Mierzwa , Apfelbaum and Haney, and others have begun to demonstrate that many of the insects, reptiles, amphibians, birds, and other animals go the same way as the plants.[9] Indeed, many of the animals that depend on the Illinois savannas or open woodlands are now on the way out. Typical examples include Kirtland's snake, Cooper's hawk, and the silvery blue butterfly—but the list could go on for pages. Many animal species that once inhabited the savannas have subsequently done fairly well for a time in artificial habitats such as woodlot edges, orchards, or even backyards. But as suggested by the experience in many parts of the country with the eastern bluebird, Bewick's wren, barn owl, and others—the changing artificial niches may not remain suitable to such species indefinitely. Without a natural habitat to fall back on, even many of today's more common savanna animals and plants may disappear.

Thus, it is critical whether the succession that eliminates the original biodiversity of the savannas is or is not to be considered "natural." Whether this succession is or is not so recognized may determine whether savanna and woodland are to be maintained by management in our preserve systems. For many species that evolved in oak ecosystems this semantic question is a matter of life or death.

With this background, let us revisit the question of whether restoration destroys nature.

If a marsh that had been ditched and was starting to drain could be unditched in time to save its plants and animals, few would quarrel with the use of bulldozer or backhoe to carry out the restoration. If the natural community were then able to hum along as before, few would dispute that the result of that mechanized restoration was more natural than the alternative.

The idea that bulldozers and backhoes could actually (though not yet very often, of course) foster nature is crucial to the new definition of nature that is emerging. Yes—for biodiversity it would have been better to leave the marsh alone in the first place. But, once the ditches have been dug, to discourage as "manipulation" the restoration which would save an ancient community of hundreds of rare species makes little sense.

According to the emerging definition of nature, people can in fact play a constructive and integral role in it. If one definition of "nature" is the rich mix of rare species and processes that in the Midwest are largely limited to "natural areas," then what people may do to protect and maintain this biodiversity becomes a part of nature.

Putting a drip torch to a fire-dependent woodland, planting the seeds of species that have been unnaturally extirpated, removing alien pigs or brown tree snakes from an oceanic island—even though highly artificial methods may be required to accomplish these tasks—must all be thought of as fostering nature, if the result is the recovery of a rich, highly evolved community with ancient lineage.

As an experiment, it may be appropriate at times to study what happens as artificial succession destroys the biodiversity of a preserve. For those who want to study the phenomena we have no shortage of such experiments. The overwhelming majority of "preserved" savannas and oak woodlands in the Midwest are following that course. In these, I suppose, we are preserving an *idea* of nature. In restored and managed sites we are preserving natural processes and thereby the species that nature produced.

THE POWER OF DEFINITIONS

Just as there is debate about the meaning of nature, there is also disagreement about how to define and label its parts. Some of the current confusion about savanna derives from the fact that there is no generally accepted definition of the word. For biodiversity purposes, the names ultimately are immaterial. In practice however, it has been helpful to try to name and define communities so that we can make sure that all major types are represented and surviving in our preserve systems (see Fig. 1).

In *The Vegetation of Wisconsin*, John Curtis provided the most detailed summary of relationships between natural plant communities that had then been done for any state. Curtis was also the first to demonstrate how significant the savanna had been as a Midwestern natural community. His chapter on the savanna is compelling and perceptive. The book was profoundly influential.

Curtis defined savanna as a native grassland with tree canopy cover ranging from one tree per acre (5 or 10 percent canopy) to a maximum cover

Fig. 1. Conceptual Model of Savanna, Woodland, and Related Communities as a Function of Canopy Cover

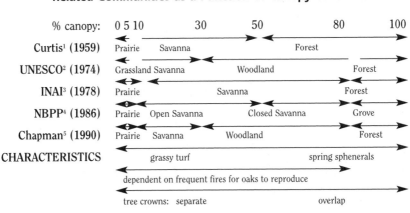

1. *The Vegetation of Wisconsin* (see references); 2. *Aims and Methods of Vegetation Ecology* (see references); *Illinois Natural Areas Inventory Technical Report* (see references); 4. North Branch Prarie Project seed mixtures designed for restoration, contact NBPP, c/o The Nature Conservancy, Chicago; 5. Kim Chapman, Crosswalk Classification of Terrestrial and Palustrine Community Types, Midwest Office of The Nature Conservancy, Minneapolis. (Gaps without arrows indicate transitions where percent of canopy coverage was not explicitly defined.)

of 50 percent. It was not a minor community. By this definition Curtis found savanna to be the most widespread community in southern Wisconsin (prairie: 2.1 million acres; savanna: 5.5 million acres; xeric (oak) forest: 4.4 million acres; mesic (maple) forest: 3.4 million acres.)

A small part of Curtis's chapter on the savanna, I believe, had the potential to be misinterpreted, however. Unfortunately for the savanna, this provided an excuse for neglecting the very part of nature that most needed help.

Natural areas conservation, an endeavor which began principally in the Midwest and which had Curtis's work as one driving force, sought to preserve and restore examples of the major ecological communities. The savanna, though originally widespread, would have been a high priority for preservation. In one way the prairies and forests were more like each other than either was like the savanna; their vegetation at any given point was more stable. The savanna community as a whole is perhaps equally stable over time, but its vegetation at any given point is highly dynamic, and the whole community is highly unstable in the absence of fire. The classic, rich savannas on good soil (called "oak openings" by Curtis) therefore deteriorated rapidly following European settlement, and by the 1950s few high-quality sites remained to study, preserve, or restore. The savanna's dynamic nature works against it.

When the Illinois Natural Areas Inventory defined community types, the ecologists recognized that a gap existed between a 50-percent-canopy savanna and closed-canopy forest. But the mission of the inventory scientists—to find *undisturbed* sites—made them think twice about such open "forests." For the canopy not to have filled in, some force, presumably fire, must have been in control (at least on sites with fertile soil). To the inventory workers such communities fit better with the fiery changeable savanna than the noble steady-state forest. So the inventory defined savanna broadly—an oak community with a canopy of 10-80 percent, fertile soil, and an understory composed principally of prairie species. What Illinois considered the 50-80 percent canopy component of the savanna, Curtis had classified as xeric forest. However the Illinois workers, like those subsequently carrying out inventories in other states, found virtually nothing that matched the definition, so this category, broad as it now was, remained an unfilled one in our preserve systems.[10]

Both Curtis and the inventory recognized that savannas are fire-dependent. But when people like myself—trying to restore remnants of this missing component in our preserve systems—sought to initiate fire management, we found ourselves butting heads with two groups: Midwestern foresters who didn't want burning in the forests, and prairie managers, who were focused on burning out or otherwise removing trees that had invaded the prairies. Both treatments gradually destroyed remaining vestiges of savanna.

Both groups seemed to believe that forests and prairies were entirely separate things. In a related community—sand savanna—fire was not anathema, perhaps because these barrens areas never develop the hallowed aura of a "forest primeval." But on good soil, where once there had been a continuum, now there was to be only the treeless, fire-maintained prairie and the closed-canopy pro-

Table 1. Number of prevalent modal species and percentage of prevalent species that are modal in eleven communities according to Curtis (1959).

		Prevalent modal species	
		Number	Percent
Prairie:	Dry	27	57.5
	Dry-mesic	8	14.6
	Mesic	19	34.6
	Wet-mesic	18	29.0
	Wet	10	22.7
Oak Openings:	(all)	1	2.1
Southern Forest:	Dry	13	24.1
	Dry-mesic	37	56.1
	Mesic	10	25.6
	Wet-mesic	4	10.2
	Wet	16	55.2

tected-from-fire forest. Although such critics, as Mendelson and colleagues demonstrate, recognized the presence of an intervening continuum when arguing that the savanna was merely an ecotone, in practice the survival of the continuum was threatened precisely by the insistence that prairie and forest be defined as discrete entities that required distinctly different management.

Enter a rationalization. Curtis had pointed out that the oak openings are "intermediate" between forest and prairie. Of the species Curtis found to be prevalent in the oak openings, all but one reached higher presence values in other communities (see Table 1). If undisturbed savannas were so difficult to find, busy conservationists reasoned, and if the savanna's species seemed to be secure elsewhere, then perhaps no great effort needed to be taken to conserve savannas. When some of us sought to get resources and change attitudes as required for savanna conservation, a keystone in the arguments of those who resisted was that the savanna was a mere "ecotone."

As Mendelson and colleagues put it, " 'Savanna' is no more than a name applied to an arbitrarily defined segment of a particular continuum . . . an eco-tone of uncertain width and uncertain stability lying between grassland and forest." The argument seems to be that the savanna's unusually "transitional" nature sets it off from more legitimate communities like tallgrass prairie and maple forest. This is essentially a definitional question; but it is an important one because of the implication that savanna is marginal. From such a per-spective there is no great urgency to save savanna since its components are adequately represented in prairie and forest preserves. If savanna were seen properly as ecotonal, wrote Mendelson and colleagues, savanna restoration activities "would lose some of their romance."

The fact that a community is part of a continuum does not diminish its significance, however. Most, if not all, communities are part of continua. Biotic continua of many types may be described: dry-wet, hot-cold, light-dark, young-old, rich soil-poor soil, and so on. The dry-wet continuum might be articulated as:

> desert . . . chaparral . . . shortgrass prairie . . . mixed grass prairie . . . tallgrass prairie . . . tallgrass savanna . . . oak woodland . . . beech maple forest . . . swamp . . . marsh . . . stream . . . river . . . estuary . . . inshore ocean . . . open ocean

Except for the end points no part of this continuum is more or less "ecotonal" than any other part. For successful conservation we would want to maintain healthy examples of all parts. Defined communities, though arbitrary, are useful in designing and monitoring fragmented preserve systems.

In fact, if we could rely on landscape-scale burning, natural processes would then maintain the whole continuum, and whether people applied one name or another to various parts of it wouldn't matter. Instead, it is precisely because managers must find and restore isolated remnant components of the continuum that we have to watch our definitions. Back when many managers thought simply in terms of prairie and forest, our preserves were being envisioned as, and managed to become, one or the other. The definition was determining the characteristics of "real" nature. It was necessary to focus on the missing part of the continuum to convince people to protect it too. In this way nature would be less imperfectly represented in our preserve systems. But priority-setting brings us back to the question, Is the savanna an especially "ecotonal" community—one with few species that depend on it?

As has been pointed out above, this idea is supported principally by data assembled and analyzed by Curtis. Curtis conducted a wide variety of mathematical analyses on his sampling data. He assessed the degree of distinctness—how much one community differs from others—by consideration of a community's prevalent and modal species. Prevalent species to Curtis were those most likely to be encountered in a stand of the community in question. They were also "the ones present in highest densities." Modal species for a community are those which were present in a higher percentage of stands of that community than in any other. As Curtis wrote, "If a high number of the most common species have optimum presence values in that community, then that community is recognized as more distinct than another community in which the common species are actually modal elsewhere."

Consider the numbers in Table 1. The oak opening (savanna) does seem to be strikingly low in prevalent modal species. Is this enough to convince us that savanna is indistinct, as Curtis implies?

For a number of reasons, however, this minor point within Curtis's work cannot support the heavy weight put on it by Mendelson and others. For one thing, Curtis's oak openings data came from relatively small, poor-quality, atypical fragments because these were all that could be found. In contrast, the prairie and forest data to which it was compared came from larger, higher-quality remnants, much more likely to have full complements of their original species.

More importantly, Curtis had divided the prairie and forest communities into five subtypes, from wet to dry. Because there was so little material to work with, the oak openings data was lumped as one type. Plant species are most likely to be found in one part of the moisture gradient. The chance of a given species reaching its highest frequency in the lumped oak openings is thus much reduced in the analysis as Curtis did it. For example, a species that is common in dry savannas will see its frequency in Curtis's analysis diluted by the fact that high presence on the dry sites is lumped with low presence on the mesic and wet sites. In other words, the lack of modal prevalent species in Curtis's oak openings data may well be an artifact of the sampling and analytic process rather than a characteristic of the savanna part of the landscape continuum.

This confusion is the source of the misconceptions about the distinctive "ecotonal" or "transitional" nature of the savanna. The confusion was amplified when Curtis's conclusions about the oak openings were generalized to include the 50–80 percent part of the continuum as defined by most state conservation programs. The "xeric forest" communities of Curtis (the oak-dominated dry and dry-mesic southern forest), having ample modal species, have not themselves been labeled ecotonal or transitional, though these would be largely "barrens" or "savanna" as defined by the Illinois inventory (compare Table 1 with Fig. 1). The problem was that, when the definition of "savanna" was expanded to include the 50–80 percent canopy part of the continuum, Curtis's assertion that there were few prevalent modal species in the savanna was applied to the more broadly defined system, even though his data showed that the 50–80 percent segment of the continuum actually had a considerable number of modal species (see table 1). In fact, if we were merely to use the Illinois definition, for one part of the savanna continuum Curtis's data confirm impressively high numbers of modal species. Accordingly, the claim that the more broadly defined savanna of Illinois, Missouri, Ohio, and so on, was unusually "transitional" is particularly inappropriate. Yet the confusion contributed to a scientific and conservation amnesia about this part of nature.

In the work of seminal thinkers like Curtis, semantic shades of meaning that are apparently minor can have major implications as that work is later applied, especially as ideas and language evolve. Consider the complex relationship between canopy cover, moisture regime and fire. Natural-area biologists understand high-quality communities to be relatively stable, having reached their present richness only over long periods of time. Curtis often made this same point, but his definitions of terms are often subtly different from the ones widely used today. On page 149 of *The Vegetation of Wisconsin*, for example, Curtis describes how "destruction" by fire permitted "retrogressive" replacement of maples and basswoods by red oaks. He points out that "the xeric forests of southern Wisconsin are seen to be a series of rapidly changing species compositions whose local complexity is the result of progressive and retrogressive processes induced by the biological characteristics of the dominant species and by the repeated interference of outside agents of destruction." Later, he projects this thinking into the future: "The indications are clear that only the climax mesic forests have the ability of ever regaining their initial composition under full protection, with all other communities certain to be permanently different under any foreseeable future treatment." These state- ments—though all perfectly true if we understand the words as he intended them—sound odd to ecological managers today because in Curtis's time "pro- tection" included protection from fire. Today a slightly degraded prairie is probably as likely as a slightly degraded maple forest to regain most of its com- position once protected. That is because today "full protection" for a prairie is understood to include prescribed burning.

The changing connotations of the word "mesic" (intermediate between wet and dry) have also contributed to the confusion. Curtis described southern dry forest as "unstable in the absence of fire. Succeeded by more mesic types." Under the heading "Succession," Curtis refers to "the natural transition from xeric to mesic forest," a process which "is most rapid on flat lands." You might easily get the misimpression from these true statements that a fine dry oak woodland preserve, full of biodiversity, would be likely to change to a fine mesic forest, full of biodiversity. Nothing could be further from the truth.

In the decades since Curtis published his work, biologists have defined and studied "natural disturbances."[11] The need for such "disturbances" (fire, dis- ease, grazing, etc.) in the survival of biodiversity is increasingly well under- stood. Today a good ecological manager would be quick to point out that a dry- mesic forest on flat ground which rapidly became a mesic forest in the absence of fire would probably be degrading and, thus, might soon no longer qualify as a natural area. It is true that, as canopies close, ground gets moister because sunlight and wind are reduced and a duff layer builds up. But does one kind of natural area succeed to another kind in this case? If a high-quality "dry forest" was growing on rich soil on flat ground, the open canopy would most likely have been the result of frequent fire. In the absence of fire, succession would most likely produce (particularly if no high-quality mesic forest was adjacent) an atypical and depauperate community—a mesic forest perhaps, but not a natural area.[12]

And what would happen to its rare species? It is common to hear ecology students say that as white or bur oak woodland succeeds to closed-canopy forest in the absence of fire, species that are "more mesic" move in. But only some of the "more mesic" species increase. The specialized, and now rare, shade-intolerant species of mesic open woodland do not; it is the shade-tol- erant species of mesic *closed* forest that win out. This distinction is important to biodiversity conservation because there are, in fact, species which depend on mesic and wet savannas or open woodlands. Such species in Illinois include swamp white oak (*Quercus bicolor*), glade mallow (*Napeaea dioica*), Kirtland's snake (*Clonophis kirtlandi*), and a great many others.

My restoration work leads me to believe that a full complement of species will be seen as prevalent, modal, and even predominantly dependent on many

Table 2. Examples of species regarded as principally savanna or woodland species by several working restorationists and the communities in which they are listed as modal by Curtis.

Scientific name	English name	Modal community
Asclepias purpurascens	Purple milkweed	wet-mesic prairie
Cacalia atriplicifolia	Pale Indian plantain	wet prairie
Camassia scilloides	Wild hyacinth	wet-mesic prairie
Gentiana flavida	Cream gentian	mesic prairie
Lespedeza violacea	Violet bush clover	exposed cliff
Muhlenbergia mexicana	Satin grass	weed communities

of the various phases of the savanna once substantial acreages have been restored. But then what happened to these lost savanna species—the ones that I believe would have been on Curtis's list of prevalent modals if he had better remnants to sample? Many of the species that restorationists have come to associate with mesic open woodland and savanna were found by Curtis to have survived best (and therefore in his data show up as modal) in dry-mesic forest. That is not surprising. As Curtis points out, unburned savanna will succeed to xeric forest. A number of species that are now considered classic savanna or woodland species by restorationists are listed as savanna ("barrens") species by Mead and dry-mesic forest by Curtis.[13] Examples include *Galium circaezans, Gerardia grandiflora, Prenanthes alba,* and *Solidago ulmifolia.*

However, many other species of mesic open woodland and savanna do not compete so well in the shadier conditions. When searching Curtis's data for these displaced species one finds them in an ill-assorted diaspora of open communities. To get a good understanding of such species it will be necessary to find, restore, and study the full array of canopy and wetness combinations.

But as a practical matter, many ecologists and managers are increasingly confident about recognizing savanna fragments and choosing species for successful restoration planting, and these people see many of the species Curtis studied in a very different light. Table 2 shows a sampling of such species. I chose these species because, in my experience, they were distinctive species of savanna and woodland remnants and restorations. I asked two restoration practitioners, Ed Collins and Tom Vanderpoel, and a field taxonomist, Gerould Wilhelm, who are familiar with the vegetation of northern Illinois and southern Wisconsin, to judge whether each of these species would most frequently be found in prairie, savanna, woodland, or forest under a natural burn regime In the judgment of these three, all six species, would most often be found on savanna or woodland sites. Their responses were consistent with each other and seemed to differ from Curtis. In fact, Curtis and these restorationists were answering differing questions. Curtis was describing a then-existing badly disturbed landscape. I do not mean to suggest that subjective data should replace Curtis's actual sampling data. Data need to be and are being gathered from recently discovered as well as restored landscapes. But even without it, I do think that there is sufficient doubt about the applicability of Curtis's modality data to natural areas like those in Illinois that we should now hold in abeyance the characterization of savannas as "transitional" and "ecotonal."

This debate may seem like much ado about a minor point, but mischaracterization has been yet another impediment in the way of the savanna getting the attention it needs to survive. This community deserves to be seen as a major conservation priority, rather than as merely a marginal mixing of species that mostly belong elsewhere.

SETTING MANAGEMENT PRIORITIES

In the founding years of the discipline of natural areas management (the 1960s and 1970s), there was typically little need for decision making about basic goals. Working only with high-quality natural communities, we wanted to remove disturbances and let natural processes restore disturbed areas adjacent to or within the natural area. It was not always easy to determine the best way to remove disturbance. But the goal was straightforward.

However, as both our knowledge and resources increased, some managers found themselves facing more difficult questions. A classic example of such a difficulty arises when a preserve remnant tenuously supports populations of endangered species that exist in less than the minimum viable numbers. Habitat size for—and thus numbers of—that species might be increased by restoration of adjacent land, but restoration necessarily replaces some species with other species. Restoration has ecological as well as financial costs. Managers must make judgments about whether the biodiversity benefits of an action outweigh the biodiversity costs.

Mendelson and his colleagues have criticized the managers of Cap Sauers Holding for burning and trying to restore savanna in the wrong place—that is, on forest soils. This criticism represents, in part, a disagreement about conservation values and in part yet another confusion of definitions. As we have seen, a portion of what was called "savanna" by the Illinois Natural Areas Inventory was called "oak forest" by Curtis and others. With tree canopy covering 50-80 percent of the ground, this is part of a nearly forgotten community called "rich open woodland"; it is rated globally endangered by the Conservancy because few or no healthy examples remain. This community, whatever it is called, is what the managers are trying to restore at Cap Sauers Holding. It is the community that was there historically.

The Public Land Survey (PLS) carried out at what is now Cap Sauers Holding in the 1830s, before European settlement, gives us a sense of the natural community at that time. Of twenty-four trees cited, twenty-three were oaks. (There was one black walnut.) In many places the oaks were widely spaced. At the quarter-section corner nearest the restoration area, the surveyor had to walk 129 feet to reach a second witness tree. People may legitimately call such a community "forest" if they prefer. But it is an error to lump such open oak woodlands with forest if this definition results in thinking that these stands are essentially like maple forest.

The distinction between (fire-adapted) oak forest and (non-fire-adapted) maple forest is critical in responding to criticism of restoration by burning. Both open and closed canopy oak communities have long been known to be fire-dependent.[14] That fire was a component of the natural landscape at Cap Sauers is indicated by the fact that scattered oaks stood on a site with good soil, and a natural ignition source is not hard to find. Both the northern (lower) and southern (higher) parts of the preserve were shown in the PLS notes to be prairie. The fires that burned the woodlands probably came from both directions. The most intense conflagrations probably came from the southwest, with the prevailing wind. The fires that maintained the prairie to the north would have ignited the bottom of the wooded slope, allowing the fire to burn up the slope and throughout the preserve area here and there as conditions permitted.

On the other hand, I share one part of the concern about prescribed burning expressed by Mendelson and colleagues. Today's carefully planned burns probably are different in many ways from the original fires with which our prairies and groves evolved. Those previously discussed "landscape-scale" burns swept indifferently across vast landscapes. Ecological managers hope to restore at least some very large preserves in which landscape-scale burning will once again reign. From these sites we will learn much that will help us mimic nature better at sites like Cap Sauers. But for the present we must make site-by-site decisions as best we can.

Parallel to the definition-induced confusion about fire is a similar confusion about soils. Mendelson and his colleagues accuse the Cap Sauers managers of trying to restore a savanna on forest soil. The simple response is that they are attempting to restore the historic community on the soils that it grew on. The open oak woodland and savanna at Cap Sauers grew on Morley soils. It would be good if we could use soil data to distinguish between forest and savanna areas as Mendelson suggests. Unfortunately we have poor information to go on. Rodgers and Anderson[15] studied this question in central Illinois. They used the PLS notes to map prairie, savanna, and forest. Then they studied how well that map corresponded to a contemporary soil map. The soil map, it turns out, accurately predicted whether a given area was prairie or wooded. But within wooded areas the soil data provided no help in distinguishing between savanna and forest. In the absence of better data, however, some managers follow Nuzzo in considering mollic hapludalfs and udollic ochraqualfs to be the savanna soils.

Given that the soil data and the PLS notes are only a part of the incomplete and complex information that is necessarily the basis of so many conservation decisions, it may be helpful to consider how the Conservancy, the Forest

Preserve District, and the Illinois Nature Preserves Commission have made such decisions for two other preserves at which all three agencies are involved.

In both of these cases, as at Cap Sauers, a volunteer group carries out most of the restoration, guided by a plan that has been approved by all three agencies. The basis for the plan in each case is an analysis of the existing vegetation, the PLS notes, and soil maps.

At Somme Woods, a 300-acre (120-hectare) preserve in northeast Cook County, the western portion of the site was entirely treeless in 1838; it is shown on the USDA soil map as having predominantly prairie soils (Ashkum and Elliott); it contains a high-quality prairie remnant. In that western third of the site our goal is to remove all trees and restore prairie. In the central portion of the site the soil map shows what may be open-savanna soils (Markham and Beecher); the PLS notes record widely scattered oaks; and today a variety of rare savanna species—plants, reptiles, amphibians, and invertebrates—persist. Here our goal is a mix of prairielike openings, areas of widely spaced trees (mostly bur, Hill's, and white oaks), and also some denser groves. The eastern portion of the site had denser oaks in the PLS notes, timber soils (Morley and Blount), and currently the most degraded ecology. Few conservative species are present. Again we seek to recover what was there—which may be called closed savanna, or woodland, or forest, depending on the classification system. Our goal is to restore it to its last known natural state and then let processes that are as natural as possible proceed. In order to allow enough light to reach the understory for the herbs to recover, so that the understory species can play their role in the recovery process, much of the flush of young trees must be removed from certain areas by fire, girdling, or cutting. Since most of the young trees are non-oaks (buckthorn, ash, basswood, elm, etc.), most of the trees being removed are those non-oaks. And since the PLS notes showed nothing but oaks and hickories in the Somme area, we believe that favoring oaks and hickories is the best restoration strategy.

In contrast, at a third Cook County site, Poplar Creek, the 250-acre (100-hectare) degraded grassland in the center of the site is being restored to prairie even though the soil map shows a Markham (savanna?) soil. The decision to restore prairie was based on the facts that (1) no oaks are now present, (2) the adjacent high-quality community is prairie, and (3) the PLS notes describe the land as prairie.

Thus although soils, presettlement vegetation, and remnant vegetation often steer management in the same direction, sometimes they do not. In such cases, how should restoration questions be resolved? There is no simple answer to this question. Typically those I would most trust to decide are people who are (1) intimately familiar with the ecological features of the site; (2) committed to assembling the best scientific advice; (3) aware of the potentials—and the limitations—of available management and restoration options; (4) aware of global and regional priorities for conserving biodiversity; (5) able to develop good rapport with preserve neighbors, users, and other politically significant forces; and (6) both humble and strong enough to do the right thing. A tall order.

In challenging our reliance on PLS data for restoration planning, Mendelson and colleagues write, "What value is it to choose a single moment in time? . . . Cutting and burning our woodlands prevents nature from doing what it does best: evolving." But it is not by any means the intention of natural area managers to return preserves to some arbitrary point in time and somehow hold them static—quite an impossibility in any event. Careful studies show, however, that the "natural" landscape we see today is often utterly transformed from the natural landscape that evolved here—the one that greeted the first Europeans.[16] The reason we took to the PLS notes is that typically they are our best single source of information on what the relatively stable, locally adapted ecosystem was like.[17] Taking the land back to 1738 or 1492 or 2000 B.C.E. would serve just as well—if we knew how. As David Brower puts it, we are in the position of lost hikers trying to relocate the last spot at which they still knew where they were; once we get back on track, the idea is not to stand still but to proceed. The restoration goal is to have natural processes, including evolution, proceed, with the bulk of the biodiversity surviving.

For conservation purposes, it is instructive to consider what is happening to the biota of the prairie region in terms of the technical definitions of "catastrophe" and "disaster" as discussed by John Harper.[18] Unlike repeating disasters, which increase fitness through natural selection, a catastrophe provides no evolutionary option for much of the biota. Rather than evolving to something new, species or populations die out. What is happening in the Midwest is, by this definition, a catastrophe. The collapse of our fire-dependent ecosystems is a one-time event in which the bulk of the biota is being eliminated from site after site and ultimately from the entire prairie region—except where managers maintain it.

It is true, as our critics suggest, that a certain kind of evolution would be favored by allowing the loss of the flora and fauna of the oak woodlands. When any catastrophe dramatically decreases the species richness and complexity of a system, the result is an increase in certain kinds of evolution. The destruction of the oak ecosystems by artificial succession is thus in a small way comparable to nuclear winter, or the rare natural catastrophes that from time to time have wiped out major components of global biodiversity, as indicated in the fossil record. After such catastrophes, the evolution of new species proceeds at an accelerated rate. But, as Edward O. Wilson points out, recovery of biodiversity takes from twenty to thirty million years. Wilson comments, "These figures should give pause to anyone who believes that what *Homo sapiens* destroys, Nature will redeem. Maybe so, but not within any length of time that has meaning for contemporary humanity."[19]

The type of evolution that follows catastrophes will flourish in the ecologically degraded and fragmented modem landscape without our help. But where will be the opportunity for evolution to continue for the thousands of species and ecotypes which are products of the fire-adapted prairies, savannas, woodlands, and wetlands that covered much of the Midwest for millennia? The only hope for many lies in managed and restored preserves.

To save any substantial part of the biodiversity of the central tallgrass prairie region will take great effort. Nor do we have the luxury of time. Gerould Wilhelm of the Morton Arboretum has likened the current pace of ecological degradation to a freight train barreling down the track at sixty miles an hour. "We hardly have to worry that we're going to exert too much force too quickly to slow this thing down," he said.

There are people who take joy in laboring to stem this tide. Our critics perceive a sinister "manipulation" and "domination" as we "perpetrate" our work. Restored savannas are, according to Mendelson and his colleagues, "limited by the imagination of the manager." But when planting seed or planning fire, every restorationist knows the ecosystem will respond in unpredictable ways that rise out of itself. That's precisely what we want to liberate. Volunteer Margo Owano put it strikingly. Comparing restoration and gardening she said, "Gardening implies control. Restoration implies surrender." The goal of restorationists is precisely to set in motion processes we neither fully control nor fully understand. A restorationist, like a parent, needs to protect an unsteady being from certain great insults to its health or existence. Similar to good parenting or coaching or teaching, the goal of restoration is to help some life go forward on its own—and in the process become more truly itself.

The intrepid volunteers who have been doing most of the work and the thinking at Cap Sauers deserve thanks more than criticism. According to volunteer steward Rich Hyerczyk, "On west-facing slopes we do cut some of the basswood and other native trees and shrubs, as Dr. Mendelson says. We also leave some uncut, especially in ravines. We have to make some areas open enough so that the grasses and wildflowers have a chance. In the long run the basswoods and maples are welcome wherever they survive a natural fire regime. But in the short run the critical problem for the ecosystem is that it's too shady for most of the species." Even the soil, which the turf has helped to build and hold for millennia, begins to wash away. Mendelson and his colleagues note the high current rate of erosion at Thom Creek Woods. As the erosion proceeds, they point out, the woods are changing to be more fire-resistant and more definitively forest. They expect an increase in species associated with maple forest, and maybe some of them will increase as the oak species die out. But from the viewpoint of conservation biology, in the unburned Thorn Creek Woods overwhelmingly more is being lost than gained. Maple forest species that increase or invade will be predominantly the ubiquitous weedy ones, not the species that need preserve protection. Thorn Creek Woods was once surrounded by prairie for miles in every direction; it is today similarly surrounded by suburbia. The only way to maintain biodiversity there is to restore natural conditions.

In contrast, at Cap Sauers the patient is for the moment recognized as being in critical condition. The wounds of the surgical brush cutting, the garish dye from the medicinal herbicide, the raw fire scars from newly resumed burning—these many evidences of the restoration work offend the aesthetic sensibilities of those who do not recognize that healing has begun, and that this intensive care is temporarily necessary. The stage is being set for real nature to recover and evolve in much the same direction that the millennia have been taking it.

One way to summarize this paper is to revisit and rewrite those bullets of conventional wisdom with which we began. As of January 1993, I would restate them this way:

- Nature has many definitions. Most important for conservation is the one that recognizes the rich, ancient, diverse communities of long-evolved species.
- Biodiversity on a human-dominated planet depends on human stewardship.
- Artificial succession is a threat to biodiversity, especially in areas where natural processes have been disrupted.
- The savannas and woodlands of the Midwest are particularly dynamic, natural communities, which need stewardship to survive.

To our critics, it seems that everything humans touch is thereby corrupted. Katz subtitles his article "Ecological Restoration Is Merely the Domination of Nature in Disguise." He opens with a quotation from William James, "The trail of the human serpent is thus over everything."

I share concerns about the impact of cutting, burning, herbiciding, and weeding in nature preserves. I share a fear that under the guise of restoration the global environment could indeed be degraded by the unscrupulous or, for that matter, by well-intentioned bungling. And I, too, once was drawn to nature as a place without people—a place for contemplation. I suppose I still am. But species and whole communities are vanishing and will disappear utterly if we just watch. The new view of nature is admittedly poorer in romantic purity and mystic detachment. Yet it's richer in participation. The values that are being lost are not entirely to be mourned; to a considerable degree they were a product of our alienation from nature. The restoration ethic allows us once again to belong in nature. Throughout most of our species' history, we were a part of nature. Our challenge now is to rediscover that role and play it well. Inherent in that opportunity are pitfalls, responsibilities, and liberations.

Michael Soulé has written, "Restoration ecology and conservation biology will tend to merge because most so-called wild places on the planet will be relatively denatured and will need intensive rehabilitation and management."[20] Some people will find this fact discouraging. Others of us find it a compelling and inspiring challenge. We will make mistakes. But they will not be the irreversible mistake that we would make by doing nothing. Challenges from critics will help sharpen our ideas and test our results.

The stakes are high. Restoration is helping redesign our species' relationship with the rest of life on this planet.

ACKNOWLEDGMENTS

Thanks are due to the following people who reviewed and helped to improve drafts of this paper: Roger Anderson, John Balaban, Martin Bowles, Kim Chapman, Don Falk, Rich Hyerczyk, Robert Jenkins, William Jordan III, Virginia Kline, Doug Ladd, Jon Mendelson, Dennis Nyberg, Michael Reuter, Laurel Ross, Jim Steffen, Ralph Thornton, and Gerould Wilhelm.

NOTES

1. Eric Katz, "Restoration and Redesign: The Ethical Significance of Human Intervention in Nature," *Restoration and Management Notes* 9, no. 2 (1991).

2. Jon Mendelson, Stephen P. Aultz, and Judith Dolan Mendelson, "Carving Up the Woods: Savanna Restoration in Northeastern Illinois," *Restoration and Management Notes* 10 (1992): 127–31.

3. Illinois Nature Preserves Commission, *Rules for the Management of Illinois Nature Preserves*, (Springfield, Ill.: n.p., 1964).

4. John Curtis, *The Vegetation of Wisconsin* (Madison: University of Wisconsin Press, 1959).

5. John Humke, "Concept of the Phrase 'Natural Area,' " *Natural Areas Journal* 2, no. 2; John Schwegman, "Concept of the Phrase 'Natural Area,' " *Natural Areas Journal* 2, no. 3.

6. O. Loucks, "Evolution of Diversity, Efficiency, and Community Stability," *American Zoologist* 10 (1970): 17–25; J. Ebinger, "Sugar Maple, A Management Problem in Illinois Forests," *Transactions of the Illinois State Academy of Science* 79 (1986): 25–30; Douglas Ladd, "Reexamination of the Role of Fire in Missouri Oak Woodlands," in *Proceedings of the Oak Woods Management Workshop*, ed. George V. Burger, John E. Ebinger, and Gerould S. Wilhelm (Charleston: Eastern Illinois University, 1991).

7. Curtis, *The Vegetation of Wisconsin*.

8. Gerould Wilhelm, personal communication, 1993.

9. S. Apfelbaum and A. Haney, "Management of Degraded Oak Savannas in the Upper Midwest," in *Proceedings of Conference of the Society for Ecological Restoration*, ed. G. Hughes and T. Bonnicksen (Oakland, Calif.: n.p., 1989).

10. V. A. Nuzzo, "Extent and Status of Midwest Oak Savanna: Presettlement and 1985," *Natural Areas Journal* 6 (1986): 2

11. S. T. A. Pickett and P. S. White, *The Ecology of Natural Disturbance and Patch Dynamics* (Orlando: Academic Press, 1985).

12. See for example, Loucks, "Evolution of Diversity, Efficiency, and Community Stability," pp. 17–25; and Gerould Wilhelm, "Implications of Changes in Floristic Composition of the Morton Arboretum's East Woods," in *Proceedings of the Oak Woods Management Workshop*.

13. S. B. Mead, "Catalogue of Plants Growing Spontaneously in the State of Illinois, the Principal Part near Augusta, Hancock County," *The Prairie Farmer* (1846); Curtis, *The Vegetation of Wisconsin*.

14. For a recent summary of the literature on this subject, see M. Abrams, "Fire and the Development of Oak Forests," *Bioscience* 42 (1992): 5.

15. C. Rodgers and R. Anderson, "Presettlement Vegetation of Two Prairie Peninsula Counties," *Botanical Gazette* 140 (1979).
16. See for example, Ladd, "Reexamination of the Role of Fire in Missouri Woodlands."
17. Reed F. Noss, "On Characterizing Presettlement Vegetation: How and Why," *Natural Areas Journal* 5 (1985): 1; M. Hutchinson, "A Guide to Understanding, Interpreting, and Using the Public Land Survey Field Notes in Illinois," *Natural Areas Journal* 8 (1988): 4.
18. J. Harper, *Population Biology of Plants* (New York: Academic Press, 1977).
19. Edward O. Wilson, *The Diversity of Life* (Cambridge: Harvard University Press, 1992).
20. M. Soulé and Kathryn Kohm, *Research Priorities for Conservation Biology* (Washington, D.C.: Island Press, 1990).

REFERENCES

Abrams, M. "Fire and the Development of Oak Forests." *Bioscience* 42 (1992).
Apfelbaum, S., and A. Haney. "Management of Degraded Oak Savannas in the Upper Midwest." In *Proceedings of the Conference of the Society for Ecological Restoration*. Oakland, Calif.: N.p., 1989.
Curtis, John. *The Vegetation of Wisconsin*. Madison: University of Wisconsin Press, 1959.
Ebinger, J. "Sugar Maple, A Management Problem in Illinois Forests." *Transactions of the Illinois State Academy of Science* 79 (1986).
Harper, J. *Population Biology of Plants*. New York: Academic Press, 1977.
Humke, John. "Concept of the Phrase 'Natural Area.'" *Natural Areas Journal* 2, no. 2 (1981).
Hutchinson, M. "A Guide to Understanding, Interpreting, and Using the Public Land Survey Field Notes in Illinois." *Natural Areas Journal* 8 (1988).
Illinois Nature Preserves Commission. *Rules for Management of Illinois Nature Preserves*. Springfield, Ill.: N.p., 1964.
Katz, Eric. "Restoration and Redesign: The Ethical Significance of Human Intervention in Nature." *Restoration and Management Notes* 9 (1991).
Ladd, Douglas. "Reexamination of the Role of Fire in Missouri Oak Woodlands." In *Proceedings of the Oak Woods Management Workshop*, edited by George V. Burger, John E. Ebinger, and Gerould S. Wilhelm. Charleston, Ill.: Eastern Illinois University, 1991.
Loucks, O. "Evolution of Diversity, Efficiency, and Community Stability." *American Zoologist* 10 (1970).
Mead, S. B. "Catalogue of Plants Growing Spontaneously in the State of Illinois, The Principal Part near Augusta, Hancock County." *The Prairie Farmer* (1846).
Mendelson, Jon, Stephen P. Aultz, and Judith Dolan Mendelson. "Carving Up the Woods: Savanna Restoration in Northeastern Illinois." *Restoration and Management Notes* 10 (1992).
Mueller-Dombois, Dieter, and Heinz Ellenberg. *Aims and Methods of Vegetation Ecology*. New York: Wiley, 1974.
Noss, Reed F. "On Characterizing Presettlement Vegetation: How and Why." *Natural Areas Journal* 5 (1985).
Nuzzo, V. A. "Extent and Status of Midwest Oak Savanna: Presettlement and 1985." *Natural Areas Journal* 6 (1986).

Pickett, S. T. A., and P. S. White. *The Ecology of Natural Disturbance and Patch Dynamics*. Orlando: Academic Press, 1985.

Rodgers, C., and R. Anderson. "Presettlement Vegetation of Two Prairie Peninsula Counties." *Botanical Gazette* 140 (1979).

Schwegman, John. "Concept of the Phrase 'Natural Area.'" *Natural Areas Journal* 2, no. 3 (1981).

Soulé, M., and Kathryn Kohm. *Research Priorities for Conservation Biology*. Washington, D.C.: Island Press, 1990.

White, John. *Illinois Natural Areas Inventory Technical Report*. Urbana: Illinois Natural Areas Inventory Technical, 1978

Wilhelm, Gerould. "Implications of Changes in Floristic Composition of the Morton Arboretum's East Woods." In *Proceedings of the Oak Woods Management Workshop*, edited by George V. Burger, John E. Ebinger, and Gerould S. Wilhelm. Charleston, Ill.: Eastern Illinois University, 1991.

Wilson, Edward O. *The Diversity of Life*. Cambridge: Harvard University Press, 1992.

11

Between Theory and Practice
Some Thoughts on Motivations Behind Restoration
Donald Scherer

The term "restoration" implies the existence of a former good, but a good that can come to exist again. "Ecological restoration" implies a process of bringing to exist again some lost good associated with ecosystems. Any process of restoration requires clarity about the good to be restored and about the obstacles and limitations to bringing it back into existence. Unfortunately, three current ideas seem to cloud the important issues of restoration: about exotics, about intervention, and about technology. Certain views, including the Society for Ecological Restoration's (SER) position on exotic species, seem misanthropic because they are not squarely ecological. In this paper I use my emphasis on ecology to urge what ecological restoration should aim to be and what the profession of the ecological restorationist should come to involve.

EXOTIC REASONING

Many restorations set the restorationist to distinguishing the exotic from the indigenous and removing the former. To accept this practice without question is misguided. In the Hawaiian Islands, for example, nothing but lichen grew seventy million years ago, immediately after volcanoes formed the islands. Only after lichen break the rock down into soil can a more complex community emerge. Thus surely not all population migration involves an introduction of exotics. So how should we distinguish migrations that introduce exotics?

Fifteen thousand years ago several animal species migrated across Beringia, a land bridge then connecting northeast Asia with northwest North

Donald Scherer, "Between Theory and Practice: Some Thoughts on Motivations Behind Restoration" *Restoration and Management Notes* 12, no. 2 (1994): 184–88. Reprinted by permission of The University of Wisconsin Press.

America, Many plant species migrated with the animals, the seed making the journey in the animals' digestive systems or on their fur or hair. In those cases the animals' frequent unawareness of providing transportation eases the thought that the plant migration is natural.

Let us accept, then, that not all migrating plant species are exotics. Does it make a difference that sometimes the transportation of the seed results from an animal's taking it to a preferred storage space? Whatever our philosophy about whether animals have minds, certainly when animals transport seeds that they (often or usually) eat at a later time, their transporting behavior has considerable coherence. If a squirrel picks up a nut, it maneuvers the nut so that its hold on it minimizes interference with the animal's movement. If it drops the nut, it does not continue moving as before. Unless chased by a predator, it regularly returns to retrieve the fallen object. Thus, while it does not intentionally plant the nut in a new area, it does mindfully transport and bury it in an area where such nuts have not been. Yet the view of nature as whatever happens when no human beings are present reinforces the idea that such seed distribution by animals is no less natural than seed distribution by wind.

What, then, shall we make of the fact that one of the migrating species fifteen thousand years ago was *Homo sapiens sapiens*? The opportunities retreating ice offered humans were not unlike those that brought other animal species east. (Since the time was preagricultural, none of the transported plants was brought to be raised.) What grounds have we, then, for declaring exotic exactly those migrants humans carried? If some mindfully transported immigrants are not exotics, what makes an immigrant an exotic?

Is a species an exotic if the ecosystem is not in equilibrium after its introduction? We may be moved to this thought because we often imagine a restored environment as remaining stable. Indeed, although I believe this thought properly moves us in an ecosystemic direction, it lacks precision. By contrast, if we postulate that a restorationist properly repairs a degradation, it does not follow that the appropriately restored environment will remain in the state to which it was restored. Consider a site in the northern lower peninsula of Michigan. In the last 125 years, since the Little Ice Age (1350 to 1870 C.E.), broadleaf deciduous trees such as the maple have again migrated north to lands they occupied for 7,000 or 8,000 years after the retreat of the glacier and before the onset of the Little Ice Age. Consider a forest of white pine cut in 1870. Even if perfectly restored at that time, that forest might well have been displaced by maples as they migrated north. The climatological determinant of their migration should clarify that an ecological restoration, even one postulated to be perfect, may still be impermanent.

Is it too fussy to make a counterargument turn on climatological change? I think not, but one can reconstruct the counterargument without using climatological change as a premise. Suppose a bird swallows some seeds, flies to a territory where no such seeds have germinated, and excretes them. The process of migration, as we have noted, will not provide sufficient grounds for calling the new population exotic.

Suppose that when the seeds grow, they displace a plant already growing in the area by competing for its light. Suppose the displacing plant, unlike the displaced plant, is not nitrogen fixing. Suppose that the soil deteriorates and the community atrophies because of the reduced nitrogen content. Because the ecological unhappiness of the resulting degradation is ample reason to call the plant an exotic, we may draw two conclusions: First, for a species to be exotic, the agent of its migration need not be human. Second, in accordance with our earlier observation that humans can cause migrations as unmindfully as other mobile animals, the fact that human beings facilitate a migration does not make the migrant exotic.

Confirm this understanding by reference to the Everglades. Discussion of exotics in the Everglades focuses on two trees, the melalcuca (*Melaleuca quinquinervia*) and the Brazilian pepper tree (*Schinus terebinthifolius*). Certainly these are not the only two nonindigenous plants in the wetlands. Yet discussion focuses narrowly on these two trees that disrupt the niches of many native life forms. Each of these invaders consumes something like fifty times the water of displaced native vegetation. The net effect is that the water other swamp plants and animals require disappears: Their niches are disrupted by the reduction of the wetland's limiting resource. Since humans are doubtless responsible for the introduction of other apparently nondisruptive species, we see that the concept of the exotic is ultimately ecological.

Conclusions: There is no essential connection between species migration and human importation of species. The explanation of how humans bring a species into an area may be no different from the explanation of how some other animal species brings a species into an area. How long a species has been in an area and what other species may have caused its arrival do not tell us that the species has harmed or will harm the community into which it has come. The ecological case for the removal of a species, as part of a restoration, is that it has caused or is itself a part of a degraded community, to be replaced because it has been degraded.

SER's policy on exotics is in clear disagreement with these conclusions, but in its own way a part of the policy is quite coherent with what I have argued. As the policy says:

> Highest priority should be given to the control of those species that pose the greatest threats, namely:
>
> * Exotics that replace indigenous key (keystone) species.
> * Exotics that substantially reduce indigenous species diversity, particularly with respect to the species richness and abundance of conservative species.
> * Exotics that significantly alter ecosystem or community structure or functions.

While the policy clearly says that an exotic species is "one that was introduced, either intentionally or unintentionally, by human endeavor into a locality where it previously did not occur," the priorities reflect an ecological, rather than a misanthropic, perspective.

My conclusions notwithstanding, I have not directly considered the case in which humans intentionally bring migrants into a system. (As far as I can see, the only reason for objecting to any migration an animal causes unintentionally is that the migration effects ecological degradation.) Let us then investigate the objection that while human beings might accidentally bring new species into a territory, on their clothes or in their hair, the intentional introduction of species is particularly troublesome.

THE ABSENCE OF THE HUMAN

For restoration to be worthwhile there must be some value in an earlier condition, a value disturbed and worth restoring. What is that value? Paul Taylor, among others, grounds that value in the condition's being natural. Contrary to my previous suggestions, Taylor proposes that what is natural exists free of human intervention. Then, in response to the question, "What is the good of existence free of human intervention?" Taylor replies that "what exists naturally is free to pursue the realization of its good according to the laws of its own nature."[1]

The concept of the laws of an organism's own nature, however, is confused. The move from Newton to Darwin is a move from an absolute concept of space to a relativized concept of environment. If the specific character of an organism's environment might have been thought irrelevant in Newtonian space, the implication of evolutionary theory is that any nature an organism has is for responding to the opportunities and dangers of a presumed environment. The positioning of the eyes of predator and prey illustrate the point. Any organism's environment, quite independent of the existence of human beings, confirms that intervention is universal. Taylor's sense is surely spurious because in it, nothing exists naturally.

Taylor's view of natural existence is problematic, therefore, because it is perversely misanthropic. Taylor says human beings are destroyers of nature because their intervention prevents nonhuman organisms from pursuing the realization of their own good. But the power of Taylor's argument rests on the concept of intervention. Yet how nearby organisms pursue (and have pursued) their own good makes every other organism's pursuit of its own good unfree in the generalized sense that the presence and behavior of other organisms condition it. Even when there were no human beings, no living thing was free of the constraints of its environment to pursue the realization of its good.

Let me state this objection in light of biological views about the origins of domesticated animals. Consider those lupine animals that thrived by becoming dogs about thirteen thousand years ago. These are typical domesticated animals, having evolved in such a way that they continue to behave, throughout adulthood, with the lack of inhibitions that typifies their juvenile period.

(Indeed, archeological practice is to distinguish the skeletons of domesticated animals from those of their wild cousins by the former's typical changes toward reduced body size, and particularly, reduced jaw and tooth size.)

Let us then accept the definition of neotony as the retention into adulthood of juvenile morphologies and behavior. Since the evolution of *Homo sapiens sapiens* earlier involved such neotony, a plausible hypothesis of evolutionary theory is that the animals we call domesticated evolved their neotony because an increasingly prominent primate species responded to neotonous animals by easing their living conditions and allowing them to achieve greater reproductive success. Human beings, in other words, were part of the environment in which those animals evolved to domesticity.

My argument here is not merely that human interference with others' pursuit of their own good is more widespread than one might have thought. My point is that the environment of an organism's evolution frames the definition of the good of the organism, and, for many organisms, a human presence conditions that environment. For any such organisms, a blatant contradiction exists in the concept "the good of this organism (whose evolution requires human beings) independent of human existence." Ultimately, then, it is not just that every species is interventionist. It is that the genetic character of each species is honed by the environments *of other species* in which it has evolved.

Let me approach this conclusion through a different argument: Once one recognizes that keystone species change their physical environment in ways that create and destroy niches, one judges a keystone species for the ecosystemic richness and diversity that its action enables or undermines. We do not argue, "Beavers help retain moisture in the semiarid Missouri River Valley. This is interventionistic. Therefore, beavers are bad." Instead we say, "The retention of water in the semiarid valley enhances ecosystemic richness. Therefore, beavers are ecologically desirable for their helpful intervention."

Conclusion: From an evolutionary perspective, human intention is irrelevant. For one species to affect the survival conditions of another and for one species' existence to constrain what another species becomes is as common as life. Human participation in this universal condition of life provides utterly no ground for treating that participation uniquely in the human case.

Perhaps, however, my conclusion about exotics is still to be resisted. Not on the broad ground of human intervention, but on philosopher Eric Katz's narrower ground that the intervention is technological.[2]

THE ABSENCE OF TECHNOLOGY

What, then, are the implications of Katz's view: "Natural behaviors of an x are those that exist as evolutionary adaptations, free of the control and alteration of technological processes"? Suppose x = "a fish living in a beaver pond." If so, the two phrases, "as evolutionary adaptations," and "free of the control and alteration of technological processes," push us in contrary directions. However many behaviors of fish in beaver ponds are evolutionarily disposed adaptations to conditions beaver dams create; dam-building is a technological process of control and alteration.

Katz actually mentions beavers' dam-building, but only to dismiss it as insignificant. While I can imagine several reasons for this dismissal, the activity has this significance: If a species evolves in response to the environment of beavers and beaver ponds, then beaver dam-building has been evolutionarily significant for the genetic definition of that species and thereby for setting significant parameters for their behavior. If the higher nutrient load of a beaver pond over a free-flowing river causes the genetic modification of what becomes a lake-bottom plant, beaver technology has provided the condition under which that plant flourishes. However much the scale of human technology dwarfs that of other organisms, the existence of species resultantly adapted to the presence of nonhuman technologies is an evolutionarily significant effect.

I do not wish, however, to overstate the analogy between nonhuman and human technologies. Human technologies have the clear potential to degrade enormous swatches of the ecosystems of millions of species. The scale of human technology gives it a disruptive potential arising both from the particular technologies it employs and from the size of the human population. Such large-scale disruptions obviously are problematic for maintaining desirable ecosystemic equilibria.

Somewhat incongruently, however, Katz's concern with human technology expresses itself as a skepticism about the very possibility of restoration. Katz correctly notes that whatever a restorationist does, the process from original through disruption to restoration destroys the historical continuity between the original and the restored ecosystem. Katz believes that this discontinuity makes restoration impossible.

Does Katz correctly analogize historical and ecosystemic restorations? If a restoration is historical, the goal is to restore what previously existed. If the home of John Muir in Martinez, California, is to be restored, our result will be imperfect if we must include pieces of furniture like those in Muir's home but from other California homes of the late nineteenth century. Even if our restoration is authentic to the period, it may not restore the house to what it was. Certainly, a curator could tell us what percentage of the very (copies of) books Muir owned and handled are now in the home's library. On the other hand, if a restoration is ecological, a restoration of Muir's orchard, perhaps, the restoration is not imperfect because, say, none of the restored trees were alive fifty years ago when the area was degraded. Ecological sameness does not require the same organisms. In other words, as Wittgenstein argued, "same" does not mean the same: criteria of identity vary, relative to purposes and the goods they involve.[3]

In other words, the case for ecological restoration differs from the case for historical restoration. In an ecosystem, historical continuity is not always required for reestablishing the equilibrium of interacting, flourishing populations that inhabited the ecosystem prior to its degradation. The reestablishment of such a functional equilibrium, far from requiring the same organisms that previously inhabited the site, does not necessarily require using organisms of the originally inhabiting genera. As restorationists know, a process that restores species of the biological families to the niches they once held often reestablishes the previous functional equilibrium. Thus, functional criteria of ecosystem identity determine whether the (*same!*) ecosystem has been restored. Because ecological restoration requires no more than a reestablished equilibrium of biologically similar, interacting, flourishing populations, ecological restoration can exist without historical continuity.

RESTORATION IN A WORLD HUMANS INHABIT

Nonecological criteria of exotics are, ecologically, arbitrary. Noninterventionistic is what life cannot be. Ecologically, technology can either enhance or degrade ecosystems. Beyond these philosophic distractions is the ecological question of what it means for human beings to be plain citizens and participants in an ecosystem.

Ecologically, human beings are scavengers. That is, materials that other species discard or ignore humans may use to their advantage. Scavenging is not, as such, an ignoble or disreputable activity. Appropriately pursued, it is an activity that benefits ecosystems by removing or transforming potential contaminants. Human scavenging becomes problematic when its scale or its by-products cause ecological degradation. Or what humans may label as scavenging is disruptive because the materials the humans use are essential resources to other populations whose decline leads to ecosystemic disintegration.

Ecologically, human beings are manipulators. Like beavers, elephants, and honeybees, humans significantly rearrange their habitat to facilitate their own ends. Manipulation, although disruptive, is not necessarily ignoble or disreputable, ecologically. Manipulation is simply the trademark of keystone species. Indeed, when we strip away whatever bias environmentalists may have for the lifestyles of native peoples, what remains of the commendation of native lifestyles is that they involve enhancing, nondegrading manipulations. When, contrary to SER's policy on exotics, the intentional as well as the unintentional interventions of native peoples are not faulted, the only nonbiased interpretation of such privileged tolerance is that some intervention does not degrade. Manipulation sometimes benefits ecosystems by increasing diversity, redundance, and resilience. Human manipulation becomes problematic only when it makes ecosystems less resilient and less capable of capturing and transforming energy into useful forms.

Ecologically, humans often displace other species when humans immigrate. Like scavenging and manipulating, displacement is in itself ecologically neutral. Leopold urges that human beings become plain citizens of ecosystems. Plain citizens should neither be glorified nor denigrated. They have their strategies, like individuals of all species. The strategies are not in themselves ecologically unacceptable, for they do not inevitably cause ecological degradation. It is not the strategies themselves, but the human success in their pursuit, the lack of competitive constraint on that success, and the scale of that success that yields ecological disaster.

Twenty-some miles from my home is a more-or-less preserved oak opening. One problem about the maintenance of that ecosystem is that the range of each of the predators indigenous to the opening is larger than the preserve. Leopold used the human removal of carnivores from ecosystems both to exemplify the degradation that unchecked herbivores can cause and to argue for human stewardship responsibilities.[4] When humans displace another species, often they alone are able to rectify the ecological instability they have caused. Instability that leads to degradation, however, is ecologically wrong. Therefore, humans bear the responsibility for avoiding the degradation.

Human activity has disabled or degraded many previously self-maintaining systems. In a social world of minutely specialized labor, a niche for teams of ecological restorationists develops in response to the stress humans effect upon ecosystems. The stewardship of teams of ecological restorationists is thus a part of the larger family of human efforts to reach an accommodation between the earth and its currently dominating species.

Consider, then, an extension of Leopold's argument. The wolf is only Leopold's example. The category exemplified is niche holders that have impeded human success but that also facilitate the continued flourishing of ecosystems. What Leopold points to is how the nonperformance of the ecosystemic function of the removed population causes some other population to become problematic to ecosystemic well-being.

Once we grasp that this is the ecologically crucial category to which Leopold's example points, the significance of the wolf is multiplied: It is not only the deer population that has become problematic of late. The population biologist tells us of the marked recent success of *Homo sapiens sapiens*: an eightfold population increase in the course of two centuries—in a population of mammals with the most prolonged immaturity of any species—that is now consuming more than 20 percent of the earth's food supply.

Human stewardship, then, cannot end simply with the human checking of herbivore populations. If, as is evident, the recent growth of human population represents the removal of ecological checks, then the application of Leopold's example is that, having removed those checks, we have taken the responsibility for the displaced work of human parasites and diseases. Otherwise, the good of flourishing ecosystems is jeopardized by an unchecked human population.

Let me be clear: This is not an argument in favor of war, parasites, or bacteria. The tension is not between human health and ecosystem well-being. The tensions are between human population size and human disablement of niche-holders on the one hand, and ecosystem well-being on the other. The removal of checks on human activity and population is the most ecologically destructive effect of modern times.

THE WORK OF THE RESTORATIONIST

Specific implications for the work of the ecological restorationist seem, therefore, to follow.

Professional Humility: The environment in which the ecological restorationist can thrive is of either of two sorts. The environment is either a society in which people pay substantial lip service to ecological well-being, hypocritically covering their collective endorsement of self-aggrandizement, or a society itself molded to respect and encourage ecological flourishing. In accordance with the latter of these goals, a publicized humility about the limits of our restorative capacities is in order to avoid the impression that stewardship simply amounts to finding the means to pay for what we feel entitled to want.

Professional Caution: Since ecosystems are much more easily maintained than restored, the ecological restorationist has a duty to promote nondegradation. When the choice is between restoring a degraded site (while developing a thriving site) versus developing a degraded site (while maintaining a thriving site), the restorationist has a professional obligation to seek the means to pursue the latter—in the face of the current structure of incentives to the contrary. As the physician's motto is "First, do no harm," so should the restorationist's code of ethics prioritize the well-being of ecosystems. Professional seriousness about the well-being of ecosystems imposes this obligation, for it is only prudent not to jeopardize that which is difficult, or impossible fully, to restore.

Educational Leadership: The promotion of respect for ecological flourishing also moves the restorationist to sponsor and encourage a widespread appreciation of flourishing ecosystems. Most of what the thriving of an ecosystem amounts to is hidden from human eyes, so little acclimatized as they are outside human-dominated environments. Humans in such societies are in no position to respect the energy, dynamism, redundance, resistance, and resilience of ecosystems. If they do not even know the reference of such terms, how can they be expected to appreciate the goods for which they stand?

Support for Supporters of Ecological Well-Being: The avoidance of degradation requires, first, that humans lower the impact of their actions. Beyond recycling lies the refusal to buy throw-away products. Knowing the externalities created prior to one's purchase decision provides a fuller accounting of the true impact of one's actions. Markets are sufficiently specialized that companies can find niches based on their reputation for environmental responsibility. Support for companies known to have such an ethic is a responsibility of the restorationist. Public support for such companies is a means of enriching human society so as to integrate the ecological goods for which restoration stands.

As a standard part of one's personal hygiene, one brushes one's teeth, not because one enjoys the brushing, not even because one despises the dentist's drill, but because it is good for the teeth. Contrarily, the habit of ecosystem maintenance is not a standard part of modern human repertoires. The degeneracy restorationists see daily is the product of a society whose assignment of responsibilities has not made a habit of ecosystem health. Restorationists who care about ecosystemic well-being should not be satisfied with being the society's institutionalized hand-waving. Instead they need to be a body that promotes widespread care for ecosystem health, even as it attempts such restoration as science, skill, and dedication make possible.

ACKNOWLEDGMENTS

The author wishes to thank Bill Aiken, Tom Attig, Mark Gromko, Chris Morris, Nancy Rubenson, and Sarah Wortham for their stimulating and helpful comments on versions of this paper.

NOTES

1. Paul Taylor, *Respect for Nature: A Theory of Environmental Ethics* (Princeton: Princeton University Press, 1986), pp. 186–92, 304–306, and chaps. 4, 6.
2. Eric Katz, "The Ethical Significance of Human Intervention," *Restoration and Management Notes* 9, no. 2 (1991): 90–96.
3. Ludwig Wittgenstein, *Philosophical Investigations* (New York: Macmillan, 1951).
4. Aldo Leopold, *Sand County Almanac* (Oxford: Oxford University Press, 1949).

REFERENCES

Katz, Eric. "The Ethical Significance of Human Intervention in Nature." *Restoration and Management Notes* 9, no. 2 (1991).
Leopold, Aldo. *Sand County Almanac.* Oxford: Oxford University Press, 1949.
Taylor, Paul. *Respect for Nature: A Theory of Environmental Ethics.* Princeton: Princeton University Press, 1986.
Wittgenstein, Ludwig. *Philosophical Investigations.* New York: Macmillan, 1951.

12

Eradicating the Aliens
Restoration and Exotic Species

William Throop

The problem of exotic species has increasingly compelled the public's attention. The zebra mussel, originally from the Caspian Sea, is endangering indigenous mussels in the Great Lakes. Gypsy moths defoliate forests in the eastern United States. Melaleuca trees brought to Florida from Australia have been changing the hydrology of the Everglades. The brown tree snake, which invaded Guam and eliminated a number of ground-dwelling birds, has hitched rides to Hawaii, where it would have similar impact if it escaped detection. In 1993 an Office of Technology Assessment report estimated that there were over two thousand exotic plant species in the United States.[1] Michael Soulé has suggested that the flood of alien species is one of the central challenges for conservation biology in the next century.[2]

Environmental restoration often aims at eliminating exotics from an ecosystem. To recreate oak savannas at Cap Sauers Holding in northeastern Illinois, basswood, black cherry, and hawthorn are cut or girdled. Parts of Haleakala National Park in Hawaii are fenced to prevent feral pigs and goats from returning after removal. Herbicides are used to control the invading molasses grass in the same region. The elimination of exotics almost inevitably brings about the deaths of many individuals. If these individuals have intrinsic value, if our causing their death is prima facie bad, then restorationists owe a defense of their elimination. This defense may not pose a significant challenge when the eliminated exotics are plants and insects.[3] When we move to mature mammals, however, the moral burden is much more severe. Increasingly people recognize some value in sentient animals. Many believe that our actions regarding them are bound by moral principles. If so, then a restoration project is justified only if the values recovered by restoration outweigh the disvalue of the individuals killed.

I

To explore the moral problems associated with the removal of exotics and assess potential justifications for such restoration, I will focus on the proposed elimination of mountain goats from Olympic National Park. In the 1920s a small number of mountain goats from British Columbia were introduced into the Olympic Mountains of Washington to establish a population for hunting. The best current evidence indicates that mountain goats were not native to the area, even though some historical reports suggest the contrary.[4] By the 1970s goats had colonized most of the mountain systems in the park and established sufficient populations outside the park to justify a bow hunting season. According to a 1983 census, there were an estimated 1175 goats on the Olympic Peninsula. The goats have a significant impact on the native ecosystems in the region. Their grazing affects species composition, as do their trail systems. They make sizable wallows that destroy vegetation and displace significant quantities of soil in fragile areas. They affect populations of several rare plants, including Olympic milk vetch, which was a candidate for the federal endangered species list.

The National Park Service has the policy of preserving "the natural abundance, diversity and ecological integrity of the plants and animals" in the parks and of eliminating exotics when they endanger park resources.[5] Management personnel began removing goats in the late 1970s using a variety of techniques, including rope snares, drop nets, and chemical immobilization. By 1989, 693 goats had been live captured, and it was estimated that 390 remained. The live-capture programs involve large costs and some risks to humans involved in the programs. As the goat populations declined, both costs and risks per goat captured increased. The mortality rate of the goats targeted for capture also increased, rising to an average 19 percent in 1989.[6] Because of the costs of maintaining the lower population densities through live capture, the difficulties of sterilization programs, and the continued impact of the goats at lower densities, the 1995 draft of the goat management plan proposed eliminating goats from the park by shooting them from helicopters.

The goats of the Olympic Mountains are a particularly tough case for the restorationist. The goats are native to neighboring mountain ranges such as the Northern Cascades, where they have similar impacts on vegetation. It seems mere chance that they did not find their way to the Olympic range. They are intelligent, highly adapted animals who are strong candidates for moral protection. Moreover, their aesthetic value and their relative rarity make them very popular with wildlife enthusiasts. It is impractical to limit their impact on native ecosystems without killing them. If it can be established that eliminating the goats is morally permissible, then the removal of exotics in many other cases will be permissible for similar reasons.

I believe that, on balance, we should eliminate the goats. We cannot do so with a clear conscience, however, because the situation approximates a moral dilemma in which important values must be compromised. I doubt that arguments can establish such a strong conclusion though. Resolving the issue requires weighting many values, and there is unlikely to be a unique, correct way to weight them. We must be content with a small set of reasonable value rankings, and hence some reasonable differences of opinion about the issue. In such situations, prudence suggests focusing on the permissibility of eliminating the goats. There are two relevant senses of "permissibility." In the stronger sense, shooting the goats is permissible if no reasonable weighting of the relevant values ranks the value of the lives of the goats over the competing values. In the weaker sense, it is permissible if some reasonable weighting ranks the competing values over the value of the goats' lives. To establish the permissibility of shooting the goats in the strong sense, one would need a careful assessment of the intrinsic value of individual wild animals, which I cannot undertake here. However, I will show that several key arguments against the elimination of goats are unconvincing. In the process of exposing their flaws, I will outline a general case for eliminating the goats and other exotics. At a minimum, the case will show that the policy of eliminating the goats is based on a reasonable weighting of the relevant values. Thus, eliminating the goats from Olympic Park is permissible.

My argument will proceed in three stages. First, I will show why it is reasonable to place negative value on exotic species merely because they constitute humanization of an environment. It is tempting to justify removal of exotics in terms of their degradation of ecosystems, but I argue that this disvalue will not justify removing the goats. Second, I will show how the removal of exotics, which involves additional human activity, can return value associated with a wild (unhumanized) ecosystem. Third, I will show how it can be reasonable to rank the value of wildness over the value of the lives of the goats.

II

The first stage requires a defense of the standard definition of "exotic species," which focuses on species introduced by humans. According to the National Park Service, "exotic species are those that occur in a given place as a result of direct or indirect, deliberate or accidental action by humans (not including deliberate reintroductions)."[7] A similar definition is embraced by the Society for Ecological Restoration. Donald Scherer argues that such definitions are unacceptably misanthropic.[8] He notes that the migration of species can be a perfectly natural event. If seeds transported beyond their previous ranges by nonhuman animals establish new populations, these are not exotics, according to the above definition. Yet there seems to be little to distinguish such cases from nonintentional human transportation of seeds to new areas. The preference for the nonhuman seems arbitrary and misanthropic. Moreover, a species migration which is not mediated by humans could significantly degrade an ecosystem by displacing species which provide essential services to the ecosystem. If restorationists repair ecosystem degradation, then it would seem that such a species should be removed. Accordingly, Scherer suggests that we should think of an exotic species as any nonnative species which harms an ecosystem.

How one defines "exotic species" depends on the purposes one has for the use of the term. Scherer starts from the assumption that "exotic species" carries a strong negative value in addition to representing a nonindigenous life form. Since he thinks human-mediated introductions of a species cannot account for the strong negative value, he locates it in the effect the species has on its new environment. An exotic species is a nonindigenous species which harms or degrades an ecosystem. I agree that it is useful to have a term that refers to species which have a negative impact on the environment, so I will reserve the term "exotic" for this purpose. I will use "nonindigenous species" for the value-neutral reference to species which have migrated by some means into a new area. I am doubtful, however, that the appeal to ecosystem harm is sufficient to account for the negative connotation of "exotic species," and I will argue that being introduced by humans is sufficient.

Do the goats harm or degrade the Olympic Mountain ecosystem? They negatively impact vegetation, but if this is harm in the Olympic Mountains, then it should also be harm in the Northern Cascades. Yet if the latter is harm, then almost any significant alteration of vegetation by animals would be harm, which seems highly implausible. Nature works through some species constraining the flourishing of other species, and one can hardly imagine it being otherwise. Of course, in the Olympic Mountains the goats are affecting somewhat different species, but why should this matter? One may be tempted to say that the goats do not "belong" in the Olympic mountains, but they certainly might have been native to the region if circumstances after the last ice age had been somewhat different. Moreover, it is not clear why merely not belonging in a region would make an animal's impact harmful.

The National Park Service puts emphasis on the threat to rare endemic species, especially the Olympic milk vetch, but it is far from clear that such threats alone constitute harm. If the goats were threatening rare plants in their native range for reasons unrelated to humans, we would see them as exerting selection pressures in a perfectly natural way. We might say that certain species were being harmed, but it would not follow that the ecosystem was being harmed or degraded. If a local population of a plant was eliminated by their activity, we would have a natural alteration of the ecosystem. If we say such an alteration is harm then we must say all such changes in ecosystem composition are harm, which again seems implausible. Almost all change impacts negatively on some species, but such impact is compatible with the ecosystem, altering it in perfectly healthy ways. There may be good political reasons to defend a potentially unpopular management plan by reference to the Endangered Species Act, but even these are evaporating, as the Olympic milk vetch was removed from candidacy for the endangered species list in 1996.[9]

Perhaps there are clear cases of nonindigenous species harming ecosystems—millefoil filling a pond or melaleucas draining regions in the Everglades. My argument is only that in many cases, harm cannot be easily distinguished from mere change. Although harm to an ecosystem does carry a strong negative value, its empirical content is quite vague. Those who define "exotic species" in terms of harm open themselves to the objection that many nonindigenous species are not exotics in the relevant sense, since the alterations they bring about are not clear cases of harm. In particular, the goats in Olympic National Park do not appear to be exotics in this sense. Although this result may be welcome to some, it is gained at the cost of significantly diminishing our capacity to evaluate ecosystem structures.

Of course, one could assess harm in terms of the particular causes of the change, such as human intervention, but then the harm account of exotics collapses into the standard account. One could also assess harm in terms of change from a particular baseline ecosystem. Steve Packard distinguishes artificial succession from natural succession, and maintains that the former changes constitute degradation of the ecosystem.[10] Artificial succession occurs when some of the "natural" processes which maintain an ecosystem are altered and the ecosystem's components shift as a result. When we eliminated fire from oak savannas and they evolved towards closed forests, we were degrading the ecosystems, not just changing them. In doing so, we also lost landscape diversity. Even if no species were endangered, historically important ecosystems were lost.

The reference to natural processes might suggest processes that existed independent of humans, but Packard does not want to separate humans from nature. For him, what is natural in an area seems to be determined by whatever "highly evolved community with an ancient lineage" has recently existed within the area.[11] This account is helpful in justifying savanna restoration, and it could be used to designate mountain goats as exotics in the Olympic Mountains. It is highly problematic, however, as a general characterization of the natural. If a "natural disaster" shifts the structure of an ecosystem, resetting succession towards a different kind of system, the result seems no less natural than the original, even if it lacks an ancient lineage in the area. More to the point, the new ecosystem need not be degraded just because it is different. Furthermore, Packard's account has the unlikely implication that an ancient Mediterranean olive grove is natural, even if it is the result of continuing intensive cultivation.

In general, preference for a particular ecosystem structure is increasingly hard to justify on ecological grounds as many ecologists move away from equilibrium models of ecosystems.[12] If, as some argue, disturbance is the norm in nature and change frequently occurs on a variety of temporal and spatial scales, then one needs special reasons for thinking the alterations caused by nonindigenous species are harms. Of course, if one selects one's baseline ecosystem in terms of its being relatively unhumanized, then one is back to a variant of the standard definition.

III

In light of the difficulties in distinguishing harm or degradation from mere change, it may seem more promising to reconsider Scherer's objection to the Park Service's definition of "exotics." Can a case be made that human changes to a relatively unhumanized environment are in themselves bad? If so, then because the goats were introduced by humans, their impact is bad. Let us say that an environment is "humanized" to the degree to which it has been altered by humans, and that it is "natural" or "wild" to the degree to which it has not been so altered. Like an increasing number of environmental philosophers, Scherer finds it evolutionarily and ecologically naive to place positive value on the wild and disvalue on the humanized.[13] He argues that from an evolutionary point of view, human manipulation of the environment is no different in kind from the manipulation of other species, though it may differ in degree. Keystone species always affect the survival conditions for other species, and there is no ecological reason for singling out humans. Thus, he concludes, views which take human alteration of the environment to be negative in itself must be based on a negative view of humans.

The premises of this argument seem reasonable enough, but the conclusion does not follow from them alone. The implicit premise seems to be that either the evaluation of human impact must be based on scientific differences between human and nonhumans or it must be a general appraisal of humans. But this claim is highly problematic. Value differences between entities can be based on a wide variety of empirical differences. They need not be tied to scientific distinctions or to inherent features of the entities. I suggest that the negative value associated with the standard definition of "exotic species" results from a widespread recognition that humans have altered so much of the environment that they have made less altered environments especially valuable.

In moderate doses, humanization of environments is good. When Native Americans crossed the Bering land bridge, their humanizations of the new environment were often improvements. Even when the first Europeans settled the new world, they found it so unhumanized, relative to their standards, that human transformation of the land was typically interpreted as improvement. The relative proportion of the nonhumanized to the humanized has shifted dramatically, however, at least in North America. In the current context, many believe that the process of humanization has gone too far. This disapproval of humanization need not involve a negative appraisal of humans per se; it need not be misanthropic. Just as one may believe that one has been eating too much without disapproving of eating, one may disapprove of increased humanization without disapproving of humans. If I am right, the degree of humanization is what makes additional humanization bad, including the introduction of exotics, and it underwrites a significant part of the negative connotation of the standard definition of "exotic species."

I cannot fully defend this suggestion here, but the following points weigh in its favor. In a wide variety of cases, many people do seem to value less humanized over more humanized entities. From purchasing natural vitamins and organic produce to hunting for one's meat and hiking for one's exercise, many preferences seem to reflect a valuing of the less humanized, among other things. The widespread appeal of wilderness is easily explained on this hypothesis. The value seems stable under conditions of increasing knowledge. In my experience, increasing the salience of our evolutionary heritage does little to diminish the appeal of the less humanized, and neither does the awareness that in other contexts, the appeal is absent.

Wild nature is also valued because it is "other" than human. Most people recognize the importance of a balance between the celebration of human achievement and the awareness of human limitations. One way to promote this balance is to posit some "other" which has great value. By appreciating what is "other," humans can put their own achievements in context and avoid hubris. Historically, divinity has played the role of the "other," but increasingly wild nature has become the "other" in secular society. Many of our transgressions are against nature. Restorationists claim to heal the breach between humans and nature, and the complexity and diversity of wild nature stimulate religious attitudes of awe and reverence. The quasi-religious concept of nature as "other" implies limits on humanization without implying any fundamental ecological distinction between humans and nonhumans.

My claim that exotic species are bad in virtue of their being increased humanization is compatible with there being other reasons why they are bad in particular cases. Exotics may harm species or alter ecosystems which we particularly value. They may reduce landscape diversity, and, as noted above, they may in obvious ways degrade an ecosystem. These additional disvalues may be used, along with considerations of practicality, to prioritize control of exotics. Some of these considerations, especially landscape diversity, play a role in the case for eliminating mountain goats from Olympic National Park. They are not required, however, for my qualified defense of the proposal.

IV

The second stage in my defense is to show how the human activity of shooting goats can decrease the disvalue of the humanization of the Olympic Mountains. This is a specific instance of the more general challenge of showing how restoration can make an area more natural, given that it seems to involve additional human alteration of the area. Eric Katz argues that restoration produces an artifact which cannot have the value that the predisturbance state had in virtue of its wildness.[14] Wildness value is determined by the particular history of an area. One cannot change this history, and one certainly cannot eliminate human alterations from the history by more human alterations. If he is right, then eliminating the goats may enhance landscape diversity and other values, but it cannot remove the disvalue which stems from their humanizing the region.

Katz's argument has the air of paradox, for it certainly seems that removing exotics diminishes human impact. The apparent paradox results from conflating two senses of "humanized," both of which are compatible with the earlier definition of "wildness." If one means by "humanized" the historical property of having been affected by humans, then human alteration cannot be removed from an ecosystem. On the other hand, if one means the property of reflecting changes made by humans in the current structure and functions of an ecosystem, then humanization can be removed by more human activity. The reasons mentioned above for associating negative value with humanization seem to apply equally well to both senses of "humanization," so they cannot be used to select one of the senses as dominant.

If we associate value only with the historical property, then we have the counterintuitive result that restoration can never diminish the disvalue related to humanization. Yet it seems that if New York State purchases land in the Adirondack Mountains for wilderness, and it tears down four-walled structures on the land, it does diminish some of the negative value that is associated with humanization. If, like Katz, we choose to frame our account in terms of the historical property of humanization, then to make the account compatible with strongly held intuitions, we must posit another value which derives from history without being defined in terms of it. I suggest that if a creative process is valuable, then, other things being equal, the contingent product of that process is also valuable. If being painted by Picasso makes a canvas valuable, then the particular images created by the process also have some value. If a Picasso painting is damaged and restored, the process is not recreated, but the valuable product is.[15] Similarly, if being created wholly through natural processes is valuable, then the product of those processes in a region—that is, the structure and functions of the predisturbance ecosystem—also has some value. The latter value derives from the value of the historical process without being created by it.[16]

We cannot eliminate the human introduction of goats from the history of the Olympic Mountains, but we could recreate an ecosystem which does not reflect that part of the history. By eliminating the goats and allowing the vegetation to regenerate, perhaps with some human assistance, the mountain ecosystem would approximate the product which had been created by wholly natural processes in the region. Thus restoration would return some portion of the value associated with the unhumanized system, and thereby diminish the disvalue of humanization.

Even if restoration can enhance the wildness value of an ecosystem, that value can also return in other ways. Typically nature renews itself after degradation, and humanization gradually washes out of a system. A forest grows back after a clear-cut and a pollutant is gradually flushed from a river. In the case of an exotic species which has become thoroughly integrated into its new habitat, we sometimes speak of its "naturalization." We might wonder whether this has taken place in the Olympic Mountains; perhaps the humanization which resulted from the introduction of the goats has washed out as they have become naturalized. If so, then eliminating them would reduce wildness.

Usually, however, restoration speeds the washing-out of humanization; this is part of its attraction. If significant signs of human impact remain, as in the case of the goats, we are often reluctant to say that humanization has washed out of a system. The criteria we use to determine naturalization seem highly variable. They may reflect our feelings about the invading species and the systems they alter, as well as empirical considerations such as the species' impact on the ecosystem, its degree of integration into the system, or the amount of time since its introduction. Our reactions to feral pigs in Hawaii and feral goats on San Clemente Island suggest that on average, mammals introduced into rare and fragile ecosystems take much longer than seventy years to become naturalized. Thus it seems likely eliminating the goats from the Olympic Mountains will significantly reduce our humanization of the region.

V

So far, we have seen reason to believe that the presence of goats in the Olympic Mountains is bad, in virtue of its being a humanization of a relatively unhumanized region. We have also seen that this disvalue can be diminished through eliminating the goats and restoring the ecosystem. Along the way, we have noted that although the goats may be harming particular species, it is far from clear that they are harming or degrading the ecosystem as opposed to merely changing it. Since we do not believe that we should protect vegetation from the harm caused by goat browsing and wallowing in their native habitats, it seems doubtful that the harm to vegetation, in the absence of other considerations, should motivate us to eliminate the goats. This leads to the third stage of my argument where I must show that the value gained by restoring the park to a prehumanized state can legitimately outweigh the disvalue of the lost lives of goats.

It is notoriously difficult to weigh values, especially values of very different sorts, for there is no way of measuring degree of value and comparing the measurements. Even if we had an acceptable measuring device, measurements would vary among knowledgeable, sensitive valuers. Nonetheless, we can often agree that some rankings are unacceptable. Someone who preferred eating puff pastries to preserving the lives of hundreds of people, supposing each were easily accomplished, would be contemptible. One of the principal ways of showing that a value weighting is permissible is to undermine arguments that it is an unacceptable weighting. Conclusions derived in this way are highly defeasible, for additional objections to the weighting may arise. Often, however, we can provide no better justification than the considerations which show why serious objections fail.

We do not have to look far to find a powerful argument that preferring wildness value over the lives of sentient animals is unacceptable. Consider the following: Wildness value is an aesthetic value; it results from our appreciation of certain kinds of landscape. The value of the lives of the goats is a moral value. It is a function of the interests of the goats, and it is independent of our liking or disliking the goats. Moral values, at least those pertaining to the lives of morally considerable beings, should have priority over aesthetic values. Thus, it is impermissible to eliminate the goats in order to return the Olympic Mountains to a less humanized state.

I agree that the goats do have intrinsic value; it matters morally what we do to them. I doubt that one of the goats has as much value as an average adult human. We would legitimately prefer preserving the life of the latter if the two lives came in conflict through no fault of either. Still, the value of the lives of hundreds of wild goats is considerable. To override that value, the value of the diminished humanization must be great indeed. Calling the latter an aesthetic value does make it unlikely to outweigh the moral value, unless we accept an aggregative theory of value, such as utilitarianism. But one of the things which makes aggregative theories seem problematic is the thought that the mere aesthetic appreciation of many people could override the value of the lives of a few. I will not assume such a theory, and I doubt that it would justify eliminating the goats, given current preferences of the human population.

By attending to other weightings of wildness, to the context in which the weighting occurs and to the significance of death in a relatively wild ecosystem, we can see how values that apply to large systems, like wildness, can override the values of individuals. Whether wildness value is an aesthetic value depends on how broadly one construes the category, but the more broadly one construes it, the less clear it becomes that aesthetic values cannot outweigh the value of nonhuman lives. Let us grant that the value of the nonhumanized is a function of the appreciation of some, but not all, human valuers. In this sense, it is like the value of particular kinds of beauty. It not a mere idiosyncratic preference, however, like the preference for chocolate ice cream or for misty mornings. Aesthetic values shade imperceptibly into spiritual values and moral values which carry much more weight than idiosyncratic preferences. Other reasonable judgments about the relative weight of wildness value in large systems suggest that it can weigh a great deal.

Those who value wildness typically think that it outweighs the nonbasic interests of many humans, while they would not think that the mere aesthetic preference for some scenery would do so. The importance of establishing wilderness areas is often thought to outweigh the disvalue of jobs lost and hardships endured as a result. As these are serious disvalues, the value of wilderness must be given significant weight. Although wilderness embodies many values, wildness is central among these, and must carry much of the value weight.

Weighting wildness over human hardship seems reasonable partially because in this context, large systems rather than individuals are the legitimate focus of interest. Just as we may justify some involuntary sacrifices on the part of humans in terms of the good of a community or nation, we may do so in terms of goods applied to large ecosystems, especially when these goods are increasingly rare as a result of humans not making voluntary sacrifices of their own welfare. In some roles, we may legitimately place systemic goods over individual goods. The primary responsibilities of heads of states who are negotiating treaties are to the states they lead, not to individual members of the states. Similarly, the primary responsibility of the U.S. secretary of the interior is for the larger ecosystems he or she oversees, not for the individual members of those ecosystems. Even if we are not in such roles ourselves, we can make judgments about how values can be weighted from within such roles. In light of the tremendous and unbalanced humanization of the planet, it often seems reasonable to weight the value of wild ecosystems over some serious human goods. Thus, if one wants to say wildness is an aesthetic property, then it can reasonably be thought to carry a much greater value than the preference for certain kinds of scenery. But can it take priority over life?

It would be very hard to justify sacrificing the lives of humans for the wildness of an ecosystem. The situation differs somewhat with the lives of wild animals, however. The death of wild animals is an important part of the functioning of a wild ecosystem. To be sure, death is an evil for the animal, but it often contributes to the good of the larger system. This does not change if the death is a result of an intentional action—say, a mountain lion's killing a goat—or even of an action for which someone is morally responsible—a human killing a goat. In this way, the death of a wild animal has a different moral status than the death of a domestic animal. Most domestic animals are no longer full participating members of relatively wild ecosystems. The process of domestication creates special relationships between animals and humans, and possibly special obligations. In this respect, the death of a domestic animal may be more like the death of a human than the death of a wild animal.

Of course, the observation that the death of a wild animal often contributes to the good of an ecosystem does not imply that any such death is a good thing. Wantonly killing wild animals is clearly wrong. It does show, however, why one might reasonably believe that the disvalue of death in the wild might be more easily overridden than the disvalue of other deaths. One might worry that death caused by humans is not wild, so it does not have diminished significance. But this confuses the cause of death with the status of the dead organism. The cause of death is not wild, and it is not valuable in itself. Indeed, it is regrettable that humans must intervene and harm innocent organisms. But the effect—the deaths—is not be as bad as deaths in other contexts.

Let us return to the situation of the goats. First, the primary responsibilities of National Park ecology managers are for the systems which they manage. Here I am not just suggesting that park policy focuses on systems, which it clearly does, but that it is appropriate for park policy to have that focus. This creates a defeasible presumption in favor of giving priority to the values of the systems they manage. We have seen reasons to believe that in the current context of an overly humanized world, significant value is created by reducing the humanization of ecosystems. By removing the goats from Olympic National Park, managers will be significantly reducing indirect humanization of the land. We have also seen that putting the death of wild animals in the context of an ecosystem can diminish its disvalue. Thus, killing the goats is not as bad as it might otherwise seem. Clearly, it would be preferable to remove the goats without killing them, but apparently this is not practical, and it significantly increases human risk.

Once relevant information has been assembled and due consideration has been given to the range of values in play, one must make priority judgments on the basis of their intuitive fit with the range of other judgments one makes. Positive argument can go no further, though one should continue to subject the priority judgment to the most severe criticism. The judgment that the increase in wildness value of the Olympic National Park weighs more than the disvalue of the death of the goats coheres well with the judgment that wildness weighs more than some serious human interests. Both give significant weight to wildness value. Since the latter judgment seems reasonable, the former should also.

We may not be required to rank the values in this way, but we do not seem to be required to adopt any contrary ranking, either. At least one serious criticism of weighting wildness more than the goats has been defused; certain aesthetic goods can take priority over important moral goods. It appears that in the weak sense, shooting the goats is permissible. If the elimination of the goats is permissible, then in general, the removal of exotics will be permissible, even if it causes the deaths of many members of the exotic species. Appeals to other values may be rhetorically useful additions to the justification for removing some exotics, but if I am right, they are not required in most cases.[17]

NOTES

1. Nancy Holloway, "Nurturing Nature," *Scientific American* 270 (1994): 102.

2. Michael Soulé, "The Onslaught of Alien Species, and Other Challenges in the Coming Decades," *Conservation Biology* 4 (1990): 223–39.

3. A strong case can be made, however, that plants and insects do have intrinsic value. See Paul Taylor, *Respect for Nature: A Theory of Environmental Ethics* (Princeton: Princeton University Press, 1986).

4. National Park Service, *Draft Environmental Impact Statement for Mountain Goat Population within Olympic National Park* (Washington, D.C.: U.S. Department of the Interior, 1995), pp. 225–40.

5. Ibid., p. 18.

6. Ibid., p. 216.

7. National Park Service, *Management Policies* (Washington, D.C.: U.S. Department of the Interior, 1988).

8. Donald Scherer "Between Theory and Practice: Some Thoughts on Motivations behind Restoration," *Restoration and Management Notes* 12 (1994): 184–88.

9. *Federal Register* 61, no. 40 (February 28, 1996): 7595.

10. Steve Packard, "Restoring Oak Ecosystems," *Restoration and Management Notes* 11 (1993): 5–16.

11. Ibid., p. 8.

12. See, for example, Daniel Botkin, *Discordant Harmonies* (Oxford: Oxford University Press, 1990).

13. For a similar version of this argument, see J. Baird Callicott, "The Wilderness Idea Revisited: The Sustainable Development Alternative" *Environmental Professional* 13 (1991): 234–47.

14. Eric Katz, "The Big Lie: Human Restoration of Nature," *Research in Philosophy and Technology* 12 (1992): 231–41.

15. There are significant disanalogies between paintings and ecosystems. The former are static products of intentional design, whereas the latter are dynamic systems which evolve spontaneously. These disanalogies do not affect the points made about valuable processes and their products.

16. I defend this suggestion at much more length in "The Rationale for Environmental Restoration," in *The Ecological Community*, ed. Roger Gottlieb (New York: Routledge, 1997), pp. 39–55.

17. I am grateful to Ned Hettinger, Steve Schwartz, and my value theory class at Green Mountain College for their comments on an earlier version of this paper.

REFERENCES

Botkin, Daniel. *Discordant Harmonies*. Oxford: Oxford University Press, 1990.
Callicott, J. Baird. "The Wilderness Idea Revisited: The Sustainable Development Alternative." *Environmental Professional* 13 (1991).
Federal Register 61, no. 40 (February 28, 1996).
Holloway, Nancy. "Nurturing Nature." *Scientific American* 270 (1994).
Katz, Eric. "The Big Lie: Human Restoration of Nature." *Research in Philosophy and Technology* 12 (1992).
National Park Service. *Management Policies*. Washington, D.C.: U.S. Department of the Interior, 1988.
———. *Draft Environmental Impact Statement for Mountain Goat Population within Olympic National Park*. Washington, D.C.: U.S. Department of the Interior, 1995.
Packard, Steve. "Restoring Oak Ecosystems." *Restoration and Management Notes* 11 (1993).
Scherer, Donald. "Between Theory and Practice: Some Thoughts on Motivations behind Restoration." *Restoration and Management Notes* 12 (1994).
Soulé, Michael. "The Onslaught of Alien Species, and Other Challenges in the Coming Decades." *Conservation Biology* 4 (1990).
Taylor, Paul. *Respect for Nature: A Theory of Environmental Ethics*. Princeton: Princeton University Press, 1986.
Throop, William. "The Rationale for Environmental Restoration." In *The Ecological Community*, edited by Roger Gottlieb. New York: Routledge, 1997.

Part IV

New Paradigm
or Old Problem?

13

A Field Guide to the
Synthetic Landscape
Toward a New Environmental Ethic

Frederick Turner

At first it looks like a big, untidy field—tall grass infested with weeds. But then, looking a little longer and a little more carefully, my mind reorders it. There is an unfamiliar, breathtaking, pale yellowish jade freshness in the green, and a preciseness and laciness in the texture that reminds me of wild-flowers, the ones I've seen along rocky seacoasts or in alpine meadows. These grasses are at home where they are: the towering bluestem and Indian grass in the damper hollows; the twisted awns of the drier stipa; the feathery offset florets of the side oats grama; the brilliant emerald clumps of hair-leaved dropseed. Then there are the broad-leaved plants. Some are giants: the compass plant, with its leathery handlike leaves; the blanched ultraviolet flowers of the downy phlox; the black-eyed susan, the hoary puccoon, and the coneflower; and below, the cold green shields of the prairie dock, the exquisite Turk's-cap lily, the leadplant thought by early miners to indicate the presence of ore, the purple-and-white prairie clovers; and look—a mottled white-violet-chocolate prairie orchid. Walking on the drier slopes that heave up sunlit into a sky darkening toward a squall, I can see wild roses, sage, horsetails. And there are seedlings from the nearby grove of savanna oaks that will, if a prairie fire does not kill them, transform these grassy hills (after a few decades) into a shadowy forest.

This *is* a prairie, then. But again, things are not always as they seem. This is Greene Prairie, planted forty years ago by the ecological restorationist Henry Greene on forty acres of degraded Wisconsin farmland. It is part of the University of Wisconsin's arboretum, which all told has more than a hundred acres of thriving prairie. Almost every prairie plant here is descended from seeds or whole specimens found in old cemeteries, along railroad rights-of-way, or on other unfarmed scraps of land in southern Wisconsin. Greene Prairie was one of the first projects of its kind in the country, but now many such restorations are under way.

How does one plant a prairie? First the existing vegetation—in Wisconsin, mostly European grasses or weeds—must be plowed under or burnt off. The height of the water table is considered. Sweating gangs of young volunteers in dungarees harvest the wild seeds or dig up clumps of virgin sod. A prairie contains over two hundred species of plants alone, not counting the bacteria, the mycorrhizal fungi in the rootweb, the insects, animals, and birds. The land is planted; then the real hard work, the weeding, begins. The volunteers must be drilled meticulously on the differences between native and alien species, a process that engenders an extraordinary familiarity with the land. Then, after a few seasons of backbreaking work, the prairie is established, and it begins to police and nourish itself.

Much has been written about the marvelous interdependence of species in the wild; the most recent thinking treats ecological systems such as prairies as if they were indeed single entities, with different organs for different functions. The Gaia Hypothesis, advanced by the visionary British ecologist James Lovelock, proposes that the entire planet is itself such an organism—a living being in the wastes of space. In the prairie, the fine network of mycorrhizal fungi that flourishes below the soil surface acts as a primitive nervous system, linking the plants and regulating the flow of nutrients. The actual soil of a healthy prairie is paradoxically very poor, because almost all the nutrients are in circulation in the living biomass—the birds and bees, plants and trees. Creating the prairie, the volunteers and the ecologists who led them created nature—man-made nature.

Nearly three years ago, in an essay in these pages,* I called for the cultivation of a new American garden—a fresh kind of ecological thinking that would bridge the deep and damaging gap in the American imagination between nature and humanity, the protected wilderness area and the exploited landscape. I came to the arboretum at the University of Wisconsin in search of that garden, and I believe that I found it—or at least one of the core elements of it—in the work of ecological restorationists. Nor are the restorationists cultivating just in Wisconsin. Wetlands are being restored around the country, and in California, redwood forests. There is the *Bosques Colón* (Forests of Columbus) project in the West Indies, and Dan Janzen's visionary tropical dry-forest restoration project in Costa Rica. It seems to me we have here the elements of a new kind of environmental ethic, one which accepts human partic-

---

*"Cultivating the American Garden: Toward a Secular View of Nature," *Harper's*, August 1985.

ipation in nature as essential for us and for the world, and which actively seeks out ways in which that participation can be deepened and extended. It could be argued that the lovely complex tissue of the biosphere, threatened as it is, needs our best talents if it is to survive.

If the restored prairie is one prototype of the American garden, it should also be understood as the culmination of a long tradition, the Arcadian tradition. What is Arcadia? One may find it in the paintings of Giorgione, Bellini, Titian; of Lorrain, Poussin, Chardin. In the Western landscape-gardening tradition it consists of a set of ideas and tastes handed down to us, beginning with the biblical gardens of Egypt and Babylon; then on to the Greek gardens celebrated by Homer in his mythical Phaiakia; to the Roman gardens of volcanic Sicily, Naples, and the Alban hills; and thence to the gardens of northern Europe—Pope's Twickenham garden, Stourhead, Monet's Clos Normand at Giverny; and then across the Atlantic to the painted landscapes of the Hudson River school, the literary ones of Thoreau, and the real ones of Frederick Law Olmstead. It took the bitter check of the Dust Bowl to bring about the last, severest, and most demanding notion of the Arcadian ideal. That notion came to Aldo Leopold, the author of *A Sand County Almanac,* one of the founders of the University of Wisconsin arboretum, and the father of its restored prairie.

Arcadia, if we may speak broadly, is a place where human beings cooperate with nature to produce a richness of ecological variety that would not otherwise exist. Arcadia undergoes continuous but mild change. It is adaptable to all sorts of minor ecological alteration; nevertheless, it works to conserve, to protect, and to preserve what is needed and what is good—it maintains itself. Perhaps it is a country of the mind only, but we can see traces of it in the hills of Tuscany, the hedgerow and beech landscape of the Cotswolds, the savannas of Africa, and on the prairies of the Midwest. We are drawn to such places, I think, because they remind us, way down in our genes, of the savannas where we achieved our definitive evolution—where human beings became human beings.

But it could be that our very instinct for Arcadia misleads us, fools us into thinking we can recreate the place of our origins; this explains why we might accept a "reproduction" for true nature itself. In my admiration of the restored prairie, am I not like a child gazing through the glass of a museum showcase? Is not the restored prairie little better than a dusty little diorama, with its perpetually brilliant sky lit dimly by the fluorescents, its claustrophobic trompe l'oeil perspective, its taxidermized specimens frozen forever in some "natural" act of forage or nest building?

The preservationists of the old fire-and-brimstone school would say just this. For them the discipline of ecology is essentially elegiac, essentially a eulogy to what we humans have destroyed; their science is a postmortem, their myth is of a primal crime by which we are all tainted: the murder of nature. We cannot expiate, let alone compensate for this crime; the best we can do is acknowledge it publicly by setting aside whatever relatively untouched places remain and keeping human beings out of them. For such perfectionists the study of nature is essentially passive and classifactory;

action and experiment would be unwarranted. A real diorama might not disturb their fundamental sense of rightness so much as would a restored prairie. A diorama, after all, does not depict nature as a corpse—*nature morte*, as the French call a still life.

One can encounter the dismal grandeur of this position, its *schadenfreude*, in many sectors of art and learning. There are political purists who reject reform as a palliative that will only delay the cleansing fires of the revolution, classicists who see only cultural decline since Homer. It is possible to sympathize with such purists; they often serve as a conscience to humankind. But human beings are just as often ill-served by them—people are not at their best when motivated by guilt or alarm. If not actually paralyzed, they act mulishly, dutifully, without the job and playfulness that liberate the imagination and start the flow of creative thought.

～ ～ ～

Still, we cannot escape the question: Is the restored prairie a fake? I have heard it said by one skeptic that to have a restored coastline instead of a "natural" one is as if a museum's Vermeer were removed and secretly replaced by a perfect replica. One is ultimately as shortchanged by the copy of nature as one would be by the copy of the work of art. A large part of the value of nature, as with a Vermeer, is that it is the original; that is, it's value depends on its origins.

A plausible and widely held idea, or *ideal*. Behind it, perhaps, we can glimpse the notion, fundamentally theological, that the world is a creation, and inferior to its creator. And underlying this notion there is, perhaps, that basic Indo-European habit of thought—a *human* habit of thought—that derives the nature of the child from the nature of the parent, and thus insists on the inferiority and subordination of child to parent. The very word "nature" is derived from an ancient Indo-European root meaning "birth," a root sounding like "gand," and giving rise also to such words as "natal," "native," "natural," and "nativity" on one branch; "gender," "genus," "generate," "general," "genital," "gentle," "gene," and "generation" on the second branch; and the Germanic "kin," "kind," "kindred," and "akin" on yet a third. (The very practice of etymology as a pedantic explanation of the meaning of a word implicitly privileges origins as determinative of outcomes.)

But is not the true role of the parent to educate the child to the point where it becomes independent of its origins and capable of creation beyond its parents' dreams? The American Revolution was a declaration of such independence from the motherland, the fatherland. And though there is one wisdom that says that we know a thing by its origins, there is another that says "by their fruits ye shall know them"— that is, we derive the identity of something not from what produced it but from *what it produces*. The kingdom of heaven may be more like a mustard seed, like a leaven or ferment, than like an achieved perfection; more in potential than in exhaustion of possibility. The branching tree of evolution brings about wonderfully new forms of life, unpredictable from their origins, or "predictable" only after they have actually appeared.

Perhaps we should compare a living landscape not with a Vermeer, but with a sonnet, which, far from losing beauty and meaning when copied, derives its very life from being printed and reprinted. Shakespeare has a sonnet that says just this:

> Since brass, nor stone, nor earth, nor boundless sea,
> But sad mortality o'ersways their power,
> How this rage shall beauty hold a plea,
> Whose action is no stronger than a flower?
> O, how shall summer's honey breath hold out
> Against the wrackful siege of batt'ring days,
> When rocks impregnable are not so stout.
> Nor gates of steel so strong, but Time decays?
> O fearful meditation! Where, alack,
> Shall Time's best jewel from Time's chest lie hid?
> Or what strong hand can hold his swift foot back?
> Or who his spoil of beauty can forbid?
> O none, unless this miracle have might,
> That in black ink my love shall still shine bright.

And it still does, unspotted by the centuries, precisely because it has been copied and recopied in "black ink"; precisely because it has taken on the ethic of the fruit and the seed, which is to give all to the future.

The analogy is a rather precise one. A landscape is not at all like a Vermeer, if by that we mean it is the same landscape year to year as a Vermeer is the same painting year by year. (And *is* a Vermeer forever the same?) A prairie recopies, reprints itself every spring, using seeds and shoots that are the books wherein are inscribed the instructions of the DNA code. I would say that a prairie is like the renewing vision of the world that Vermeer began in our culture, that tradition of the revelatory power of light that is reborn in us every time we see a girl in a room lit by a tall window.

In reproducing a prairie, then, the ecological restorationists do but take a leaf out of nature's book. Nature itself copies; it is an *uncopied* prairie, if such could exist, that would be unnatural. When the retreat of icecaps, the silting up of lakebeds, or devastation by volcanic ash lays bare a new environment suitable for prairie, the prairie species are seeded by natural vectors—wind, birds, insects—and copy themselves onto the empty page. Is not *Homo sapiens* in this case just another vector that the prairie biome employs to reproduce itself? A flower uses the aesthetic preferences of the bee to attract its pollinator; likewise our aesthetic attraction for the prairie causes us to carry its germs to a new environment.

But perhaps even this conception is too conservative. It is the job of the scholar to ensure that the sonnet remains utterly uncorrupted by copying or printers' errors; but nature's copying is not exact. Though the copying process is entirely natural—and thus the preservationists' argument against the "fake" is without substance—nature itself goes beyond copying to innovation, and allows copying "errors" into its sonnets in an attempt to improve them.

Let us be precise about this. Prairie grass can propagate in one of two ways: by cloning itself with runners or rhizomes or by mating and sexual reproduction, using flowers, fruits, and seeds. When it sends out a new shoot, whether vertical, parallel to the ground, or under it, every biomolecular precaution is taken that the DNA in the new cells is identical to that in the originals. Redundancies in the code, periodic checks for exact matching in the complementary nucleic strands, and an immune system on guard against cancerous or virus-induced revisions of the code—all protect the integrity of the copy. But when a plant reproduces itself sexually, the policy is utterly changed. The twin strands of the chromosomes are separated from each other, the naked strands are paired with those of an alien individual, the genes are chopped up and reshuffled, the copies are conflated and thus corrupted.

What is sex for? Why should plants go to the extraordinary expense of complex energy-using reproductive systems—flowers and fruit and the rest—when they could simply use their built-in growth system and bud themselves a clone? It's all for one purpose: variation. To put this more precisely, it is to create true genetic individuals. And the function of individuals is to act as experimental tests of various possibilities in body conformation, chemistry, and behavior that fall within the range of variation for the species. If the individual survives to reproduce, then its particular traits are perpetuated in the gene pool of the species. If it reproduces itself more abundantly than its parents, then it has probably found a better fit to the vicissitudes of its environment. In biological terms, the offspring can better represent its species than the parent. What this means is that, at least when dealing with the phenomenon of life and all phenomena derived from it (culture, technological development, religion, history, etc.), we must allow for the possibility that we can only understand something truly by knowing its future, its fruits, its consequences.

Even more revolutionary is the implication that the injunction to know things by their fruits and not only their origins might also apply to the inorganic world of physics and chemistry. The physical universe itself should then be characterized as a life-producing universe. "Life-producingness," to follow this logic, is an essential trait of that "species" we call the universe. This is a version of what physicists call the Anthropic Principle, which stipulates that one of the constraints on the initial state of the cosmos was that it should be the kind of cosmos that could bring about through evolution observers of it that could confirm its existence and compel it to actualize itself by being observed. Quantum theory treats reality as a product of both whatever is "out there"—in itself only a probability—and the act of observation or registering that forces the probability to collapse into actuality. Without observers no universe can exist. We are a far cry here from the ideas of the purists, who want us to leave Nature alone and who deplore the corruptions of human reflexiveness.

But let us press on and see where the argument takes us. Our meditation upon flowers is not yet over; for variation by sexual recombination, which is the function of flowers, is not enough by itself to keep the breed adaptively abreast of its competition. Another element is required, and that is death. If death does not cull out of the species those individuals whose genes are not adapted to the environment, the defective genes themselves will remain to contaminate the more vigorous strains. It may seem paradoxical to describe death—which is after all the opposite of survival—as a tool in the process of evolution, whose mainspring is survival. But this is exactly the magnificently risky policy to which the sexually reproducing organisms have committed themselves. Most sexual organisms even contain a programmed aging system on the cellular or genetic level to ensure that the individual does not outstay its time. Sex and death; the two great forces at work.

Aging, though, is not enough in many cases to clean out the deadwood of genetic failure. Many species rely on their predators to cull the unfit, and if this kind of "death" is not longer available for some reason, the system begins to break down. An example: The deer population of the Wisconsin arboretum recently began to exceed the capacity of the land; in the long run such an unchecked population explosion would endanger the genetic vigor of the herd. The effects of the overpopulation unlimited by predation are similar to the effects of incest and inbreeding in a human community: Individuals are born feebler, more susceptible to hereditary diseases, and sometimes even deformed. The arboretum prepared to shoot some of the deer to relieve the population pressure.

But then what some park managers call the "Bambi syndrome" set in. Public outcry against the deer kill was overwhelming, and the arboretum was forced to call it off. (This phenomenon is not confined to Wisconsin. Recently there was so much fuss about the deer kill at a national zoological park in Maryland that congressional hearings were held, with the result that federal money was appropriated to evacuate the deer and build a ten-foot steel fence around the park to keep them from coming back. Democracy is a beautiful thing.)

But not even predators are enough to keep an ecosystem balanced. The old prairies were dependent on periodic fires to clear the thatch, fertilize the soil, and above all to kill the tree saplings that would otherwise quickly cover the ground. The richest mix of species occurs only on burnt prairies. Before the settlers came, a prairie fire could burn all the way from Illinois to the banks of the Wabash. As William R. Jordan, the editor of *Restoration & Management Notes*, once told me, "Remove the fires caused by lightning or set by Indians, and you have to replace them, or the prairie will quietly vanish, not in a roar of machinery, but into the shadows of a forest." Accordingly, the Wisconsin arboretum burns its prairies—every two years at first, but now more irregularly, as nature might. It is said to be an unforgettable sight, with flames leaping up thirty feet, and it is gradually taking on the status of a ritual for the professionals and volunteers who set and manage the fire. I myself can remember from my childhood in central Africa the spring burning practiced by the Ndembu tribe, and the air of festival in conveyed; it is associated for me with the smell of grass smoke, harsh native honey beer, the hunters' rites and dances, and the delicious little ground-fruits that we village boys would find among the burnt grass roots. Perhaps one day prairie burning will be one of the great ritual occasions of the Midwest, a sort of festival of Dionysus, the god of inexhaustible life—an occasion for drama, music, poetry, and storytelling.

It is remarkable how passionate the true prairie restorationists are on the subject of burning. The discovery of the need to burn, I believe, emancipated the naturalist; burning can even be seen as a sacrificial rite of redemption for our ecological guilt. The patient, careful labor of copying the natural prairie called for the medieval virtues—humility and obedience to nature, poverty and chastity of the imagination, sensitivity, self-abnegation, self-effacement. Burning showed that nature needed us, needed even those most Promethean and destructive elements of ourselves symbolized by fire.

～ ～ ～

Let us approach ecological restoration—its value, its moral necessity, its *naturalness*—from another angle. In a very different field of endeavor, the search for extraterrestrial intelligence, a shocking conclusion is beginning to suggest itself, catalyzed by the awkward question blurted out a few years ago at a conference of astronomers: "Where is everybody?" Given the sensitivity of our signal-detection instruments, the ease with which radio signals can be propagated to great distances, the huge number of planetary systems within probable range of us, and the certainty that any other technological civilization must be employing radio frequencies for communication, the airwaves should be filled with interstellar chatter. Instead, the silence is deafening. There is no sign that *anyone* is out there. And the moment one begins to think about this fact, it appears more and more plausible that we are alone in the universe. For instance, it is now generally accepted that the universe is only about twelve to twenty billion years old, but estimates of how long it will remain in existence in such a form as to support life range well over a hundred *trillion* years. In other words, the universe has seen only a tiny fraction of its existence; it is brand new. Why should we not be the first? There has to be a first.

And consider this: Given the present age of the universe, there has only just been enough time, under the most favorable conditions, for us to have evolved. First, the universe had to cool enough to make possible ordinary stars. Then there had to have been at least one previous generation of stars—having lived out its life cycle, burned up its nuclear fuel, collapsed, and then exploded—to have produced the heavy-element ash out of which our own solar system is made and without which no likely form of life could exist. Then the solar system had to form. Almost immediately after the earth cooled down enough to support life, the first living organisms appeared, about four billion years ago, perhaps less than ten billion years after the Big Bang. Earthly life has been around for nearly a third of the universe's history. And yet all that time was needed for life to transform the atmosphere from a methane-nitrogen–water vapor–hydrogen sulfide–ammonia one to a nitrogen-oxygen one, and to graduate from the very slow evolution of asexual organisms to the rapid evolution of sexual ones and the still more rapid evolution of social animals, whose communities can, to an extent, evolve themselves. It would be hard to imagine a faster evolutionary scenario than the one that brought us into being on this planet.

If we are alone, then we carry a gigantic responsibility. We are the custodians of life in the universe, and the only plausible vector by which life may propagate itself to other worlds and thus escape the risk that some minor cosmic accident—the impact of a stray asteroid, or a disturbance of the sun's activity—should snuff forever out the first shoots of life. It is becoming clear that we cannot survive, psychologically or physically, without the rich web of other lives around us. If we leave this planet we must take our biosphere with us.

❦ ❦ ❦

The great class of the angiosperms—the flowering plants that appeared in the mid-Cretaceous period and came in a mere five million years to dominate the ecology of the planet—owes its existence to its insect assistants and the new ecological niches they opened up. The simultaneous explosion of land vertebrates, of which we are one, may in turn be due to the richer carbohydrate and protein content of angiosperm seeds and fruits. The work of the bee and the bird in spreading angiosperm pollen and seed across the continents was not merely a conserving activity. Rather, it actively promoted the creation of new habitats and ecologically richer regimes. The ecological restorationists are taking the first step toward being able to reconstitute on some alien soil the elements of an earthly forest or prairie. Their distant successors will be like the bees, serving as the gentle pander and reproductive vector of other species—participant-gardeners of nature.

At present the restorationist bee is more necessary as a preserver than as a colonist; and the restorationist ethic is, as I have pointed out, mostly one of medieval self-effacement. This is as it should be. But the time may come when we, and our sister species of this planet, may seed ourselves across the solar system and beyond, as once the pelagic species colonized the land, and the insects and the birds the air. The task will be enormous, and will be too much for the relatively slow and unreflective processes of genetic adaptation. Who will write the *Georgics* of this new Arcadia? It will take wise bees, seed vectors of great exactness—forces able to provide the right environment for infant growth until the growth itself has altered those harsh environments into something hospitable to human beings. But one day the long discipline of restoration may bear a strange and unexpected fruit, and an alien sun may shine on miles of blowing prairie.

14

"Sunflower Forest"
Ecological Restoration as the Basis for a New Environmental Paradigm
William R. Jordan III

I first encountered the writing of Fred Turner, my partner in this dialogue, in the summer of 1985, when I read his essay "Cultivating the American Garden" in the August issue of *Harper's* magazine. The essay made a profound impression on me, and since then Fred's thinking has contributed immeasurably to my own work at the University of Wisconsin–Madison Arboretum, and in particular to my thinking about the process of ecological restoration and its implications for the environment and for our relationship with nature.

Briefly, what Fred was suggesting was that the act of gardening offers a model for a healthy relationship between human beings and the rest of nature. His argument, in part, was that the gardener handles nature with respect but without self-abnegation—that is, he or she manipulates nature intelligently and creatively, benefiting and nurturing plants (and of course animals as well, we are speaking of "gardening" in a broad and even metaphoric sense here), while at the same time exercising a wide range of human aptitudes and leaving a distinctively human mark on the landscape. This struck me immediately, both because Fred's idea was in accord with my own experience as an amateur gardener and beekeeper (activities that I had long felt provide a basis for communion with other species) and also because it was close to my own thinking about ecological restoration and its implications for the environment and our relationship with it. By the time I read Fred's essay, I had already identified restoration as a form of gardening, and had begun to think that it represented a model for a healthy relationship between human beings and the natural landscape. The weakness of Fred's conception, from an environmentalist's point of

---

William R. Jordan III, " 'Sunflower Forest': Ecological Restoration as the Basis for a New Environmental Paradigm," in *Beyond Preservation: Restoring and inventing Landscapes*, ed. A. Dwight Baldwin, Judith De Luce, and Carl Pletsch (Minneapolis: University of Minnesota Press, 1994). Reprinted by permission of the University of Minnesota Press.

view, was that it placed little emphasis on that natural landscape, but this was where my own idea of ecological restoration came in. If gardening provides a model for a healthy relationship with nature, then restoration is that form of gardening concerned specifically with the gardening, maintenance, and reconstitution of wild nature, and is the key to a healthy relationship with it.

Shortly after reading Fred's essay I called him and we began a conversation that has continued, on and off, ever since. One result has been the linking of our two lines of thought into the more comprehensive idea that the more general process of *ecosystem construction* provides the basis for healthy interaction between human beings and the rest of nature. The key idea here is that we can best come to understand ecosystems, and to enter into a relationship with them that engages the full array of human activities, by attempting to reconstruct them. Like all forms of agriculture, however, the process of ecosystem construction has two poles: a creative pole, most clearly represented by traditional forms of agriculture, which not only construct ecosystems but create or invent new ones; and a conservative pole, exemplified by the form of gardening we term ecological restoration, the attempt to create ecosystems that resemble as closely as possible natural or historic models.

My purpose in this chapter is to explore the left limb of this axis, and to make a case for the idea that ecological restoration provides a basis—actually, a paradigm—for a healthy, mutually beneficial relationship between ourselves and the natural landscape. I will begin by stating what I consider to be at least some of the essential elements of such a relationship.

First, in order to have a relationship with anything we need the thing itself—in this case the natural or historic ecosystems, the forests, prairies, wetlands, lakes, rivers, dunelands, reefs, and so forth, and all the plants, animals, and abiotic elements, all of which comprise the natural landscape.

Second, we need an ecological relationship with these systems. By this I mean an economic transaction that entails a genuine exchange of goods and services between ourselves and the natural community. This must be reciprocal, or, as Aldo Leopold and others have said, mutually beneficial, involving both taking and giving back.

Third, this relationship must engage all our abilities—those that are innate or "hardwired" into us by evolution and those that have emerged in the course of cultural evolution. These include our physical, mental, emotional, and spiritual capacities.

Fourth, because one of these abilities is a sense of history, and of history as a kind of progress, or at least change, the relationship must acknowledge and deal with the past—the history of our interaction with a particular landscape, and the deeper history of the general relationship of our species with the rest of nature.

Fifth, because our relations with nature continue to change as a result of ongoing intellectual advances and cultural evolution, the paradigm defining that relationship must also be flexible and capable of a creative expansion and development.

Sixth, we are a language-using, social, and highly self-conscious species, so we need a way not only to explore and redefine the terms of our relationship with nature, but also to articulate and celebrate that relationship in a personally and socially satisfying way.

Now let us turn to the question of how ecological restoration provides a paradigm that satisfies each of these criteria.

1. *The object.* Restoration is difficult and uncertain at best, and the craft of restoration is in its infancy. Even the highest-quality examples, such as parts of Greene Prairie at the University of Wisconsin–Madison Arboretum, or Ray Schulenberg's tallgrass prairie at the Morton Arboretum near Chicago, are defective—that is, they are not precise replicas of their natural counterparts. In fact, some environmentalists insist that restoration is impossible and argue that conservation of natural systems depends, ultimately, on preserving those that already exist. Yet if restoration in the strictest sense is impossible, so is preservation. It is impossible either to stop a living ecosystem from changing or to prevent its change from reflecting our influence. Restoration, however, holds out at least the possibility of conserving the system, not by stopping change, but by directing it, and not by ignoring human influences, but by acknowledging and seeking to compensate for them.

In this sense, then, preservation is impossible and restoration merely more or less difficult. All systems are constantly changing, and as this change reflects at least some degree of human influence, all systems must be supposed to be moving continually toward some novel condition. This effect is especially dramatic here in the Midwest on our tallgrass prairies and oak openings, where the entire native ecosystem has been virtually eliminated as a direct or indirect result of new kinds of human activities. This situation is actually paradigmatic, however, and is true in the final analysis of all ecosystems everywhere—not because we are a peculiar or pernicious species, but simply because, as John Muir said, everything is hitched together so that everything interacts with everything else. Acknowledging our membership in the land communities is the first crucial step toward our reenfranchisement in it.

The consequence is that in the long run the best natural areas—the ones most closely resembling their historic counterparts—will not be those that have simply been protected from human influences (complete protection is impossible) but those that have been in some measure restored through a process that recognizes human influences and then effectively compensates for them. This is already evident for the Midwestern prairies and oak openings, and sooner or later will be true of all ecosystems.

This being the case, it is encouraging to keep in mind that this does not necessarily imply a gradual decline in the quality of these systems through the process of copying and recopying. The criticism that restoration is impossible generally applies only in the strictest sense. One cannot duplicate a natural system root hair for root hair and bird for bird, but there is no reason to try to do this. What is called for, rather, is the reassembly of a system that *acts* like the original. This implies not only complete species lists and the reproduction of crucial aspects of community structure, but also the reproduction of function and of dynamics—both ecologically and in the evolutionary sense. In other words, it means not just setting the system up, like a diorama, but actually setting it in motion. It also means, however, setting certain limits to this motion: The system conserved in this way may be supposed to be moving around in a defined zone of change judged to be appropriate for the system. This does imply a certain conservatism (we are concerned, after all, with the conservation of the historic system), which implies continual monitoring and specific measures to, as it were, nudge the system back toward its historic condition. But this approach by no means implies a static conception of the system, or of our relationship with it. In fact, quite the contrary: This approach involves a kind of dynamic equilibrium (within certain, often rather wide, limits) and a perpetual effort to sustain the system against the pressure of change in response to new influences. In the long run, this will be the only way to ensure the existence of classic (and in a sense obsolete) ecosystems in the landscape of the future. This is real conservation, something we will want to do not everywhere, but in some places. The result, of course, as we invent novel ecosystems, in certain cases including new, genetically engineered species, will increase rather than decrease biological diversity and richness.

2. *The ecological dimension.* The real challenge of environmentalism is not to preserve nature by protecting it from human beings or rescuing it from their influence, but to provide the basis for a healthy relationship between nature and culture. What this means most obviously is a working relationship with the natural landscape in which a human individual or community can achieve full citizenship in the biotic community. This is what Leopold had in mind when he called for a "mutually beneficial relationship" between nature and culture, but exactly what such a relationship would actually look like has remained unclear.[1] Presumably it would include an actual ecological interaction with the natural landscape that benefits both it and us—and would do so without requiring us to repudiate the achievements or abandon the accoutrements of civilization. From the point of view of modern environmentalism, however, with its strong sense of distance between humans and nature and its idealization of wilderness as nature "untrammeled by man,"[2] such a relationship has proved inaccessible. What environmentalism has offered instead is a severely limited relationship characterized by an ethic of "minimal impact" and the admonition to "take nothing but pictures; leave nothing but footprints." The concern here is almost exclusively for the landscape and hardly at all for the human participant, and the resulting relationship, though valuable as far as it goes, is extremely attenuated. It is largely nonparticipatory, and engages only a small fraction of human interests and skills. The person is confined to the role of visitor—an observer of nature rather than an active element of the land community. Ironically, such a perspective turns us all—hiker, birder, and strip miner alike—not into members of the community, but into users and consumers of the natural landscape.

This may be useful as *part* of a healthy relationship with the natural landscape, but it falls far short of what we have to accomplish if we are to save the classic ecosystems and share the landscape with them. A comment in Thoreau's *Journal* illustrates the point. Thoreau was deeply concerned with achieving an intimate relationship with nature, and most of his writing is the account of his attempt to do so. Not infrequently he imagines himself literally rejoining the natural community by taking the part of one of its members. In an early entry in his journal he wrote: "Would it not be a luxury to stand up to one's chin in some retired swamp for a whole summer's day, scenting the sweet-fern and bilberry blows, and lulled by the minstrelsy of gnats and mosquitoes? . . . Say twelve hours of discourse with the leopard frog."[3]

Here Thoreau is seeing himself as a turtle or muskrat. The problem is that he doesn't push his own figure far enough—this is not what muskrats or turtles do in a marsh. They don't sit there, watching the sun go overhead. They go about their business, which is the construction and maintenance of the marsh. This, of course, is precisely what the restorationist does. He or she is not merely an observer of the marsh or prairie, but, like the muskrat, a maker of the marsh, a direct participant in its ecology, carrying out business there in the fullest—in fact, in the Thoreauvian sense of that word, exercising skill and ingenuity, exchanging goods and services, influencing and helping to shape the community, communicating with nature in nature's terms.

Thus the restorationist resolves a dilemma that has troubled—and weakened—environmentalism since Thoreau's time. Through the constructive process of restoration he or she breaks out of the essentially negative relationship with the natural landscape implicit in the preservationist program and establishes a relationship with that landscape that is both positive and mutually beneficial—and does so, moreover, without leaving civilization behind. This leads to a way of solving the practical problem of overuse of natural areas. The traditional approach to this problem is to discourage use and place restrictions on activities, a policy based on the presumption that "use" is destructive or consumptive and necessarily compromises the natural landscape. From this point of view the visitor is just that: a visitor and a consumer at best, and at worst an out-and-out destroyer. The more such visitors there are in a natural area, the more "pressure" will be placed on it, and the more it will decline in quality.

Limiting use is one way to address this problem, but it is only a stopgap measure that does nothing either to satisfy the human hunger for immersion in nature or to deal with the unavoidable problem of ecosystem drift in response to human influence, however subtle. The real key to conservation is not restricting human participation, which is merely another way of fighting nature, but to find a constructive way of participating. Much better than proscribing involvement, then, is to change its sign, so to speak, from positive to negative. The visitor then becomes a positive and contributing rather than a negative, consuming force in the landscape. The range of experiences available in the landscape increases dramatically, and the situation shifts from having too many people using up nature to not having enough to keep it in shape.

I mean this quite literally. For years we at the University of Wisconsin Arboretum believed that our greatest problem was overuse. Too many people were, in that ugly and desperate phrase, "loving us to death." Today we have the opposite attitude: We don't have enough people to keep up with the restoration we could be doing. This is also true in the suburbs of Chicago, where the recovery of prairies and oak openings in the splendid system of preserves surrounding the city has depended almost entirely on a growing cadre of volunteer restorationists.[4] Both of these examples are from heavily used areas, but the principle applies everywhere. Eventually it will be applied to our national parks and other wilderness areas, and it will be their salvation. In my view this restoration will become the principal outdoor activity of the next century, and the result will be the conversion of nature—in its classic forms—from all "environment" into a habitat for human beings.

Briefly, then, restoration is the key to the reinhabitation of nature and, in the long run, to its preservation. In its absence our influence on nature is necessarily consumptive; in the context of a restoration program, however, use becomes the first step in achieving a reciprocal relationship, which is completed in the act of restoration. Restoration in this sense is nothing but the acknowledgment of human influence on the landscape and the attempt to compensate for it in a precise way so that the classic landscape may be maintained.

3. *The gamut of human abilities.* In his book *The Invisible Pyramid*, Loren Eiseley wrote that human beings must not only reenter the "sunflower forest" of original nature, but they must do so without abandoning the lessons learned "on the pathway to the moon."[5] Eiseley's assertion underscores a crucial weakness of the traditional environmental response to the challenge of reinhabitation: its failure to deal with the full range of human abilities, interests, and values, including those that are the achievements of culture. It is relatively easy to imagine reentering nature destructively on the one hand, or by shedding the accoutrements of civilization, on the other, or by simply leaving behind most of what makes us who we are when we step into the forest. But when we do this we limit our relationship with nature; we cease to be fully ourselves, and this makes nature not our habitat but some "other place"—not a whole world in which we "go and come with a strange liberty in Nature, part of herself," as Thoreau wrote,[6] but just another facility with a specialized purpose, like a bank or car wash.

Restoration meets this problem head-on. As a comprehensive process, it includes traditional nature-oriented activities such as hiking, birding, and botanizing, but also a wide range of other, more participatory activities, including hunting, fishing, gathering, and cultivating. All of these are integrated into an event that is constructive rather than consumptive—as each of these particular activities is in its traditional form. Restoration engages a range of physical, intellectual, social, and emotional faculties and actually entails a kind of recapitulation of cultural evolution, a redeployment of all the skills exercised and achieved by human beings, in Eiseley's phrase, "on the pathway to the moon."

Of special interest is the observation that restoration challenges our understanding of the ecosystem being restored, and so is an effective research technique, a way of raising questions and testing ideas about the systems under construction and (not incidentally) about our relationship with them. This notion is embedded in ecological thinking and practice, and has recently been explored and given the name "restoration ecology."[7] This recognition of restoration as a form of dialogue with nature has important implications. First, restoration then does for ecology what the indeterminacy principle did for physics: It recognizes the researcher as an active participant, interacting with and influencing the system being studied. It also places us in a position to develop restoration as a powerful tool for exploring the ecological aspects of our interaction with nature because, although we can change nature without knowing what we are doing, it is virtually impossible to change it *back* without comprehending in some detail both the system and the precise ways in which we have influenced it. Thus restoration brings to our attention aspects of our relationship with nature that otherwise we might not recognize.

4. *The past.* Civilization is characterized by the sense of history and the discovery of cultural change. Archaic peoples, according to Mircea Eliade, had a past that was largely mythic, and they devoted considerable energy to world renewal rites and other activities that had the effect of obliterating history.[8] We, however, know something of history and realize that our relationships with particular landscapes and with nature generally have undergone dramatic changes, especially during the past few thousand years.

Because this awareness is integral to our worldview, presumably it is also an important component of our relationship with nature, and our paradigm must accommodate this. We need the modern equivalent of the world renewal rituals of archaic peoples, not merely to renew the earth in a literal sense (which, in fact, restoration does, offering a fascinating parallel to these classic rituals), but also to explore the past and have access to the experiences of nature that have shaped us as a species, as a culture, as a community, and as individuals.

Ecological restoration offers this opportunity in various ways—or, perhaps more accurately, it provides access to several octaves[9] of historic experience: the immediate experience of the individual in a particular place; the usually longer history of the community and of a particular society or civilization; the still deeper history of cultural evolution; and ultimately the "history" of nature as chronicled by students of evolution and biogeography.

In the first instance, the restorationist revisits history while trying to reverse it. Restoration is, in fact, a form of time travel. To carry it out the restorationist first has to understand the historic system he or she is trying to restore, and then must understand the various influences that have brought about change in order to reverse them. In some cases the lessons involved may be trivial or obvious. But they may also be subtle and may lead to a more complete comprehension of the system and its history; a convenient example is the rediscovery of the role of fire in the ecology of tallgrass prairies, which emerged from early attempts to restore these systems during the 1930s and 1940s.[10] In either case, the process involves the revisiting of history and the acknowledgment, at a practical level, of its implications for the present. Thus restoration is an exploration of change and its implications, and one of its lessons is the cost of change, as well as the crucial distinction between change that is reversible and change that is not.

Restoration explores history, but it also explores the slower rhythms of prehistory and cultural evolution. The restorationist not only attempts to reverse history but also to a certain extent recapitulates the major phases of cultural evolution, from hunting and gathering, to gardening and farming, to science. All the varieties of human experience of nature are repeated. The restorationist approaches a species of plant, for example, first as a gatherer, with an economic motive and a sense of appreciation for the plenitude of nature, not as "other" exactly, but as "given"; then as a gardener or nurturer of nature, who repays what he or she takes in kind as well as in gratitude; and finally as a scientist, who observes and manipulates nature in order to satisfy curiosity, and gives back to the world the gift of its greater self-awareness.

In this way the restorationist may travel back ten thousand years in a single afternoon. Of course to benefit fully we would like to know more about the classic relationships with nature that the restorationist revisits. For this we will be depending on anthropologists for precise descriptions of the subjective experience of nature characteristic of other cultures, but from what I have been able to discover so far, anthropology has little to say on this point. Anthropologists seem to have concentrated almost exclusively on the objective aspects of the nature-culture relationship—on calories and foraging patterns and the like, which are useful but only part of the information that we need. Perhaps the task of restoration will challenge anthropology as it has challenged ecology, and maybe restoration itself will allow us to test directly ideas about the subjective experience of nature by reducing these ideas to practice.

5. *Change and adaptation.* The reason underlying all so-called environmental problems, and in fact the general human sense of alienation from nature, is simply the speed of cultural change. Culture, like nature, evolves; but while the rest of nature evolves slowly, stuck, as it were, in the old, slow lane of chemical-based Darwinian evolution, cultural change has shifted into a computerized mode faster by many orders of magnitude than most of the ecological or evolutionary changes we see—or can barely see—going on in the world around us. Thus culture is always diverging from nature, and at increasingly higher speed as the rate of cultural change accelerates.

This causes considerable despair within the old environmental paradigm, with its defensive posture toward the conservation of natural areas. The problem, however, is not that change within the human community is necessarily inimical to the classic landscape, but that environmentalism, in its necessary defense of nature, has stressed protection from human influence and has by and large failed to come to grips with the problem of human interaction with nature. As a result its whole agenda, based on the idea of minimizing impact, becomes less and less tenable as human influence on wild nature becomes more pervasive and exotic. Because the fundamental problem is not influence, which is inevitable, but a failure to acknowledge this influence and a tendency to wish it away, the solution is not more protection and the erecting of higher and higher fences in a fruitless attempt to isolate nature from culture, but a program that frankly recognizes human influence on the natural landscape and then sets out to compensate for it.

Restoration does precisely this. The salient point is that whereas environmentalism has tended toward a kind of idealism in its conception of nature, restoration is relentlessly pragmatic. It asks not how nature may be kept pure and uncontaminated but rather just how it is actually being affected by human activities, and how this influence can be reversed. What is involved is a continual dialogue rather than a program, paralleling in our dealings with the biotic community the dialogue that sustains a democratic society and makes it adaptable to change. The restoration-based paradigm reenters nature from the vantage point of any kind of culture and works out a new relationship in practical and psychological terms as change continues and as a culture diverges further and further from its native landscape.

6. *Celebration.* Environmentalism is a complex movement, embodying a wide variety of attitudes and ideas, but I think it is fair to say that the environmentalism of the past generation has generally not been optimistic about the prospects for a positive relationship with wild nature. This follows from the assumption that humans stand somehow outside nature, and that nature is therefore irreversibly compromised by the influence of culture.

There are valid reasons for this attitude. Culture is encroaching on nature nearly everywhere, and threatens both the biotic richness and the normal functioning of the biosphere. Yet it seems obvious that as the fate and well-being of the biosphere depend ultimately on us and our relationship with it, we must find out not only how to have a healthy ecological relationship with the world but also how to articulate and celebrate that relationship in a personally and socially effective manner.

Restorationists have discovered in recent years that the act of restoration can achieve and celebrate this relationship. An excellent example is the burning of the prairies in many areas of the Upper Midwest each year, usually in the spring. These prairies are in many ways the birthplace of the idea of ecological restoration. The dependence of these systems on fire was an early discovery of restorationists and one of their first fundamental contributions to the science of ecology. The burns are really the quintessential or emblematic act of prairie restoration. They have even become a rite of spring, eagerly anticipated by the growing number of "prairie people" involved in restoration efforts in the Midwest, and are often surrounded by a festive, joyful, atmosphere. Reflecting on this development, several years ago, Fred Turner put forward what I believe is a good explanation for it. It is not, he pointed out, just that burns are often spectacular, exciting events, tinged even with an element of danger, or that the fire is a powerful tool that can change the landscape drastically; the need of the prairie for fire dramatizes *its* dependence on *us*, and so liberates us from our position as naturalists or observers of the community into a role of real citizenship.[11]

The burning of the prairies is more than a process or a technology, it is an expressive act—and what it expresses is our membership in the land community. The implication is that we have a role here: We belong in this community, and so perhaps we belong on this planet after all. This, quite simply, is good news that makes people happy.

The implications obviously go far beyond the conservation of the prairies, offering an escape from the excessive and unrelieved negativism that is a kind of occupational hazard of environmentalists. This new perspective is revealed in the response of Steve Packard, a restorationist with The Nature Conservancy in Illinois, to *The End of Nature*, by Bill McKibben. This book is a classic variation on the theme of human alienation from nature and the hopelessness of our present situation. Very briefly, his theme is that nature is everything in the world except people and their works, and that because all nature—including the atmosphere, McKibben's special concern—has been touched and contaminated by human beings, nature has actually come to an end. In reading this gloomy and destructive book, I hope that the elaboration of the logical consequences of its initial premises will at least serve the purpose of emphasizing how desperate and paralyzing these hypotheses are. In one particularly ugly passage, McKibben predicts, and in a sense even offers a justification for, a growing despair over the future of nature: "The end of nature," he writes, "probably also makes us reluctant to attach ourselves to its remnants for the same reason that we don't usually choose new friends from among the terminally ill."[12] Packard, reflecting on his experience with the prairies and oak openings of the Chicago area—terminally ill ecosystems if there ever were any—replies simply, "Our experience is the opposite. Unprecedented numbers of people are becoming passionately involved with the environment. It's an honor to be among the first to have a nurturing relationship with wild nature."[13]

Packard knows what he is talking about. He has direct experience as a pioneer restorationist and as the leader of a growing army of restorationists—now numbering over four thousand—who are reversing more than a century of deterioration in the forest preserve system of Chicago, rescuing the preserves from preservation, as it were, and bringing them back to nature. The work of Packard and others like him now points toward what I believe will prove to be most important about ecological restoration: its value not just as a process or a technology or a strategy for conserving bits and pieces of the natural landscape, but its significance as a performing art and as the basis for a new ritual tradition for mediating the relationship between nature and culture.[14]

This brings us to a crucial point in the development of the restoration-based environmental paradigm—the role of performance or ritual in mediating the relationship between nature and culture. This aspect of restoration has remained invisible to environmentalism for at least two reasons. First, in its preoccupation with nature as object, environmentalism has been concerned exclusively with the products of restoration (the restored communities themselves and their quality) and has paid little if any attention to the process of restoration and its implications for people, both those carrying out the restoration and those looking on—the audience, as it were. Environmentalism has then missed restoration's value as a way of reentering nature. The second reason is environmentalism's blindness to the performative or expressive aspect of restoration—to what might be called its ritual value—and to the crucial role of ritual in mediating relationships.[15]

Of course this is not peculiar to environmentalism but rather is characteristic of our entire society, with its reduced sense of the efficacy of ritual. Perhaps this is another "root" of the so-called environmental crisis that has developed in the West since the sixteenth and seventeenth centuries. Surely the emergence of science, and later the technologies based on it, played a role by increasing the distance between nature and culture. Even as that gap widened, however, the Reformation mounted an explicit attack on symbolism and ritual, and largely did away with the ritual traditions that human beings had always depended on in their contact with nature. The result, it may be, was a worldview within which real union with nature is impossible.

This blindness to the performative experience and its implications may be understandable in historic terms, but it is a deficiency in environmental thought and could prove to be fatal. Certainly it is at the root of much of the debilitating pessimism that environmentalism generates, because perhaps, from its own puritan point of view, environmentalism has been right. A fully satisfactory relationship with nature actually may be impossible, and accessible only through recourse to another dimension, that of performance, ritual, and make-believe.

The underlying mistake here may be the perception that indigenous cultures are "natural" people who live more or less unselfconsciously in harmony with nature. (Perhaps this is why we have traditionally put them, along with evidence of their often-impressive technologies and other cultural achievements, in our natural-history museums.) This seems to be a fairly widespread notion within environmentalism, where it serves as a kind of ideal and as the foundation for much thinking about the proper relationship between humans and the rest of nature. This view is by no means universally accepted by anthropologists, however. Indeed, it is my impression that most anthropologists see in all cultures evidence of a tension between nature and culture, which is then mediated or dealt with in various ways that to a considerable extent define the culture and lend it its distinctive characteristics. On this ground, then, I put forward the following premises as the basis for a new paradigm for the relationship between nature and culture:

1. Though ourselves the products of nature, and in this sense natural, we do differ in certain fundamental ways from the rest of nature, notably with respect to our level of self-awareness. Thus we may be citizens of the world, but we are not "plain citizens," and any attempt to overlook this is simply wallpapering over a major feature in the structure of the world, and is bound to have unfortunate consequences. People have never regarded themselves as "plain citizens" of the world; instead they have always—at

least since the development of language—distinguished between nature and culture and have felt a measure of tension between themselves and the rest of nature. Moreover, though it may vary in intensity, this tension is irreducible. It cannot be avoided simply by living in a simpler or more primitive way, "closer to nature." It is part and parcel of being human; it comes with our genes.

2. Although this tension cannot be resolved in purely literal terms, it can at least be dealt with in a psychologically effective way through performance and ritual. This, then, is one of the functions of ritual, and humans have used ritual techniques from time immemorial to mediate their relationship with nature.

3. The process of ecological restoration provides an ideal basis for the development of a modern system of rituals for negotiating our relationship with the rest of nature.

This, then, is the outline of a new environmental paradigm based on a sense of the crucial role of ritual in any satisfactory relationship between ourselves and the rest of nature, and on the observation that the act of restoration provides an excellent foundation for the development of a new ritual tradition. I should stress that what I have in mind is not simply the addition of performative techniques such as music, poetry, and so on, *to* the process of restoration, but a conception of restoration itself as both an effective process and an expressive act. The idea is not merely to *decorate* restoration, but to develop it to enhance its expressive power.

This conception is at the heart of Earthkeeping, a program being developed by the University of Wisconsin–Madison Arboretum and the Society for Ecological Restoration to provide opportunities for people to participate in restoration efforts at selected sites as a way of learning about a healthy relationship with nature. In my view this is a step toward the emergence of restoration as a major cultural event, comparable with other social rituals such as elections, sporting events, festivals, and holidays—and toward Aldo Leopold's "civilized society" living not in harmony, but at least in in ongoing dialogue with the natural landscape.

CONTEXT, DEFINITIONS, AND CLARIFICATIONS

The ideas presented in this essay are the result of some fifteen years of reflections and discussions concerning the development of a collection of restored ecological communities at the University of Wisconsin–Madison Arboretum. This project was undertaken in 1934, under the leadership of a handful of ecologists and conservationists that included Aldo Leopold, Ted Sperry, John Curtis, and Henry Greene. It was a pioneering project from the first, and today the resulting collection of restored prairies and forests is considered the oldest and most extensive such collection in the world. It is widely regarded as a model for the idea of ecological restoration in its strictest sense, and has served as an inspiration—and in some cases even as a source of seed—for numerous projects at other locations.

Today the arboretum has begun to serve as a symbol of ecological restoration, and in my view it will one day rank with places such as Walden Pond or Yosemite National Park as a landmark in the development of the modern environmental sensibility. For purposes of this essay, what is important about the arboretum is its demonstration of the methods and objectives of ecological restoration. A good example is the John T. Curtis Prairie, a restored tallgrass prairie that was the first major restoration project at the arboretum and which now occupies 64 acres in the center of the 1,280-acre teaching and research facility.

Survey records from the 1830s indicate that this site was covered by a mixture of tallgrass prairie at the time of European settlement, but when the arboretum was dedicated in 1934 the original vegetation had been nearly eliminated and the site had been under cultivation for about three-quarters of a century. Restoration at that time meant attempting to return the historic grassland vegetation to a site occupied mainly by exotic grasses and weeds. Work began on a large scale in 1936 under the supervision of Dr. Theodore Sperry and has continued at varying levels of intensity ever since. Curtis Prairie and the slightly younger and smaller Henry Greene Prairie about one-half-mile away are currently regarded as the oldest restored prairies, and quite possibly are the oldest restored ecosystems anywhere. They have been the subject of many scientific studies over the years, and some parts of these prairies, especially of Greene Prairie, are considered among the highest-quality replicas of a natural prairie ever achieved.

The effort that led to the restoration of these prairies, though novel in certain respects, was not altogether unprecedented. It drew in part from related activities in areas as diverse as forestry, landscape design, and wildlife management. What set it apart from earlier efforts, however, was the commitment not just to manage the land, or even to rehabilitate it in a general sense, but to re-create, deliberately, a faithful replica of a historic ecosystem.

This activity, with this explicit purpose, is what is meant here by the term "ecological restoration." It is important to keep in mind that this can be carried on at several levels. The work at the arboretum was relatively dramatic because it involved an attempt to replace virtually an entire ecosystem wholesale on a site from which it had been almost completely removed. This makes for a clear illustration of the principle behind ecological restoration, which is simply the active attempt to compensate for human influence on an ecological system in order to return the system to its historic condition. This continual effort to sustain the system against the pressure of our own influence makes restoration such a powerful tool for exploring and defining our relationship with the system, and for achieving what might be called an ecological definition of who we are—that is, a definition written in terms of our impact on other species and ecosystems.

The degrees of influence involved in this process may vary enormously, from very great, as with the University of Wisconsin–Madison Arboretum, to subtle. When the influence is subtle many prefer the term "management" to "restoration." But there is no clear distinction between restoration and management in these senses: They are simply parts of a continuum. In my view it is important to reject the false distinction between them and to refer to activities across the entire continuum as restoration because this explicitly acknowledges the role of the human in the process and opens it to the subjective benefits explored in this essay. To do otherwise is to avoid the responsibility of biotic citizenship or perhaps to reserve this responsibility and the satisfactions and benefits associated with it to a professional elite, an approach to conservation that I believe will inevitably fail in a democratic society.

NOTES

1. Interestingly, Leopold used this phrase in a speech at the dedication of the University of Wisconsin–Madison Arboretum in which he outlined the then-novel plan for a large-scale ecological restoration project on the property. Two versions of this speech survive in written form. The longer, which contains this phrase, was printed in a booklet commemorating the fiftieth anniversary of the arboretum in 1984. The other, shorter version first appeared in *Parks and Recreation* magazine and is included in an anthology of Leopold's writings; see *The River of the Mother of God and Other Essays by Aldo Leopold*, ed. S. L. Flader, and J. B. Callicott (Madison: University of Wisconsin Press, 1991), pp. 209–11. The versions are quite different, and the latter refers to "harmonious relationship" instead of "mutually beneficial relationship."

2. The phrase is from the Wilderness Act of 1964, one of the early achievements of the modern environmental movement, and arguably one of its most characteristic, at least as far as the natural landscape is concerned.

3. Henry D. Thoreau, *The Journal of Henry D. Thoreau*, 2 vols., ed. Bradford Torrey and Francis H. Allen (New York: Dover, 1962), 1:53 (entry for June 16, 1940).

4. See Steve Packard, "Just a Few Oddball Species: Restoration and the Rediscovery of the Tallgrass Savanna," *Restoration and Management Notes* 6, no. 1 (1988): 13–22. For another example from the west coast, see Rich Reiner and Tom Griggs, "Nature Conservancy Undertakes Riparian Restoration Projects in California," *Restoration* 7, no. 1 (1989): 3–8. These early projects have demonstrated the value of restoration by volunteers to the natural-area conservation efforts of an organization such as the Nature Conservancy. Though novel when first undertaken within the past half-dozen years, these projects are now regarded as models, and such work is expected to play a central role in a new plan for the Conservancy that some insiders have called "revolutionary."

5. Loren Eiseley, *The Invisible Pyramid* (New York: Charles Scribner's Sons, 1970). The references are to passages from chapter 7, "The Last Magician."

6. The phrase is from the opening paragraph of the chapter on "Solitude" in *Walden*.

7. William R. Jordan III, Michael E. Gilpin, and John D. Aber, ed., *Restoration Ecology: A Synthetic Approach to Ecological Research* (Cambridge: Cambridge University Press, 1987), especially the introductory chapter.

8. Mircea Eliade, *The Myth of the Eternal Return* (Princeton: Princeton University Press, 1954).

9. The use of this term is borrowed from Paul Shepard, *The Tender Carnivore and the Sacred Game* (New York: Charles Scribner's Sons, 1973).

10. See J. T. Curtis and M. L. Partch, "Effect of Fire on the Competition between Blue Grass and Certain Prairie Plants," *American Midland Naturalist* 39, no. 2 (1948): 437–43.

11. Frederick Turner, "A Field Guide to the Synthetic Landscape: Toward a New Environmental Ethic," *Harper's* 276 (April 1988): 49–55.

12. Bill McKibben, *The End of Nature* (New York: Random House, 1989), p. 211.

13. Steve Packard, "No End to Nature," *Restoration and Management Notes* 8, no. 2 (1990): 72.

14. William R. Jordan III, "A New Paradigm," *Restoration and Management Notes* 9, no. 2 (1991): 64–65. See also my editorials in other issues of *Restoration and Management Notes*, including 5, no. 1; 7, no. 1; 7, no. 2; and 10, no. 2.

15. An interesting example occurs in the report on the management of the national parks prepared by a commission headed by Starker Leopold in 1963. While prescribing what is essentially a program of ongoing restoration for the parks, even describing them in theatrical terms as vignettes of the presettlement landscape maintained to create an illusion of original wilderness, the report insists that the work of restoration itself be kept out of sight—backstage, as it were. This is a classic expression of the conception, characteristic of modem environmentalism and distinguishing it from conservation movements earlier in this century, of nature as a collection of objects in the landscape—in fact, literally an "environment." Though the Leopold report sees restoration as a performance in a sense, its interest at least so far as the public is concerned is exclusively in the product of restoration: the "finished" ecosystem as an object in the landscape (that is, more an art like painting or sculpture, with their emphasis on the creation of concrete artifacts, than like the performing arts, with their ecologylike emphasis on process and relationship). This, however, deprives the public of the experience of restoration—either as audience or as participant, and excludes the people from the very process that defines our relationship with nature. The result is an illusion of nature as pristine and apart. Our relationship with it then becomes the responsibility of a corps of experts working behind the scenes. The elitism implicit in this formulation, though obviously unintended, would in my view prove fatal to conservation in a democratic society.

REFERENCES

Curtis, J. T., and M. L. Partch. "Effect of Fire on the Competition between Blue Grass and Certain Prairie Plants." *American Midland Naturalist* 39, no. 2 (1948).

Eliade, Mircea. *The Myth of the Eternal Return*. Princeton: Princeton University Press, 1954.

Eiseley, Loren. *The Invisible Pyramid*. New York: Charles Scribner's Sons, 1970.

Flader, S. L., and J. B. Callicott, ed. *The River of the Mother of God and Other Essays by Aldo Leopold*. Madison: University of Wisconsin Press, 1991.

Jordan, William R. III. "A New Paradigm." *Restoration and Management Notes* 9, no. 2 (1991).

Jordan, William R. III, Michael E. Gilpin, and John D. Aber, ed. *Restoration Ecology: A Synthetic Approach to Ecological Research*. Cambridge: Cambridge University Press, 1987.

McKibben, Bill. *The End of Nature*. New York: Random House, 1989.

Packard, Steve. "Just a Few Oddball Species: Restoration and the Rediscovery of the Tallgrass Savanna." *Restoration and Management Notes* 6, no. 1 (1988).

————. "No End to Nature." *Restoration and Management Notes* 8, no. 2 (1990).

Reiner, Rich, and Tom Griggs. "Nature Conservancy Undertakes Riparian Restoration Projects in California." *Restoration* 7, no. 1 (1989).

Shepard, Paul. *The Tender Carnivore and the Sacred Game*. New York: Charles Scribner's Sons, 1973.

Thoreau, Henry D. *The Journal of Henry D. Thoreau*. 2 volumes. Edited by Bradford Torrey and Francis H. Allen. New York: Dover, 1962.

Turner, Frederick. "A Field Guide to the Synthetic Landscape: Toward a New Environmental Ethic." *Harper's* 276 (April 1988).

15

Restoration or Preservation?
Reflections on a Clash of Environmental Philosophies

G. Stanley Kane

Ours is an era in which there is little left of nature that has not been extensively altered by the activities of human beings. Among proposed remedies are preservation, setting aside areas that still remain undisturbed and protecting them against human encroachment, and restoration, bringing degraded areas back to something resembling an unspoiled condition. On first thought one might suppose that preservationists and restorationists would make natural allies, but even a cursory reading of the relevant literature shows that all is not harmony and peace between the two groups. The writings of William Jordan and Frederick Turner, for example, include some surprisingly sharp criticisms of preservation. In this essay I wish to assess the dispute between the restorationists and preservationists, centering my discussion around two basic philosophical issues: the concept of nature and the relation of humankind to nature, and the character of human knowledge.

Throughout this essay I use "restoration" to refer to the work explained and interpreted under that heading by Jordan and Turner. There are other restoration projects, and doubtless other ways of interpreting restoration, but these fall outside my purview.

G. Stanley Kane, "Restoration or Preservation? Reflections on a Clash of Environmental Philosophies" in *Beyond Preservation: Restoring and Inventing Landscapes*, ed. A. Dwight Baldwin, Judith De Luce, and Carl Pletsch (Minneapolis: University of Minnesota Press, 1994). Reprinted by permission of the University of Minnesota Press.

THE RESTORATIONIST CRITIQUE
OF PRESERVATION

The nub of the restorationist critique of preservation is the claim that it rests on an unhealthy dualism that conceives nature and humankind as radically distinct and opposed to each other. Jordan and Turner offer little evidence to support this indictment, but others have, sometimes pointing to the Wilderness Act of 1964 as especially telling.[1] According to this act, a wilderness is an area where "in contrast to those areas where man and his works dominate the landscape . . . the earth and its community of life are untrammeled by man, where man himself is a visitor and does not remain. . . . [It is] an area . . . retaining its primeval character and influence, without permanent improvement of human habitation, which is protected and managed to preserve its natural conditions and which generally appears to have been affected by the forces of nature, with the imprint of man's work substantially unnoticeable."[2]

Dissatisfaction with dualism has for some time figured prominently In the unhappiness of environmentalists with mainstream industrial society.[3] Jordan and Turner turn the critique of dualism against preservation-oriented environmentalists themselves. In their view preservationists are imbued with the same basic mindset as the industrial mainstream, the only difference being that the latter exalts humans over nature while the former elevate nature over humans. According to the restorationists, neither position is healthy. One underwrites exploitation, with devastating environmental consequences; the other effectively takes human beings out of nature altogether and makes wilderness of it.[4]

In the judgment of the restorationists, the exclusion of humans from nature deforms both. Set off against nature, humans can only work harm in the world. Any possibility of constructive stewardship is denied them, and the best they can do for nature is depart it and leave it alone.[5] But nature suffers as well in this separation from human beings, because it is deprived of the services that humans render as rightful citizens of the biotic community. Dramatic testimony to this is seen in Turner's statement that wilderness areas from which humans are systematically excluded are "the most astonishingly unnatural places on earth."[6]

What are we to make of this criticism of environmental preservation? In answering this question we need to distinguish the issue of the merits of dualism as a philosophical outlook from the question of whether preservationists are really dualists. I am persuaded that many of the faults found with dualism by its detractors not only are real but have been fateful. But is the preservation program really committed to these errors? There is good reason, I believe, for thinking not. We can see this if we look in two places: first, at the complete environmental program supported by most preservationists; and second, at the logic of preservation itself.

It might make sense to ascribe the nature-humanity dualism to preservationists if wilderness preservation were the whole of their environmental program. It would make even more sense if in addition their principal reason for seeking wilderness preservation were the conviction that nature can be fully itself and thus have full value only when left undisturbed by human beings. Though there are exceptions, preservationists typically do more than just sponsor wilderness preservation. They also work actively on a broad array of environmental issues, such as air and water pollution, toxic waste, soil erosion, global warming, and so on. To think that such preservationists are fundamentally inspired by the nature-humanity dualism and a misanthropic view of human beings is not at all a necessary, or even a very reasonable, inference. To be sure, they *are* worried about the impact that humans are now having on natural systems, and they do think that human activity at the present time is alarmingly destructive of nature. But so do many others, including our restorationists, who would not think of solving the problem through a policy of apartheid for humans and nature. It makes more sense to think that these preservationists are driven not by the notion that human contact and commerce with nature should be kept to a minimum, but by the desire that humans avoid the kind and the magnitude of interaction with nature that destroys the health of the world and the beings, human and nonhuman, to which it is home.

The definition of wilderness in the Wilderness Act, as land kept free from the influence of human beings, might seem to count against this conclusion. This is a definition of wilderness, however, not of nature in general; that a person support the protection of wilderness and still recognize a legitimate need for other types of land devoted to other purposes is wholly consistent with this definition. It is hard to see how someone willing to accept multiple land uses in this way is a victim of nature-humanity dualism.

In any event, there is no logic that requires dualism as a philosophical underpinning for preservation. Dualism might support preservation, but it is not the only outlook that would do so. Preservation could be grounded just as securely on the much more innocuous premise that there are limits to the freedom of human beings to use nature solely for their own purposes.

There seems, then, no compelling reason for thinking either that dualism is implicit in preservation or that its practitioners generally think it is. It is perhaps puzzling that Jordan and Turner do not see this, but more puzzling, I think, is the sharpness and relentlessness of their attack on the preservationists, accentuated by the fact that they offer little, if any, criticism of those who have plundered the natural world and left it standing so desperately in need of the healing powers of their own art of restoration. They pay no attention to the obvious point that in our present situation still-untouched lands not accorded legal protection will sooner or later almost certainly suffer the fate that has historically overtaken virtually all untouched lands in the path of industrial progress. The value of preservation as means of limiting further ecological destruction is not once acknowledged. We see here a curious phenomenon: A movement that desires to restore the earth to a more natural condition singles out, from all the parties active in public life today, a group that wishes to preserve some lands in their natural condition, and belabors them for unhealthy attitudes toward nature.

RESTORATIONISM ON NATURE AND HUMANITY

The first principle of restorationism is that nature and humanity are fundamentally united rather than separate. Humans are a natural part of nature. The familiar distinctions of the natural and the artificial, of nature and culture, of ecology and economy, are not oppositions but a series of diverse and interrelated elements within a rich and unified whole. Human life, in all its manifestations, depends on nature and is an outworking of the same forces that are at work throughout the biosphere, indeed throughout the universe. But equally, because humans are an integral part of the natural order, nature also depends on humanity, and cannot maintain full health and integrity without the activities of human beings. Nature and humanity are thus interdependent, and as a consequence their proper relation is cooperative, not adversarial. When each carries out its own proper functions, they work together to produce results that are wholesome and beneficial for both.

Compared with the dualism considered earlier, this scheme of understanding allots a much more positive role to humans in their interactions with nature. No longer are we either excluded from the world or condemned to exploit it. Instead, human participation is essential both for our own good and for that of the world. We can now feel at home in the world, full-fledged citizens of the land community, beings who belong where we are, in a place that requires of us the vital work of stewardship—a critical form of which is restoration.

In this outlook human nature is not something to be decried. Humans have a wide range of legitimate needs, all of them bred into us by nature itself. Our instincts and capacities for satisfying these needs, including the astonishing intellectual and technical abilities our species has acquired over the centuries, are also products of nature. Nothing is intrinsically amiss or unnatural when we use these abilities in our dealings with nonhuman nature. To be sure, we often bring about substantial change in the nonhuman world, but that is fully natural and not to be deplored. Nature is a dynamic realm, a domain of incessant change sustained by the actions and reactions of its constituent parts. This does not mean that humans cannot do serious ecological damage or that we should not try to prevent or control such damage, but it does mean that humans need feel no hesitation about manipulating nature solely on the grounds that it leaves its mark on the world.

When it comes to assessing this restorationist outlook, the most serious issue, in my judgment, does not concern the merits of this conception of the relation of nature and humanity. Rightly understood, I believe this conception is markedly superior to that in dualism. The crucial question about the restorationist outlook has to do instead with the degree to which the restorationist program is itself faithful to the more unified vision of the relation of humans to nature it claims as its own. Rejecting the old domination model, which sees humans as over nature, endowed with authority to dominate and control it, restoration theory champions a model of community participation. Yet some of the descriptions that Jordan and Turner give of what restorationists are actually up to in the overall economy of nature do not cohere well with the community participation model.

For example, Jordan thinks that "the fate and well-being of the biosphere depend ultimately on us and our relationship with it."[7] These words might mean only that we should discontinue or scale back the activities that threaten the biosphere, but for restorationists they signify considerably more. Turner explicitly states that it is time for us to renounce what he calls false ecological modesty, recognize that we are "the lords of creation," and "take responsibility for nature"[8]—a responsibility, he thinks, that extends to creating "man-made nature."[9] Restoration is part of this project of creating man-made nature. (Some might think that the capacity of human beings to damage the ecosystems of the earth automatically gives them a controlling role in the biosphere. But this is a mistake. That humans can harm the biosphere no more gives them special authority over it than the fact that I can injure or kill my neighbors makes me lord of the neighborhood. Special authority depends on something other than mere ability to destroy.)

It is hard to square the description of humans as the lords of creation with the community model of the relation of humans to nature. Indeed, Turner's comments seem to fit better into the domination model. Lords of the world, exercising responsibility for the fate and well-being of the biosphere, even to the point of creating man-made ecosystems, and beings who thus hold literal life-and-death power over the nonhuman realm, surely occupy a position of dominance, and everything else holds a place of subservience. Fellow members of a community, in contrast, are on more equal footing; they enjoy more independence and autonomy than any of the nonhuman participants in the lords-of-creation scenario. A lord of creation is not just one of many members in a community.

Another holistic model might be more serviceable to the restorationists, namely that of nature as an organism. As with the community model, this pictures nature as a system of interconnected parts. A fundamental difference, however, is that in an organism the parts are wholly subservient to the life of the organism, whereas members of a community have lives of their own apart from their functions in the community, thus possessing a measure of independence that parts of organisms do not have. The major parts of an organism are its organs; the members of a community are not organs, but are themselves organisms. They stand to the community, therefore, in a relation very different from that of organs to organisms.[10]

If we could think of the biosphere as a single living organism and could identify humans with the brain (or the DNA), or control center, of the biosphere, we would have a model that fits the restorationists' view of the role of humans in nature much more closely than does the community model. But just how plausible is such a model? Is there any credible evidence that humans are indeed the control center of the biosphere, or any compelling reason for thinking that they have the ability to carry out this function well?

The evidence is, to put it mildly, not strong. If we were the biosphere's control center, then the extinction of the human race would mean the death of the biosphere. Mass extinctions of the past have not had such a catastrophic consequence. It is difficult to see why the biosphere could not just as easily withstand similar extinctions now, even if humans were included in the die-off. What makes the human species so much more vital to the living earth than other species? According to one prominent analyst, the biosphere would be able to withstand even nuclear war followed by nuclear winter.[11]

But let us suppose, contrary to the evidence, that humans really are the control center of the biosphere and that we really do have responsibility for directing its progress and ensuring its well-being. Why should we believe that we are up to the task? The prospects are not encouraging. The difficulties that would have to be overcome are just too great. For example, how could we expect to acquire the knowledge that would be required? The biosphere is too large and complex, too much the product of a long and intricate history of natural development, and too many of its processes are marked by an intrinsic indeterminacy, for us to comprehend it thoroughly enough to control its fate.

Even if we could acquire the necessary knowledge, we would have to face the problem of how to find the wisdom and moral will to employ that knowledge to beneficial rather than harmful effect. The record of history inspires little confidence that humans in positions of responsibility will use their power generally to improve the health and well-being of those under their authority. Granted, some of the harm done has been a consequence of ignorance, and is thus correctable by advances in knowledge, but much of the damage takes place when people in authority use their positions to further their own interests at the expense of those in their charge. If that state of affairs is not remedied, gains in knowledge and power will only increase the potential for social and ecological disaster; for the more powerful our technologies are, the less tolerant they are of human error or ill intentions.

To consider humans as the control center of the living earth (or as lords of creation) is to ascribe to them a dominating role in nature. Is this significantly different from the old-fashioned domination model? If not, then restoration, notwithstanding its genuine concern for ecological wholeness and well-being, may be unable to make good on its promise to bring healing to nature.

Striking parallels exist between the old domination program and restoration. The most basic is that in both systems humans hold the place of highest authority and power within the world. Also, neither view recognizes any limits to the scope or range of legitimate human manipulation in the world. Everything is fair game for our manipulations if useful to our work. This does not mean that there are no constraints—only beneficial manipulations should be undertaken—but it does mean that nothing is intrinsically off-limits. A further parallel is that because the fate of the world rests on humans, they must have a clear idea of what needs to be done. They must know what conditions are good (or at least what conditions are better) and then work to bring them about. Their activity, then, requires them to shape the world after ideas in their own mind.

There are, of course, important differences between the two theories. First, restorationists no longer view the world in the old dominationist way as a passive and inert object; instead it is a system that is alive, dynamic, creative, and one that has a history. Second, restorationists consider humans to be continuous with nature rather than separate from it. Third, though both assign to humans a controlling role in the world, dominationists conceive this in terms of conquest while restorationists conceive it in terms of healing. In restorationist doctrine humans are physicians to the biosphere who, through their special knowledge and skill, aid nature as it drives to maintain and develop itself. A fourth difference is that restorationists recognize that needs and interests other than exclusively human ones have a claim upon us. Fifth, the ideas that must serve to guide our work in the world are drawn not solely from a consideration of human needs and purposes, but from an understanding of the biosphere—the beings, the systems, and the interconnections that make it up, and the values embedded therein. Sixth, in the restorationist program, humans' controlling role in nature is not to be used solely for their own good, as dominationists thought, but for the health and well-being of the biosphere. Finally, because restorationists believe that the biosphere has needs and interests beyond narrowly human ones, they are more conscious than dominationists of our capacity to harm nature.

These differences are significant, but the continuing parallels raise troubling doubts about whether restoration is sufficiently removed from domination. The degree of anthropocentrism and human control that still remains in restoration, although not as crude as in domination, could still make restoration more a part of the environmental problem than its solution.

If the community model is best, we are seriously misguided if we act as the lords of creation, believing that if we don't make things happen for the well-being of the biosphere then the job won't get done. Community members hold responsibility jointly for the health and integrity of the community, and community values are not enhanced by one member taking on what others are better suited for. In the community of nature, nonhuman entities have their own stakes in the well-being of the biosphere and their own contributions to make in furthering it. The good of the biosphere requires that they be given the freedom to play their special parts. It they are deprived of opportunity to do this, the community suffers.

In situations of ecological breakdown, it is tempting for humans to think that they can save the biosphere by seizing control and restoring things back to order and health. But if the community model is correct, yielding to this temptation is self-defeating. There are constructive possibilities for the use of power, but only within limits. Beyond these limits a member simply has to trust the system—the process and arrangements by which the community lives and on which it depends—to be sufficiently self-regulating, self-adjusting, and self-maintaining to survive the challenges and assaults that come its way. If the system becomes too impaired to survive, power grabs on the part of the individual members will not save it. (I hope it is clear that, in speaking about trusting the system, I am not saying anything that would encourage submission to repressive political regimes. I am speaking here of community, not political systems inimical to community.)

Trust of this type is, of course, risky. It puts one at the mercy of forces beyond one's control, which may explain the appeal of the domination model. But life is inherently risky. A system in which there are no risks is a system in which there is no life. Beyond a certain point, the effort to control and eliminate risk does more harm than good, and taken far enough becomes deadly. Humans are incontrovertibly creatures of forces they do not control. If the forces that brought forth life in the first place cannot be trusted to maintain it—provided they are given the leeway to do so—there is little basis for thinking that anything humans can do will save the situation. (Trust need not, indeed should not, be naive or uncritical.)

The argument for trust, however, is not just that we may as well bow to the inevitable. In a community trust is a positive good—even when relations are not going smoothly. We need only consider family life to see that this is so. When conflicts arise within a family, maintaining trust and respect for individual autonomy, though risky, is not thereby made less valuable or less necessary to family survival and prosperity. If community is the best model for our basic relations in the world, the quality of human life, and of life generally, will ultimately depend more on trust than on control.

From the point of view of the champions of community, the unwillingness of restorationists to make room for an ethic of trust in our dealings with nature, and their reliance instead on a program of control, is precisely what makes them fellow travelers with the old-fashioned dominationists. Like the dominationists they give humans a larger role than they are suited for, one for which they have neither the knowledge nor the moral wisdom to carry out well. They do, of course, propose to redirect human control from the final end of the dominationists, that of human empire over nature, to that of the health of the biosphere, but they do nothing to scale back the role of humans in the world, and nothing to correct the mismatch between their unlimited task and their limited qualifications. As a consequence, restoration offers the world no realistic protection against continuing social and ecological disasters of our own making.

The restorationist might respond that this criticism underestimates the significance of the shift in ultimate end. The crucial problem with domination, the response might go, is that it had no interest at all in the health of the biosphere. It is not surprising, then, that when Western civilization mobilized national economics to promote human empire, ecological values took a beating. Restorationists, however, recognize the supreme importance of ecological values. If the global economy were now to become reorganized around the principles and values of the restorationist program, humans could be expected to do much better in avoiding further ecological destruction and in restoring the health of the biosphere.

There is some validity in this response, but it does not meet the basic force of the objection. It is on solid ground in holding that the chances of hitting a target are better when we are aiming at it than when we are not. But the dispute is whether we can act without mischievous consequences, no matter how unexceptionable the ends we seek, if we do not know very fully what we are doing. To the critic of restoration, the limitations of our knowledge are emblematic of our holding a more humble position in the biosphere than that of its lords. If we step out of our proper role and presume to take responsibility for the well-being of the whole biosphere, not really knowing what we are doing, we will as certainly produce havoc under the restorationist regime as we did under the aegis of domination. We could profit from the salutary reminder that the projects of domination spawned by the old model were all boosted with extravagant promises of beneficial results, were motivated by what were considered the noblest intentions, and were backed by the best science of the day—just as the new programs of control are touted now. For these reasons the restorationist rejection of the old domination model seems not nearly complete enough to restore a healthy relation between humans and nature. From this perspective, the restorationist shift to a new end in view does little more than dress up the old domination program in a currently fashionable green.

None of the foregoing implies that actual efforts of restoration should not be undertaken. This essay is not focused on ground-level projects of restoration but on philosophical principles in terms of which restoration is conceived and justified. If the philosophical principles of Jordan and Turner are defective, that does not entail that particular restoration projects are unsound. Individual projects—just because they are ground-level and do not reach out to encompass the entire biosphere—may have a potential for good that the philosophies used to justify them do not. Indeed, it seems to me that in our own day restoration is an inescapable obligation. Not, however, for the grandiose reason that we have ultimate responsibility for the health and well-being of the biosphere, but on the more homely grounds that when we make a mess we should do what we can to clean it up. This is more pedestrian and less exciting, but much more befitting members of a community that share the same neighborhood with others.

RESTORATION AND MAKER'S KNOWLEDGE

One of the signal advantages claimed for restoration by its enthusiasts is that gives us the highest kind of understanding. The idea, as Jordan explains, is that we understand something to the degree that we can assemble and control it.[12] As the practice of assembling (or reassembling) ecosystems, restoration provides us at once with the fullest knowledge and the ultimate test of our understanding of them. This involves more than just knowing the actions that will in some particular circumstances result in bringing about restoration, for restoration accomplished in this fashion may be no more than a case of triggering natural processes that then, apart from anything one knows or controls, get the job done. Restoration in its most thoroughgoing sense is a matter of full control, and only the most complete knowledge gives that to us.

In certain ancient disputes about knowledge, a distinction was drawn between beholder's knowledge, user's knowledge, and maker's knowledge; and a question was asked, triggering a debate that continued into the modern era, about who understands a thing the best: its maker, its beholder, or its user.[13] Restorationists take their stand unequivocally with maker's knowledge.

This stand has become almost an article of faith in the modern scientific West. It can no longer be taken for granted, however, for the question of the supremacy of maker's knowledge is an issue we are forced to reopen as part of the profound rethinking of basic assumptions prompted by the environmental crisis. We may start a reexamination by noting that in many cases it is highly questionable that maker's knowledge provides us the best understanding. Take pain and torture, for example.[14] Who understands better what these are: the person who causes them or the person who suffers them? Or a child: does the physician who produces the baby through in vitro fertilization understand this child better than the parent who loves it, cares for it, and nurtures it to maturity? Or even consider a technical instrument—the computer, let's say—the type of thing for which the claim for the superiority of maker's knowledge seems most compelling. Does the one who designs and manufactures the computer really understand it better than the historian or sociologist who sees the wide variety of its uses and effects in the lives, the activities, the thinking, and the satisfactions of individuals, and in all the manifold and complex transformations it brings to the world of work, to business, to social and economic structures, politics, international relations, military policy, education, science, demographic patterns, human self-understanding, philosophical worldview, cultural ideals, and so on? In each of these instances it would be difficult to make out the case for maker's knowledge. This is not to suggest that maker's knowledge never provides the best understanding, but only to show that whether maker's knowledge really gives us the best understanding of a thing is related to two factors: what kind of thing it is, and how it fits into a broader context.

Another point to note is that the kind of knowledge we can have of anything is influenced by the relation we take to it and the purpose we have for it. This is evident in the fact that the three forms of knowledge in question so far are named after relations. We can easily imagine other relations that yield their own forms of knowledge, such as lover's knowledge, disciple's knowledge, parent's knowledge, enemy's knowledge, worshiper's knowledge, partner's knowledge, and so on. There is a different form of knowledge for every different relation a would-be knower may have to what he or she wants to know.

Combining the results of two preceding paragraphs, we are led to the conclusion that the kind of knowledge that constitutes the deepest understanding of something depends on what the thing is, how it fits into a larger picture, and what our proper relation to it is. When we apply this conclusion to nature—to the biosphere and its systems and subsystems—we are brought back to the topics of the previous section, the nature of nature and the character of our relation to it. The same issues are at stake both here and there, only now we are looking at their epistemological side instead of their metaphysical side. Whether maker's knowledge can provide us the best understanding of living ecosystems depends on whether the biosphere is best represented as a community or by some other model.

These themes have already been presented in their metaphysical guise; now it may be valuable to point out some epistemological equivalents. First, because maker's knowledge and its close associate, controller's knowledge, are the epistemology of the old domination program, it's hard to see how the restorationists' conception of knowledge takes them away from this in any significant way. To be sure, restorationists stress the importance of ecological relationships, but that in itself does not represent abandonment of domination as the goal; it may signal only an adjustment of the old domination program to the new order of nature disclosed by the ecological sciences. Jordan argues, for example, that forms of restoration that proceed by making a few key adjustments and then allowing nature to take its course are not the most valuable, as "the essential idea is control—the ability not only to restore quickly, but to restore at will, controlling speed, altering its course, *steering* it, even preventing it entirely. . . ."[15] He also writes that full understanding of a system can be gained only when we see what happens when it is disturbed, and, he adds, "the perturbations must be extreme."[16] What is this if not a continuation of the Baconian domination science that studies "nature under constraint and vexed," on the premise that "the nature of things betrays itself more readily under the vexations of art than in its natural freedom"?[17] Indeed, domination is so much the overriding objective of the research Jordon describes that the actual restoration of nature is not a final end after all, but a means to gaining control.

As we saw earlier, this does not fit in with what seems to be the best model of nature, because domination and control are radically contrary to the spirit of community and violate the independence and autonomy of its members. What we need to note here is that independence and autonomy have their epistemological counterpart in mystery. Any entity marked by a degree of autonomy has within it a level of being that is inscrutable. It has a dimension of itself, all inner reality, a unique element of what it is to be the thing it is, that is inaccessible to anything else, perhaps even (so some extent) to itself. It has an identity, a value, a purpose, a creativity that escapes reduction to the categories of objective knowledge and to the uses of human beings. Such a dimension, though not beyond destruction, is beyond mastery (including intellectual mastery) and control by others. Perhaps the fact that as our knowledge of nature has grown ignorance has grown apace[18] is eloquent testimony to the element of mystery at the heart of things. If humans indeed live in a great community of being, our lives are governed by mystery more deeply than they are governed by knowledge, and we need an ethic of the mysterious—appropriate means for approaching and responding to mystery and autonomy—more than continual increase of maker's knowledge. (An ethic of the mysterious is of a piece with the ethic of trust discussed earlier.)

A good beginning in the development of such an ethic is the recognition and preservation of places where the autonomy and mystery of things is respected, and where creatures are allowed to be themselves, without the disturbing intrusions of those who would dominate them. People coming into such places will set aside the quest for knowledge and control that has become normal today, and they will find opportunity instead for quiet and undisturbed encounter with the mysteries. In these places we may open ourselves up to the wonder of the great community of being, we may admire the marvelous forces of evolution or God (or both) that have brought forth the intricate structures of our world and its biosphere, and experience the paradox of being at once humbled and uplifted. In the process we may gradually grow in our ability to see and hear and understand, not as controlling knowledge understands, but in ways that beings who care for each other and depend on each other—parents, children, friends, lovers—understand. This experience has the capacity to fill, inspire, change, and invigorate people—and empower them for a return to daily activity, bearing a sense of the awesomeness of Life and Being that gives meaning and definition to everyday pursuits while at the same time placing the needed constraints upon them.

Legally designated wildernesses are not the only possible places of this type. They certainly have their importance in serving the values indicated, and they may be particularly crucial as refuges for species that do not get along well with humans in the same habitat.[19] But these tend to be far away from the centers of human population. We also need many smaller areas scattered here and there—especially in our cities and suburbs, where undisturbed nature tends to be squeezed out of the environment. These would be places more accessible to the average city dweller. In addition, we need places in our own souls, and in the whole range of the relations we maintain, that have not been submitted to the procedures and the uses of maker's knowledge, which can serve as points of contact with a level of being and a richness of life that is not of our making or our control.[20] If wholeness in the nature of things and in ourselves is to be recovered, we need these points of contact everywhere.

We are now in a position to see why the tone of the criticism that restorationists direct against preservation is so harsh and visceral. Because initially it strikes one that there is no incompatibility between restoration and preservation, and that the two could well join hands in a powerful environmental alliance, it is tempting to seek explanations in ad hominem terms: as a matter of polemical style, competition for public support, or even congenial dyspepsia. The issue, however, goes deeper than any such factor. By holding that humans are lords of creation, restorationist metaphysics tolerates no enclaves anywhere kept free of human domination and control; by maintaining that maker's knowledge gives us the best understanding of things, restorationist epistemology tolerates no mystery. But mystery and the preservation of places kept free of human domination are at the heart of the preservationist program and philosophy. Preservation thus presents a direct challenge to the most fundamental assumptions and aims of the restorationist program, and vice versa. The disagreements between the two groups go all the way down to the foundations, to the level of basic philosophies concerning who we are, what nature is like, and what human life is about. This being the case, short of philosophical conversion on one side or the other, the disagreements are irreconcilable.

NOTES

1. J. Baird Callicott, "The Wilderness Idea Revisited: The Sustainable Development Alternative," *Environmental Professional* 13 (1991): 240.

2. Bill Devall and George Sessions, *Deep Ecology* (Salt Lake City: Peregrin Smith Books, 1985), pp. 114–15.

3. Carolyn Merchant, *The Death of Nature: Women, Ecology, and the Scientific Revolution* (San Francisco: Harper & Row, 1980); Theodore Roszak, *Where the Wasteland Ends* (Garden City, N.Y.: Anchor Books, 1973); Morris Berman, *The Reenchantment of the World* (Ithaca and London: Cornell University Press, 1981).

4. Frederick Turner, "Cultivation of the American Garden: Toward a Secular View of Nature," *Harper's* 271 (1985): 48.

5. Frederick Turner, "The Invented Landscape," in *Beyond Preservation: Restoring and Inventing Landscapes*, ed. A. Dwight Baldwin, Judith De Luce, and Carl Pletsch (Minneapolis: University of Minnesota Press, 1994).

6. Turner, "Cultivation of the American Garden," p. 45.

7. William R. Jordan III, " 'Sunflower Forest': Ecological Restoration as the Basis for a New Environmental Paradigm," in this volume.

8. Turner, "Cultivation of the American Garden," p. 51.

9. Ibid., p. 50.

10. Eric Katz, "Organism, Community, and the 'Substantial Problems,' " *Environmental Ethics* 7 (1985): 241–56.

11. James Lovelock, *The Ages of Gaia: A Biography of Our Living Earth* (New York: W. W. Norton & Co., 1988), p. 232.

12. William R. Jordan III, Michael E. Gilpin, and John D. Aber, "Restoration Ecology: Ecological Restoration as a Technique for Basic Research," in *Restoration Ecology: A Synthetic Approach to Ecological Research* (Cambridge: Cambridge University Press, 1987), pp. 12; Jordan, "Sunflower Forest."

13. Antonio Perez-Ramos, *Francis Bacon's Idea of Science and the Maker's Knowledge Tradition* (Oxford: Clarendon Press, 1988), chap. 5.

14. Ibid., p. 51.

15. Jordan, Gilpin, and Aber, "Restoration Ecology," p. 17; emphasis in original

16. Ibid., p. 12.

17. Francis Bacon, *The New Organon* (Indianapolis: Bobbs-Merrill Educational Publishing, 1960), p. 25.

18. J. R. Ravetz, "Usable Knowledge, Usable Ignorance: Incomplete Science with Policy Implications," in *Sustainable Development of the Biosphere*, ed. William C. Clark and R. E. Munn (Cambridge: Cambridge University Press, 1986), pp. 415–32.

19 Callicott, "The Wilderness Idea Revisited," p. 236.

20. Wendell Berry, "Preserving Wilderness," in *Home Economics* (San Francisco: North Point Press, 1987), pp. 137–51.

REFERENCES

Bacon, Francis. *The New Organon*. Indianapolis: Bobbs-Merrill Educational Publishing, 1960.

Berman, Morris. *The Reenchantment of the World*. Ithaca and London: Cornell University Press, 1981.

Berry, Wendell. "Preserving Wilderness." In *Home Economics*. San Francisco: North Point Press, 1987.

Callicott, J. Baird. "The Wilderness Idea Revisited: The Sustainable Development Alternative." *Environmental Professional* 13, no. 3 (1991).

Devall, Bill, and George Sessions. *Deep Ecology*. Salt Lake City: Peregrin Smith Books, 1985.

Jordan, William R. III, Michael E. Gilpin, and John D. Aber. "Restoration Ecology: Ecological Restoration as a Technique for Basic Research." In *Restoration Ecology: A Synthetic Approach to Ecological Research*. Cambridge: Cambridge University Press, 1987.

Katz, Eric. "Organism, Community, and the 'Substantial Problems.'" *Environmental Ethics* 7, no. 3 (1985).

Lovelock, James. *The Ages of Gaia: A Biography of Our Living Earth*. New York: W. W. Norton & Co., 1988.

Merchant, Carolyn. *The Death of Nature: Women, Ecology, and the Scientific Revolution*. San Francisco: Harper & Row, 1980.

Perez-Ramos, Antonio. *Francis Bacon's Idea of Science and the Maker's Knowledge Tradition*. Oxford: Clarendon Press, 1988.

Ravetz, J. R. "Usable Knowledge, Usable Ignorance: Incomplete Science with Policy Implications." In *Sustainable Development of the Biosphere*, edited by William C. Clark and R. E. Munn. Cambridge: Cambridge University Press, 1986.

Roszak, Theodore. *Where the Wasteland Ends*. Garden City, N.Y.: Anchor Books, 1973.

Turner, Frederick. "Cultivation of the American Garden: Toward a Secular View of Nature." *Harper's* 271 (1985).

———. "The Invented Landscape." In *Beyond Preservation: Restoring and Inventing Landscapes*, edited by A. Dwight Baldwin, Judith De Luce, and Carl Pletsch. Minneapolis: University of Minnesota Press, 1994.

Epilogue

In its broadest outlines, the future of restoration practice seems clear. We will be devoting increasing time to restoring the earth to some preferable state after the exploding demands of human cultures have caused its degradation. In many cases, we cannot afford the luxury of allowing the earth to heal itself, as the time required would be too great and the impact on those we care about, too immediate. What remains obscure is how we will think about restoration and how our thoughts and values will fill in the details of its practice. The preceding articles sketch a broad range of approaches to restoration, but these may be fruitfully clustered into two camps. One allies restoration with the values and assumptions implicit in the ideal of sustainability, and the other links it more closely with wilderness preservation. How restoration theory evolves may depend on which of these two key features of the landscape of environmentalism takes priority in the twenty-first century.

If wilderness preservation continues to be a dominant force in environmentalism, then views of restoration that emphasize the goal of predisturbance structures, place limitations on invasive means, and express a deep ambivalence towards restoration are likely to remain widespread. The predisturbance structure goal links restoration with wilderness preservation, for it seems best justified in virtue of the wildness returned to the ecosystem. If natural processes proceeding independent of human intervention have no special value, it is not clear why we should prefer some prior structure of an ecosystem to a new healthy state which reflects more human impact. Similarly, the arguments for metaphysical and evaluative differences between restored and undisturbed landscapes typically rely on the value of the non-humanized. Perhaps other historical features of ecosystems could justify the difference claims, but it is not clear that such features would carry sufficient evaluative weight. These arguments contribute to the deep ambivalence toward restoration that is likely to accompany an ideal that prefers land undisturbed by humans.

If the value of sustainable living eclipses the ideal of wilderness, a rather different view of restoration is likely to be prevalent. In the past, sustainable lifestyles have evolved where people are deeply embedded in local ecosystems which have been transformed to meet their needs. Such people can see firsthand the impact of overuse, and they are more likely to avoid degrading the land. This image is one source of the perceived tension between sustainability and wilderness preservation. A view of restoration associated with the ideal of sustainability is likely to permit a variety of responses to degradation, any of which return health to an ecosystem. New ecosystem structures may be more sustainable than predisturbance structures which evolved under very different conditions, so often the former would be preferred. An unmixed enthusiasm for the practice of restoration is likely to accompany an ideal of sustainably integrating humans into ecosystems, for restoration is one of the most salutary means of integration.

Naturally, those who value the less humanized should be more concerned about invasive methods used in restoration, since these may actually make an ecosystem less wild than it would have been had nature been allowed to heal itself. Those who see human alterations as no different in kind from those of other species may not fault a means for involving too much alteration, though they may still worry that certain means cause unacceptable harm to individuals. Different approaches to exotics follow the same pattern. Any human introduction of a species to a relatively wild area will be problematic for the former group, whereas introductions which affect health and sustainability are likely to be the focus of the latter group.

Some authors have defended positions that do not fit neatly into either of the above orientations. William Jordan criticizes the wilderness preservation paradigm, but advocates the goal of a predisturbance structure. He seeks ways of reconnecting humans with nature, but seems to prefer a state of nature which reflects little human connection. Often the most compelling positions unite the best parts of opposing orientations; Jordan may have this kind of an attractive synthetic view. The apparent tension seems unresolved, however, and the feeling remains that enthusism for the human benefits of the process of restoration ill accords with the results sought in the "natural past" paradigm.

The associations among restoration, sustainability, and wilderness preservation are loose and flexible. Environmental policy in the twenty-first century will undoubtedly include versions of each of these ideals. The details of their presentation and their justification are likely to become more interdependent because of the pressures of internal consistency. The deep tensions that exist today have prompted calls for unity among environmentalists. One of the primary tasks of environmental philosophy is that of forging a coherent approach to the current ecological crises. Although such an approach is not essential to the political consensus required to solve large environmental problems, it is often very helpful. Since restoration theory is draws to a focus many of the tensions in contemporary environmentalism, it should attract increasing philosophical attention.

Notes on Contributors

Stephen P. Aultz is chief naturalist of the Forest Preserve District of Will County, Illinois.

Robin Attfield teaches in the philosophy department at the University of Wales at Cardiff. He has written widely in the field of ethics, and he is coeditor of *International Justice and the Third World* and *Philosophy and the Natural Environment*.

Susan Power Bratton is an ecologist who has written numerous articles on philosophical and religious attitudes towards the environment. She is the author of *The Original Desert Solitude: Wilderness and Christianity*, and she has taught in the Department of Philosophy and Religion, University of North Texas.

Robert Elliot teaches in the philosophy department at Sunshine Coast University College in Queensland, Australia. His has written several influential articles on philosophical issues in environmental restoration and his new book is *Faking Nature: The Ethics of Environmental Restoration*.

Eric Katz is associate professor of philosophy and director of the Science, Technology and Society Program at the New Jersey Institute of Technology. He is author of *Nature as Subject: Human Obligation and Natural Community* and many articles in environmental ethics.

Marguerite Holloway is a staff writer at *Scientific American*.

William R. Jordan III is on the faculty at the University of Wisconsin Arboretum. He has written widely on environmental restoration, and he is the founder and editor of *Restoration and Management Notes*.

G. Stanley Kane is professor of philosophy at Miami University in Oxford, Ohio. He is author of *Anselm's Doctrine of Freedom of the Will* and of articles in the history of philosophy, philosophy of religion and environmental philosophy.

Andrew Light is assistant professor of philosophy at Binghamton University. He has edited numerous anthologies in environmental philosophy, including *Environmental Pragmatism*, and *Social Ecology after Bookchin*. He also coedits the annual *Philosophy and Geography*.

Jon Mendelson is a professor of environmental science at Governors State College.

Judith Dolan Mendelson is a member of the Illinois Endangered Species Protection Board.

Stephanie Mills is a writer whose books include *Whatever happened to Ecology?* and *In Service of the Wild*. She was honored as a 1996 *Utne* visionary.

Steve Packard is director of science for the Nature Conservancy of Illinois. He has written numerous articles on environmental restoration.

Holmes Rolston III is University Distinguished Professor and professor of philosophy at Colorado State University. He has authored seven books and many articles in environmental ethics. He is the founder and associate editor of *Environmental Ethics* and past president of the International Society for Environmental Ethics.

Donald Sherer is professor of philosophy at Bowling Green State University. He is editor of *Upstream/Downstream: Issues in Environmental Ethics* and coeditor of *Ethics and the Environment*.

Frederick Turner is Founders Professor of Arts and Humanities at the University of Texas at Dallas. A Renaissance scholar and poet by trade, Turner has published eleven books, including two epic poems, *The New World* and *Genesis*.